INDESTRUCTIBLE HULK

Agent of S.H.I.E.L.D.

WRITER: MARK WAID

PENCILS: LEINIL FRANCIS YU

INKS: LEINIL FRANCIS YU
& GERARDO ALANGUILAN

LETTERS: VIRTUAL CALLIGRAPHY'S CHRIS ELIOPOULOS
COLOURIST: SUNNY GHO

ASSISTANT EDITOR: JON MOISAN
EDITOR: MARK PANICCIA
EDITOR IN CHIEF: AXEL ALONSO
CHIEF CREATIVE OFFICER: JOE QUESADA
PUBLISHER: ALAN FINE
EXECUTIVE PRODUCER: DAN BUCKLEY

COVER: LEINIL FRANCIS YU

TM & © 2013 Marvel & Subs. Licensed by Marvel Characters B.V. through Panini S.p.A., Italy. All Rights Reserved. First printing 2013. Published by Panini Publishing, a division of Panini UK Limited. Mike Riddell, Managing Director. Alan O'Keefe, Managing Editor. Mark Irvine, Production Manager. Marco M. Lupoi, Publishing Director Europe. Brady Webb, Reprint Editor. Angela Gray and Charlotte Harvey, Designers. Office of publication: Brockbourne House, 77 Mount Ephraim, Tunbridge Wells, Kent TN4 8BS. This ... the condition that it shall not be sold or distributed with any par... ...BN: 978-1-84653-535-2. Do you have any comments or queries abo... ...roup at Panini/Marvel Graphic Novels.

MARVEL GRAPHIC NOVEL

INDESTRUCTIBLE HULK #1

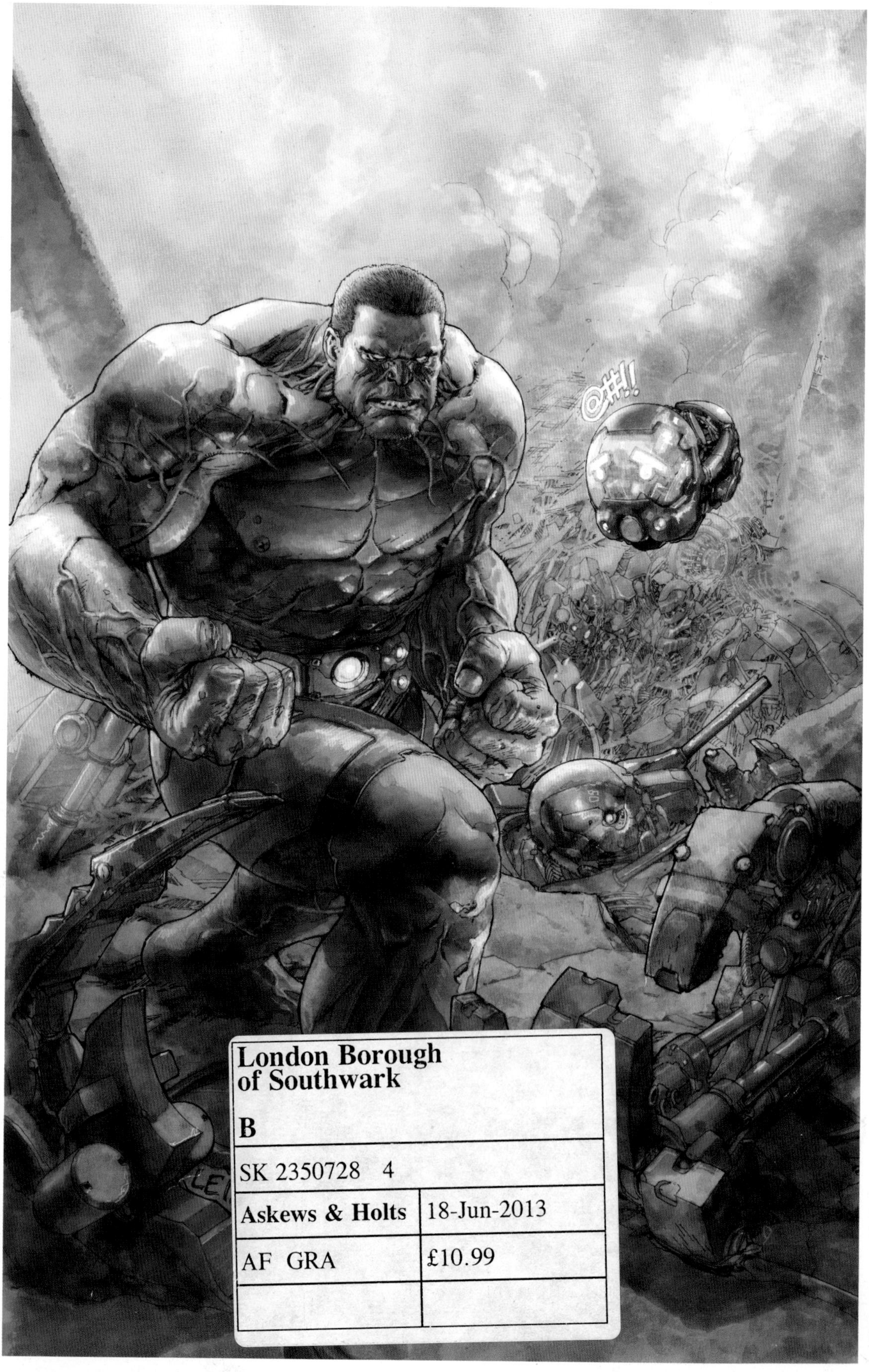
@#!!

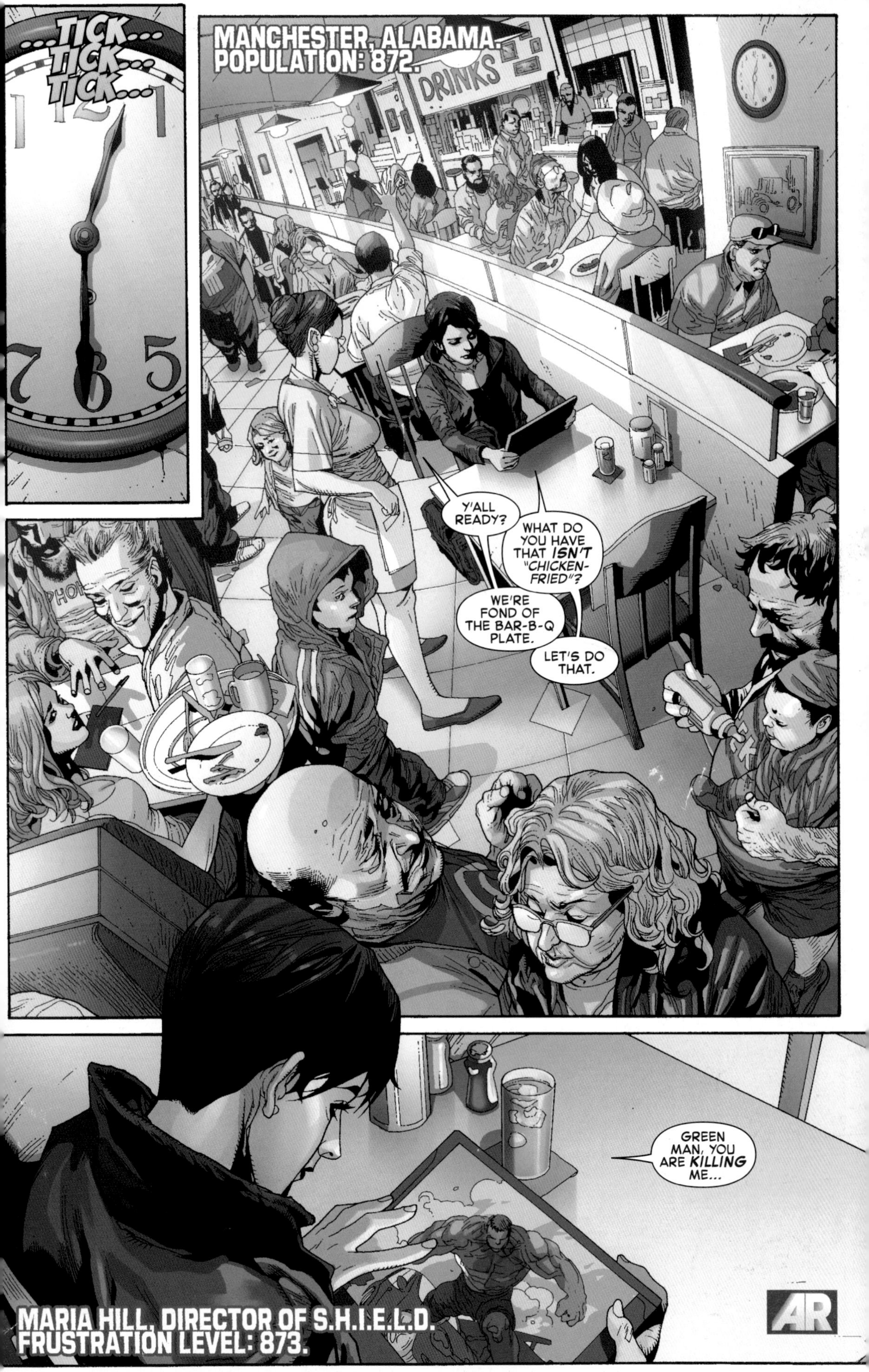
...TICK... TICK... TICK...
MANCHESTER, ALABAMA. POPULATION: 872.
DRINKS
Y'ALL READY?
WHAT DO YOU HAVE THAT ISN'T "CHICKEN-FRIED"?
WE'RE FOND OF THE BAR-B-Q PLATE.
LET'S DO THAT.
GREEN MAN, YOU ARE KILLING ME...
MARIA HILL, DIRECTOR OF S.H.I.E.L.D. FRUSTRATION LEVEL: 873.

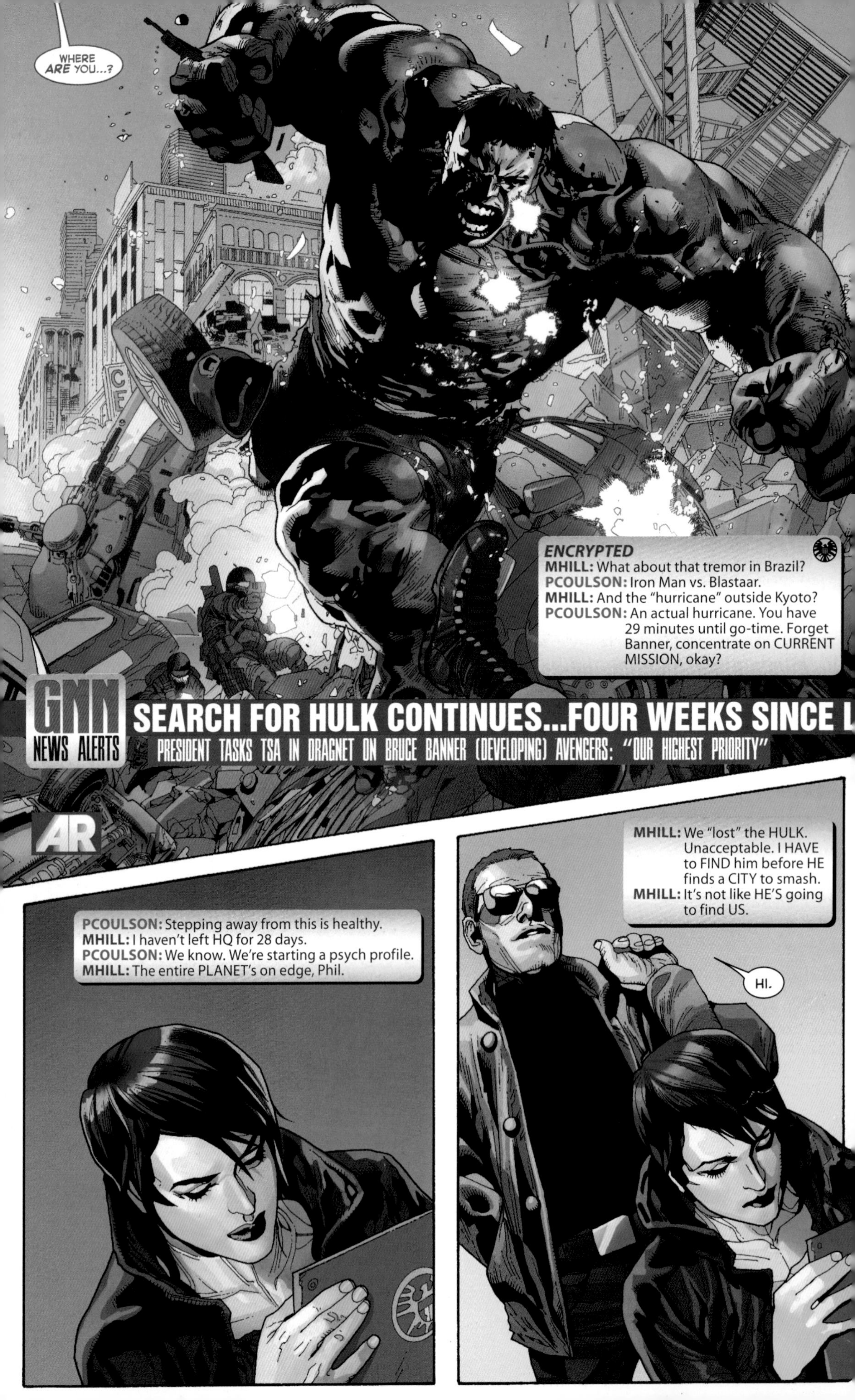

WHERE ARE YOU...?
ENCRYPTED
MHILL: What about that tremor in Brazil?
PCOULSON: Iron Man vs. Blastaar.
MHILL: And the "hurricane" outside Kyoto?
PCOULSON: An actual hurricane. You have 29 minutes until go-time. Forget Banner, concentrate on CURRENT MISSION, okay?
GNN NEWS ALERTS
SEARCH FOR HULK CONTINUES...FOUR WEEKS SINCE L
PRESIDENT TASKS TSA IN DRAGNET ON BRUCE BANNER (DEVELOPING) AVENGERS: "OUR HIGHEST PRIORITY"
AR
PCOULSON: Stepping away from this is healthy.
MHILL: I haven't left HQ for 28 days.
PCOULSON: We know. We're starting a psych profile.
MHILL: The entire PLANET's on edge, Phil.
MHILL: We "lost" the HULK. Unacceptable. I HAVE to FIND him before HE finds a CITY to smash.
MHILL: It's not like HE'S going to find US.
HI.

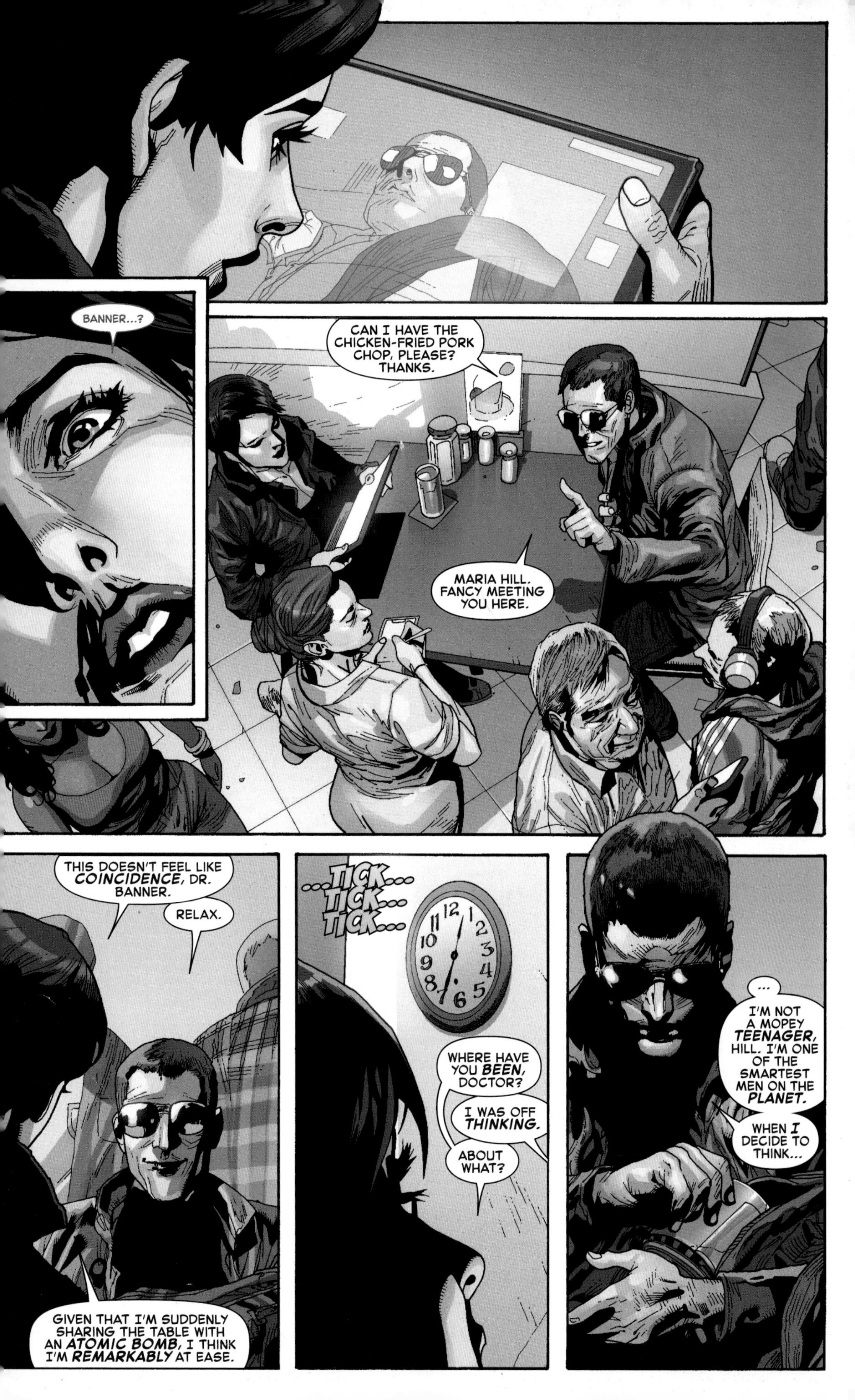
BANNER...?
CAN I HAVE THE CHICKEN-FRIED PORK CHOP, PLEASE? THANKS.
MARIA HILL. FANCY MEETING YOU HERE.
THIS DOESN'T FEEL LIKE COINCIDENCE, DR. BANNER.
RELAX.
GIVEN THAT I'M SUDDENLY SHARING THE TABLE WITH AN ATOMIC BOMB, I THINK I'M REMARKABLY AT EASE.
...TICK... TICK... TICK...
WHERE HAVE YOU BEEN, DOCTOR?
I WAS OFF THINKING.
ABOUT WHAT?
...
I'M NOT A MOPEY TEENAGER, HILL. I'M ONE OF THE SMARTEST MEN ON THE PLANET.
WHEN I DECIDE TO THINK...

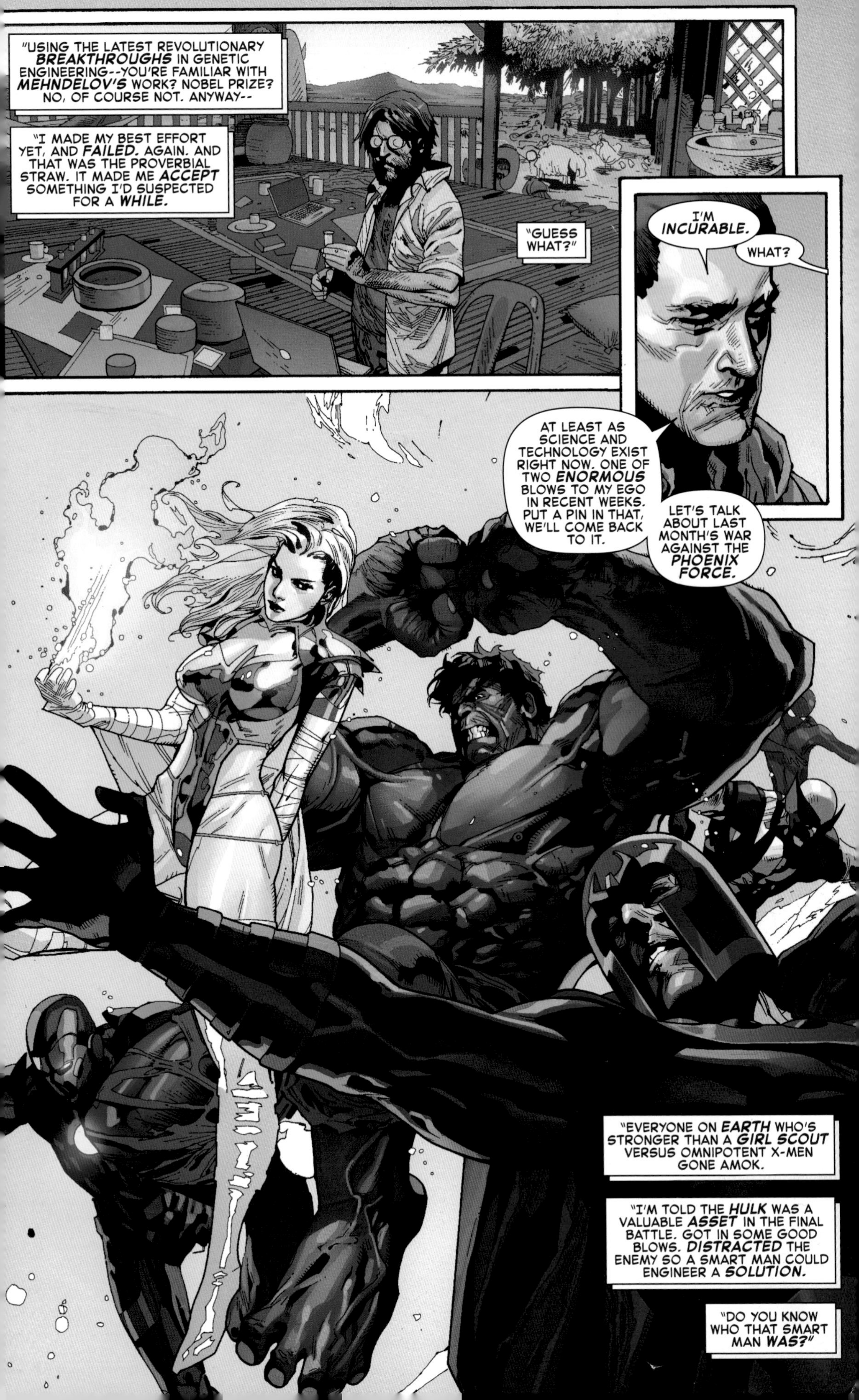
"USING THE LATEST REVOLUTIONARY BREAKTHROUGHS IN GENETIC ENGINEERING--YOU'RE FAMILIAR WITH MEHNDELOV'S WORK? NOBEL PRIZE? NO, OF COURSE NOT. ANYWAY--
"I MADE MY BEST EFFORT YET, AND FAILED. AGAIN. AND THAT WAS THE PROVERBIAL STRAW. IT MADE ME ACCEPT SOMETHING I'D SUSPECTED FOR A WHILE.
"GUESS WHAT?"
I'M INCURABLE.
WHAT?
AT LEAST AS SCIENCE AND TECHNOLOGY EXIST RIGHT NOW. ONE OF TWO ENORMOUS BLOWS TO MY EGO IN RECENT WEEKS. PUT A PIN IN THAT, WE'LL COME BACK TO IT.
LET'S TALK ABOUT LAST MONTH'S WAR AGAINST THE PHOENIX FORCE.
"EVERYONE ON EARTH WHO'S STRONGER THAN A GIRL SCOUT VERSUS OMNIPOTENT X-MEN GONE AMOK.
"I'M TOLD THE HULK WAS A VALUABLE ASSET IN THE FINAL BATTLE. GOT IN SOME GOOD BLOWS. DISTRACTED THE ENEMY SO A SMART MAN COULD ENGINEER A SOLUTION.
"DO YOU KNOW WHO THAT SMART MAN WAS?"

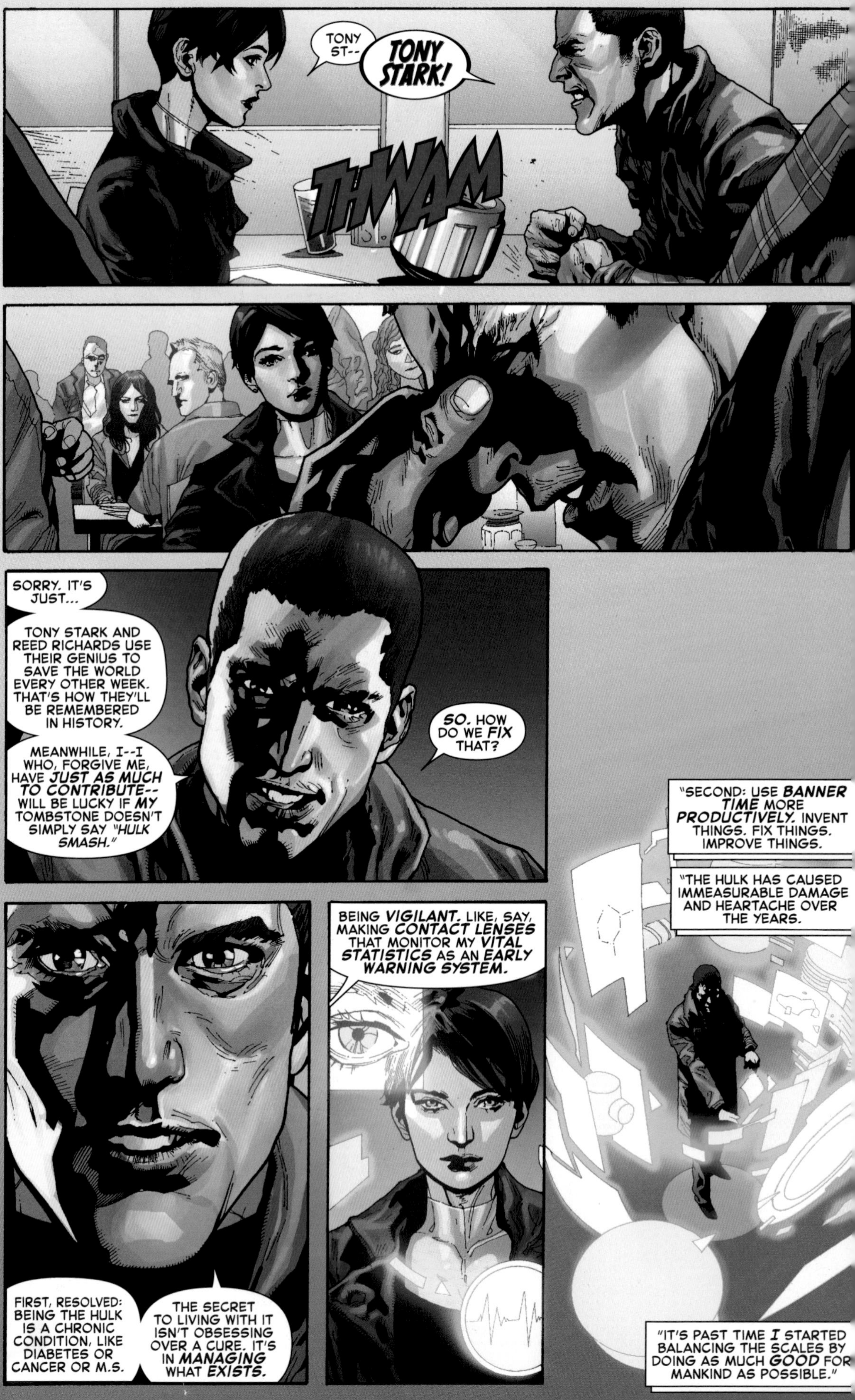
TONY ST--
TONY STARK!
THWAM
SORRY. IT'S JUST...
TONY STARK AND REED RICHARDS USE THEIR GENIUS TO SAVE THE WORLD EVERY OTHER WEEK. THAT'S HOW THEY'LL BE REMEMBERED IN HISTORY.
MEANWHILE, I--I WHO, FORGIVE ME, HAVE JUST AS MUCH TO CONTRIBUTE-- WILL BE LUCKY IF MY TOMBSTONE DOESN'T SIMPLY SAY "HULK SMASH."
SO. HOW DO WE FIX THAT?
FIRST, RESOLVED: BEING THE HULK IS A CHRONIC CONDITION, LIKE DIABETES OR CANCER OR M.S.
THE SECRET TO LIVING WITH IT ISN'T OBSESSING OVER A CURE. IT'S IN MANAGING WHAT EXISTS.
BEING VIGILANT. LIKE, SAY, MAKING CONTACT LENSES THAT MONITOR MY VITAL STATISTICS AS AN EARLY WARNING SYSTEM.
"SECOND: USE BANNER TIME MORE PRODUCTIVELY. INVENT THINGS. FIX THINGS. IMPROVE THINGS.
"THE HULK HAS CAUSED IMMEASURABLE DAMAGE AND HEARTACHE OVER THE YEARS.
"IT'S PAST TIME I STARTED BALANCING THE SCALES BY DOING AS MUCH GOOD FOR MANKIND AS POSSIBLE."

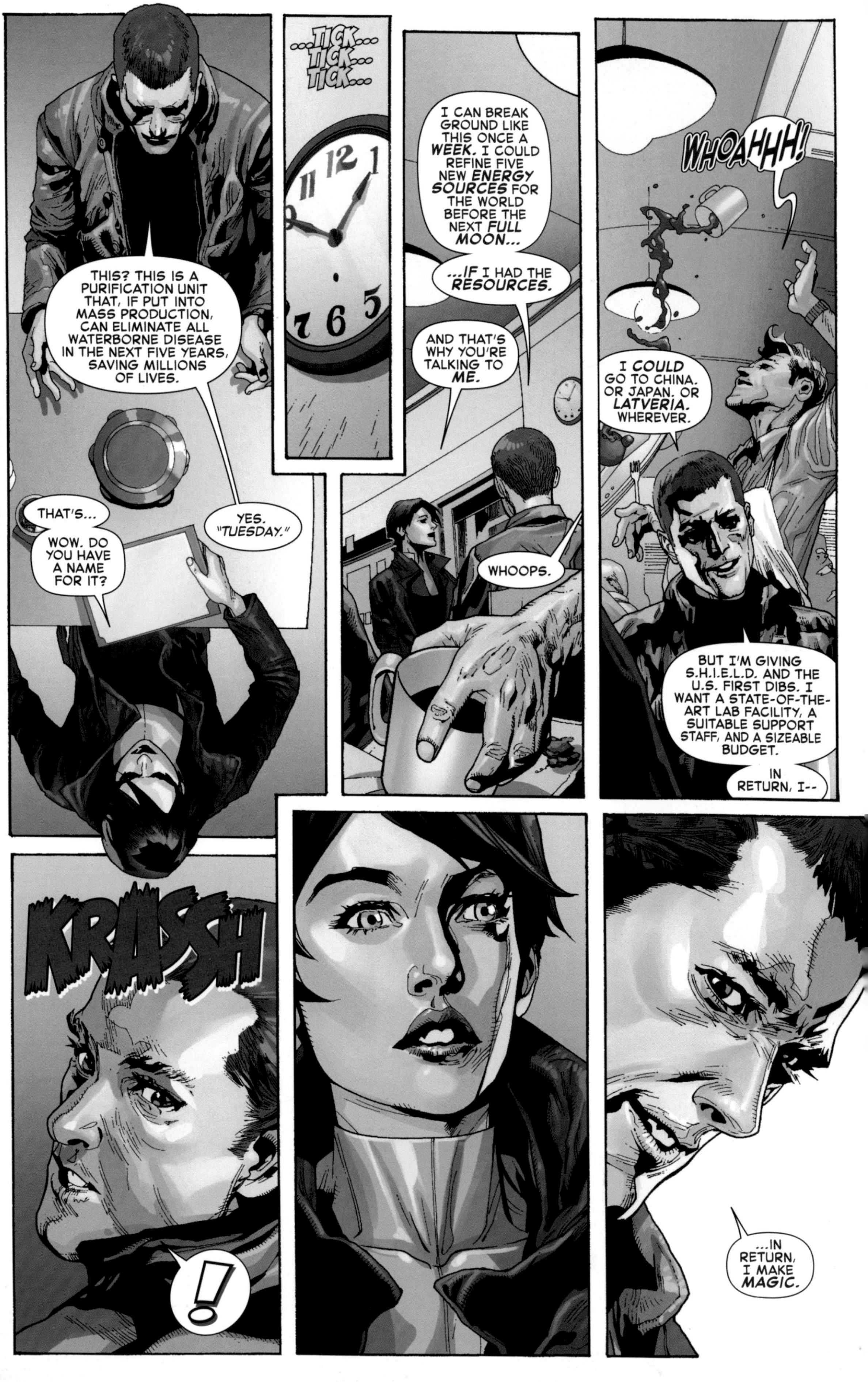

THIS? THIS IS A PURIFICATION UNIT THAT, IF PUT INTO MASS PRODUCTION, CAN ELIMINATE ALL WATERBORNE DISEASE IN THE NEXT FIVE YEARS, SAVING MILLIONS OF LIVES.
THAT'S...
WOW. DO YOU HAVE A NAME FOR IT?
YES. "TUESDAY."
...TICK... TICK... TICK...
I CAN BREAK GROUND LIKE THIS ONCE A WEEK. I COULD REFINE FIVE NEW ENERGY SOURCES FOR THE WORLD BEFORE THE NEXT FULL MOON...
...IF I HAD THE RESOURCES.
AND THAT'S WHY YOU'RE TALKING TO ME.
WHOOPS.
WHOAHHH!
I COULD GO TO CHINA. OR JAPAN. OR LATVERIA. WHEREVER.
BUT I'M GIVING S.H.I.E.L.D. AND THE U.S. FIRST DIBS. I WANT A STATE-OF-THE-ART LAB FACILITY, A SUITABLE SUPPORT STAFF, AND A SIZEABLE BUDGET.
IN RETURN, I--
KRASH
!
...IN RETURN, I MAKE MAGIC.

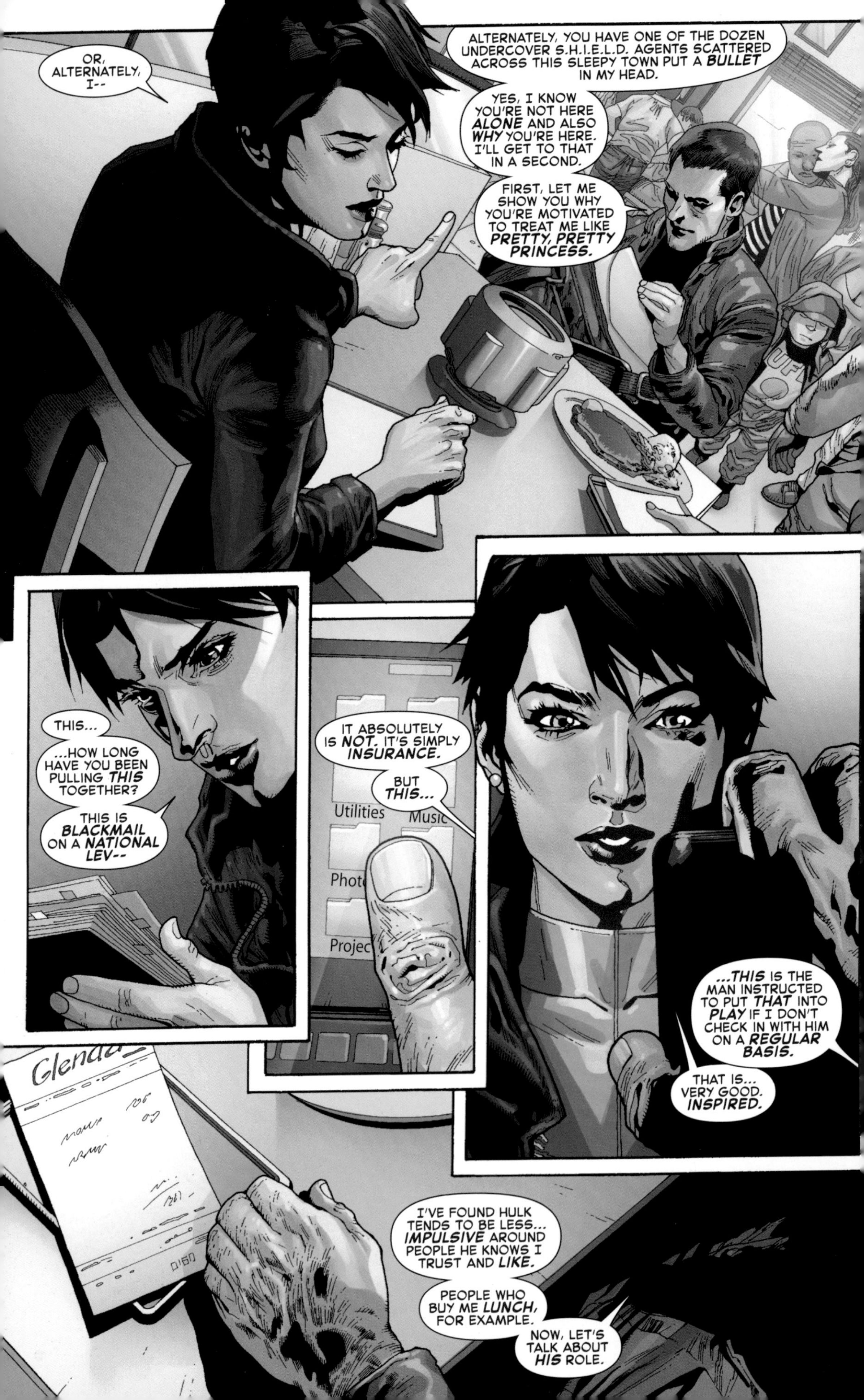
OR, ALTERNATELY, I--
ALTERNATELY, YOU HAVE ONE OF THE DOZEN UNDERCOVER S.H.I.E.L.D. AGENTS SCATTERED ACROSS THIS SLEEPY TOWN PUT A BULLET IN MY HEAD.
YES, I KNOW YOU'RE NOT HERE ALONE AND ALSO WHY YOU'RE HERE. I'LL GET TO THAT IN A SECOND.
FIRST, LET ME SHOW YOU WHY YOU'RE MOTIVATED TO TREAT ME LIKE PRETTY, PRETTY PRINCESS.
THIS...
...HOW LONG HAVE YOU BEEN PULLING THIS TOGETHER?
THIS IS BLACKMAIL ON A NATIONAL LEV--
IT ABSOLUTELY IS NOT. IT'S SIMPLY INSURANCE.
BUT THIS...
Utilities
Music
...THIS IS THE MAN INSTRUCTED TO PUT THAT INTO PLAY IF I DON'T CHECK IN WITH HIM ON A REGULAR BASIS.
THAT IS... VERY GOOD. INSPIRED.
I'VE FOUND HULK TENDS TO BE LESS... IMPULSIVE AROUND PEOPLE HE KNOWS I TRUST AND LIKE.
PEOPLE WHO BUY ME LUNCH, FOR EXAMPLE.
NOW, LET'S TALK ABOUT HIS ROLE.

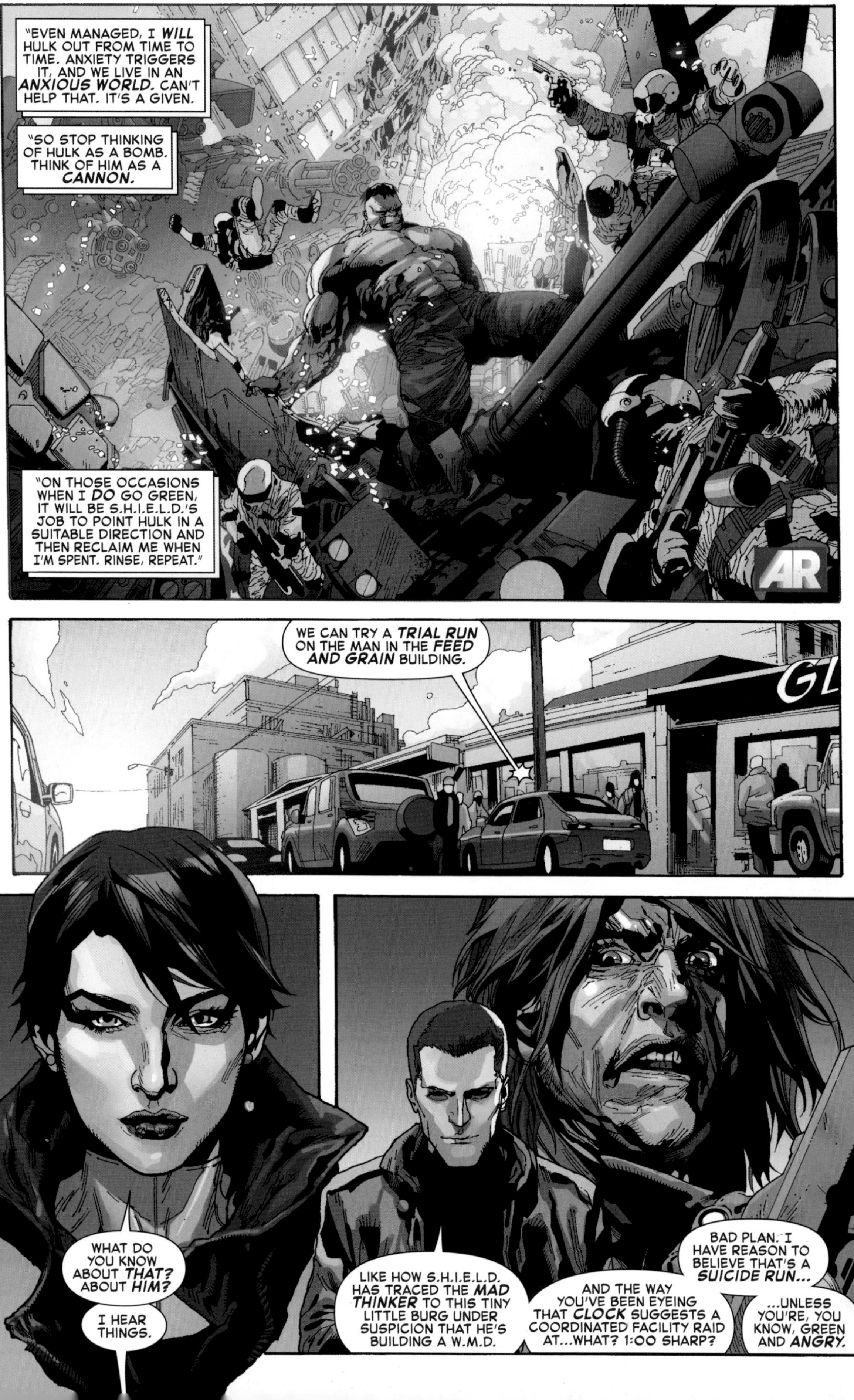
"EVEN MANAGED, I WILL HULK OUT FROM TIME TO TIME. ANXIETY TRIGGERS IT, AND WE LIVE IN AN ANXIOUS WORLD. CAN'T HELP THAT. IT'S A GIVEN.
"SO STOP THINKING OF HULK AS A BOMB. THINK OF HIM AS A CANNON.
"ON THOSE OCCASIONS WHEN I DO GO GREEN, IT WILL BE S.H.I.E.L.D.'S JOB TO POINT HULK IN A SUITABLE DIRECTION AND THEN RECLAIM ME WHEN I'M SPENT. RINSE, REPEAT."
AR
WE CAN TRY A TRIAL RUN ON THE MAN IN THE FEED AND GRAIN BUILDING.
BAD PLAN. I HAVE REASON TO BELIEVE THAT'S A SUICIDE RUN...
...UNLESS YOU'RE, YOU KNOW, GREEN AND ANGRY.
WHAT DO YOU KNOW ABOUT THAT? ABOUT HIM?
I HEAR THINGS.
LIKE HOW S.H.I.E.L.D. HAS TRACED THE MAD THINKER TO THIS TINY LITTLE BURG UNDER SUSPICION THAT HE'S BUILDING A W.M.D.
AND THE WAY YOU'VE BEEN EYEING THAT CLOCK SUGGESTS A COORDINATED FACILITY RAID AT...WHAT? 1:00 SHARP?

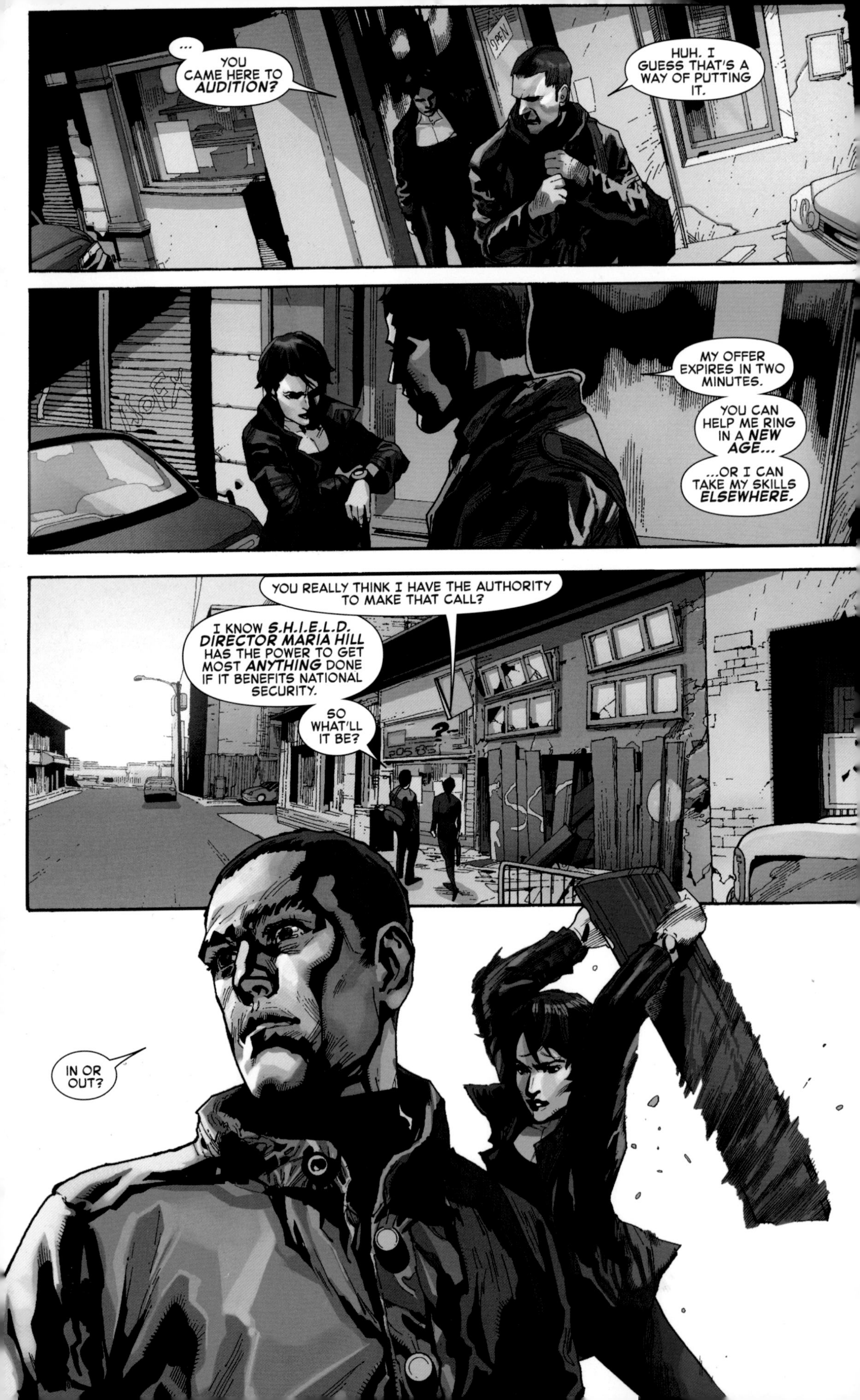
...
YOU CAME HERE TO AUDITION?
HUH. I GUESS THAT'S A WAY OF PUTTING IT.
OPEN
MY OFFER EXPIRES IN TWO MINUTES.
YOU CAN HELP ME RING IN A NEW AGE...
...OR I CAN TAKE MY SKILLS ELSEWHERE.
YOU REALLY THINK I HAVE THE AUTHORITY TO MAKE THAT CALL?
I KNOW S.H.I.E.L.D. DIRECTOR MARIA HILL HAS THE POWER TO GET MOST ANYTHING DONE IF IT BENEFITS NATIONAL SECURITY.
SO WHAT'LL IT BE?
IN OR OUT?

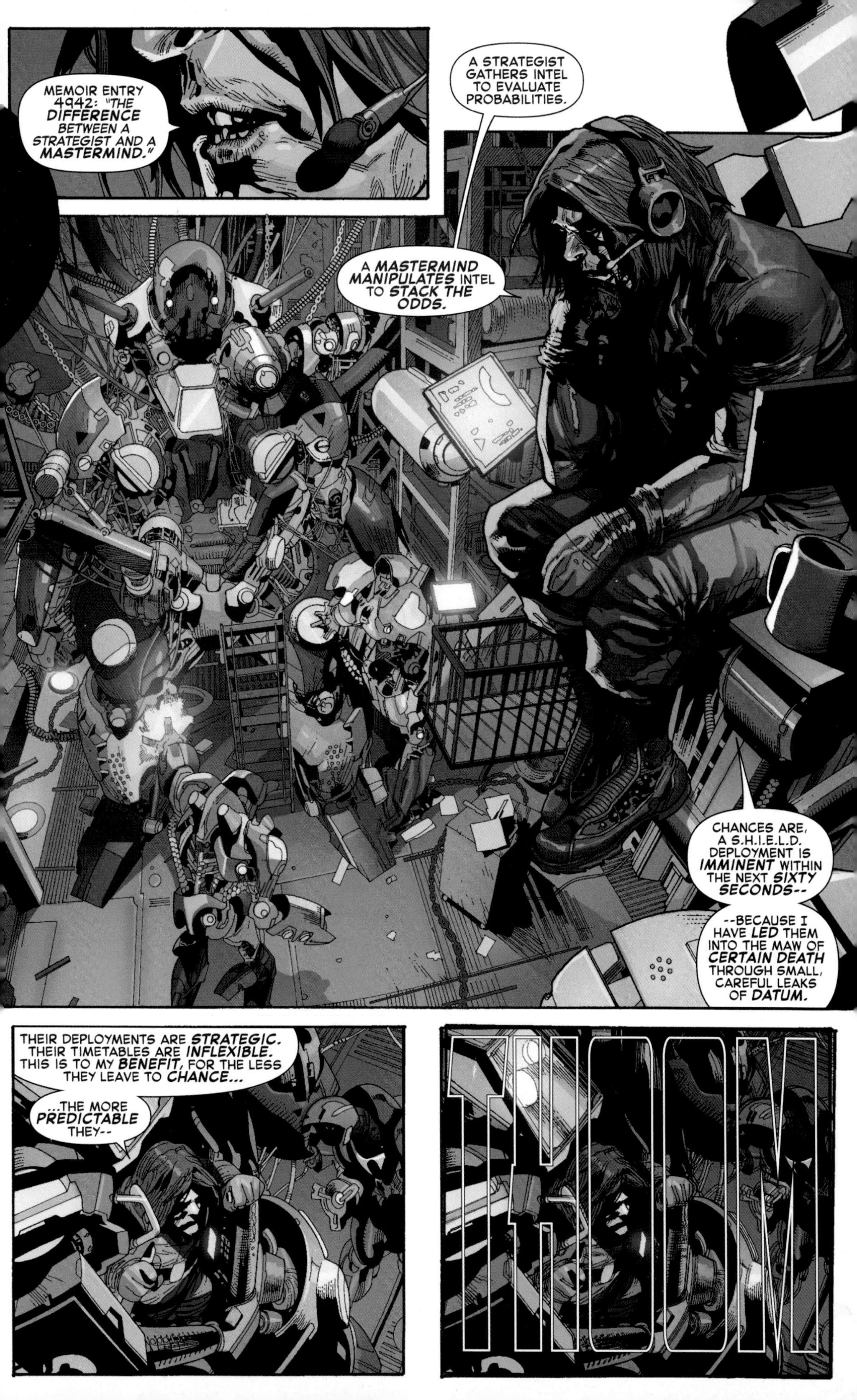
MEMOIR ENTRY 4942: "THE DIFFERENCE BETWEEN A STRATEGIST AND A MASTERMIND."
A STRATEGIST GATHERS INTEL TO EVALUATE PROBABILITIES.
A MASTERMIND MANIPULATES INTEL TO STACK THE ODDS.
CHANCES ARE, A S.H.I.E.L.D. DEPLOYMENT IS IMMINENT WITHIN THE NEXT SIXTY SECONDS--
--BECAUSE I HAVE LED THEM INTO THE MAW OF CERTAIN DEATH THROUGH SMALL, CAREFUL LEAKS OF DATUM.
THEIR DEPLOYMENTS ARE STRATEGIC. THEIR TIMETABLES ARE INFLEXIBLE. THIS IS TO MY BENEFIT, FOR THE LESS THEY LEAVE TO CHANCE...
...THE MORE PREDICTABLE THEY--
THOOM

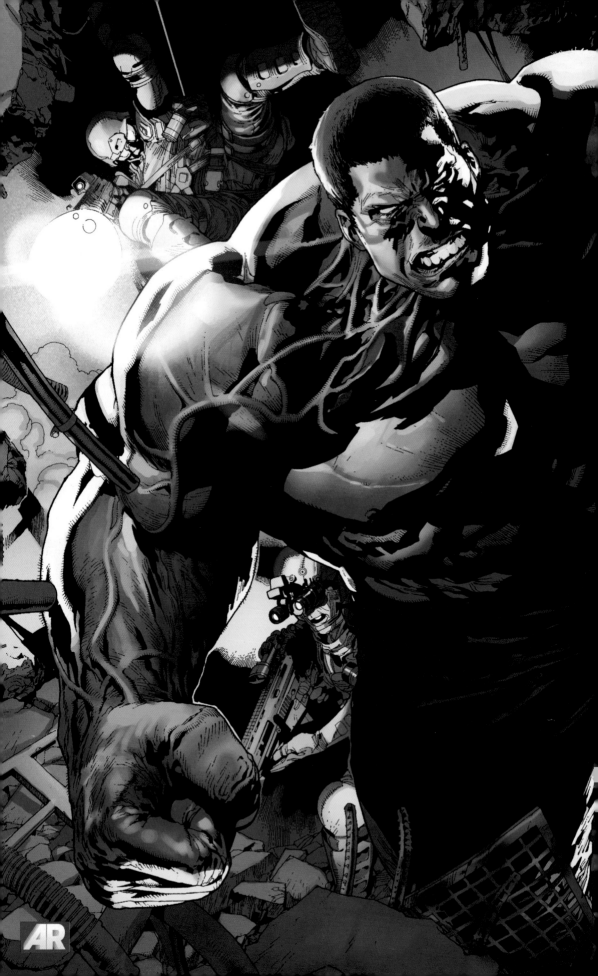

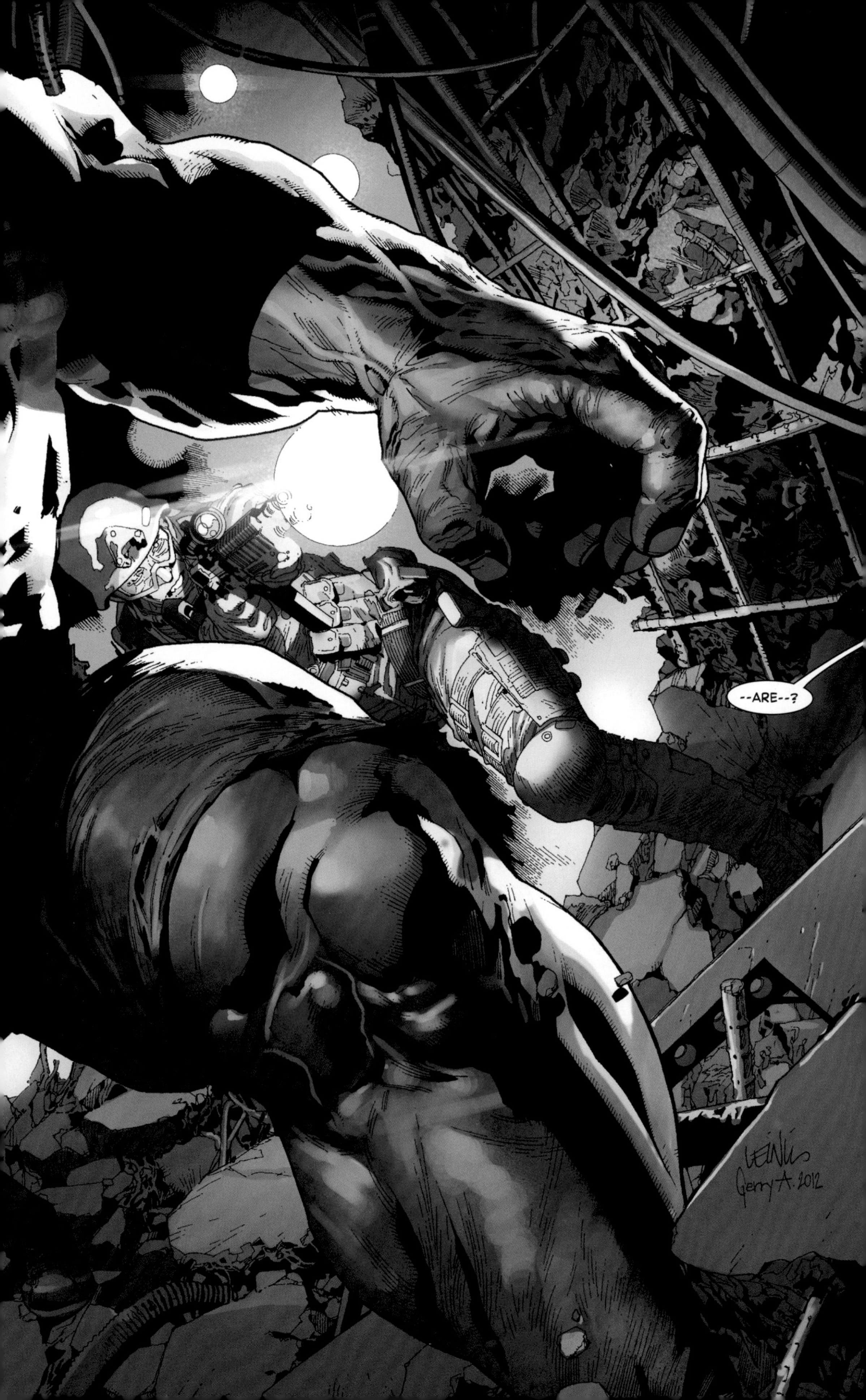
--ARE--?
Gerry A. 2012

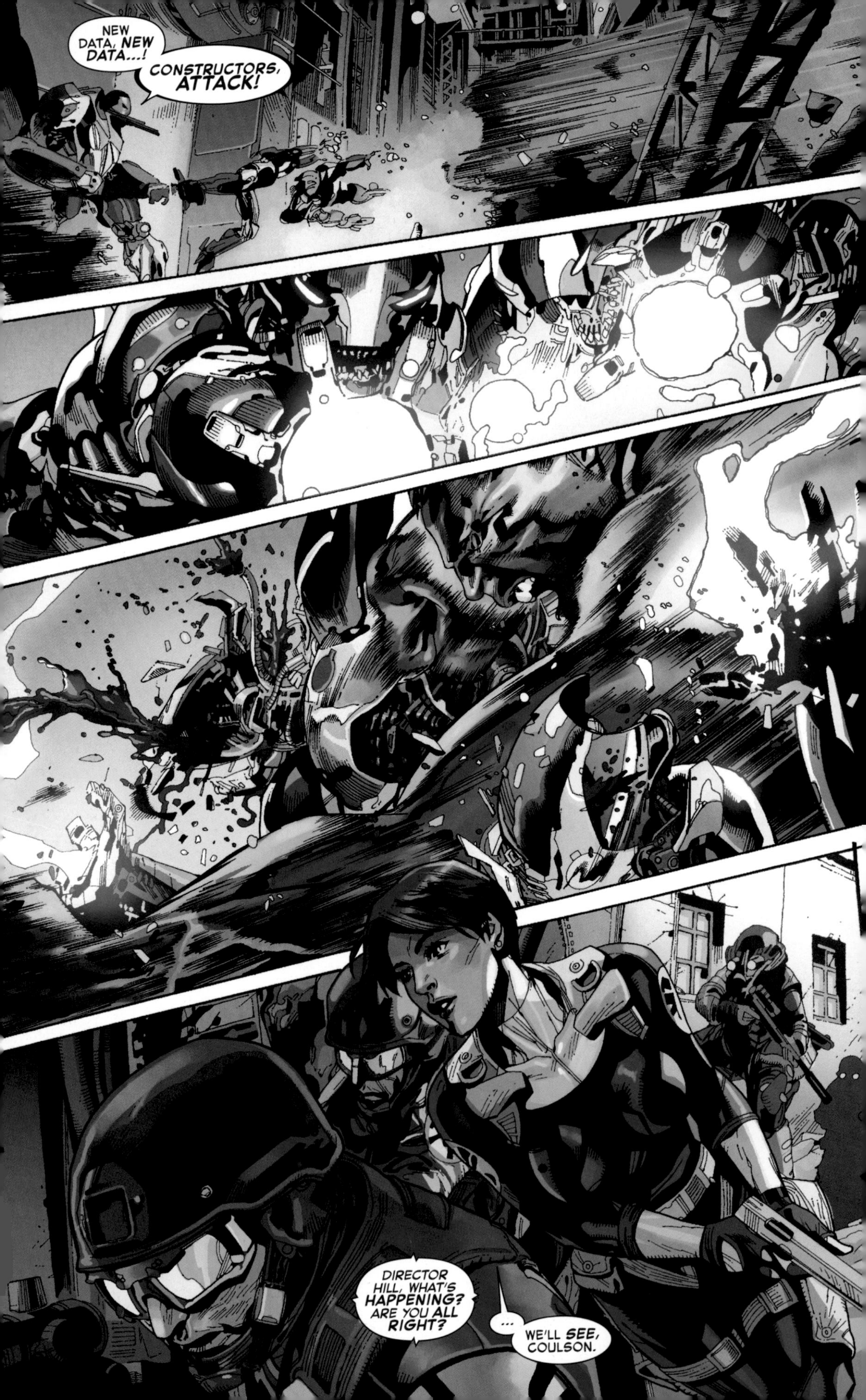
NEW DATA, NEW DATA...!
CONSTRUCTORS, ATTACK!
DIRECTOR HILL, WHAT'S HAPPENING? ARE YOU ALL RIGHT?
...
WE'LL SEE, COULSON.

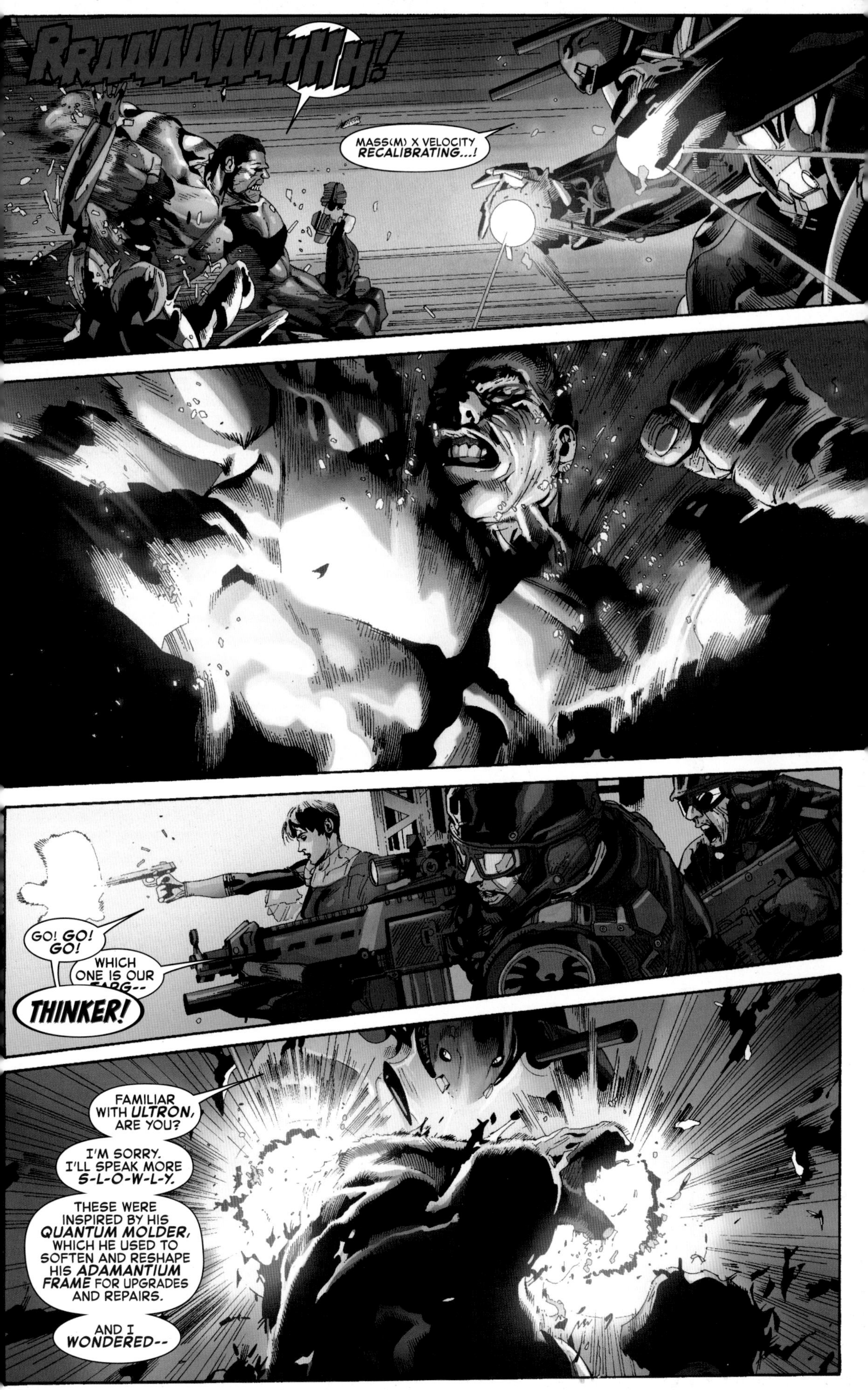
RRAAAAAAAHHH!
MASS(M) X VELOCITY RECALIBRATING...!
GO! GO! GO!
WHICH ONE IS OUR TARG--
THINKER!
FAMILIAR WITH ULTRON, ARE YOU?
I'M SORRY. I'LL SPEAK MORE S-L-O-W-L-Y.
THESE WERE INSPIRED BY HIS QUANTUM MOLDER, WHICH HE USED TO SOFTEN AND RESHAPE HIS ADAMANTIUM FRAME FOR UPGRADES AND REPAIRS.
AND I WONDERED--

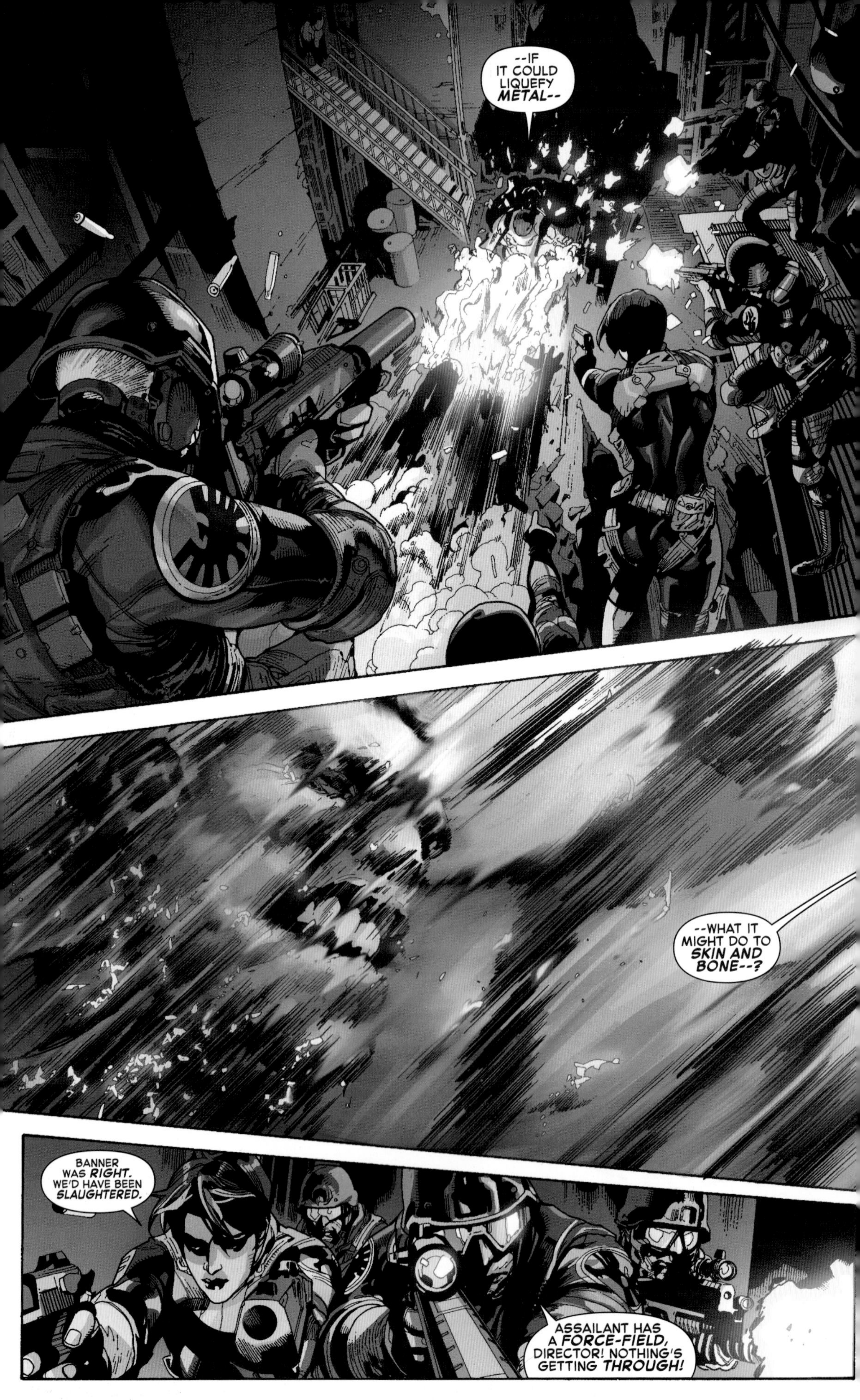
--IF IT COULD LIQUEFY METAL--
--WHAT IT MIGHT DO TO SKIN AND BONE--?
BANNER WAS RIGHT. WE'D HAVE BEEN SLAUGHTERED.
ASSAILANT HAS A FORCE-FIELD, DIRECTOR! NOTHING'S GETTING THROUGH!

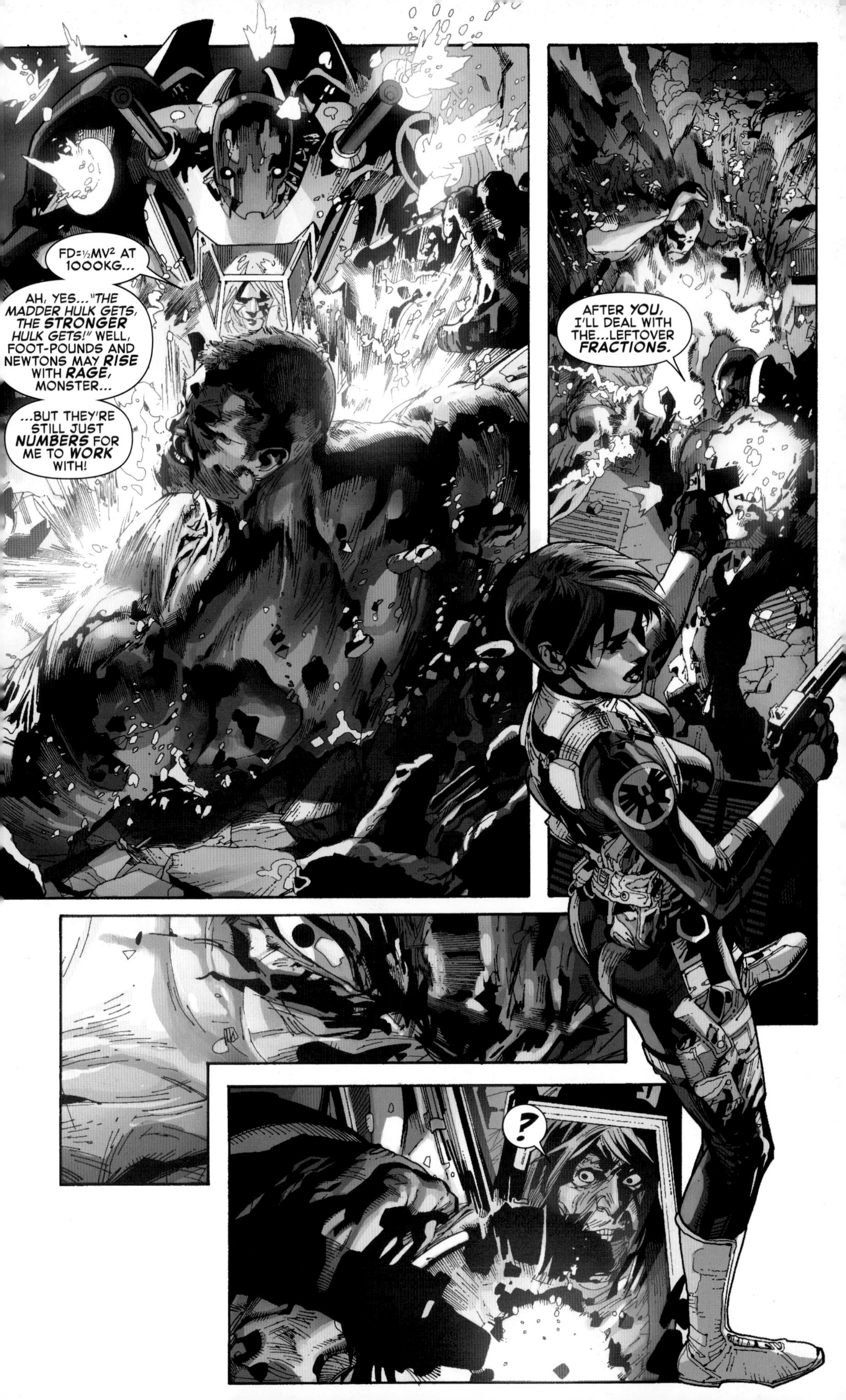

FD=½MV² AT 1000KG...
AH, YES... "THE MADDER HULK GETS, THE STRONGER HULK GETS!" WELL, FOOT-POUNDS AND NEWTONS MAY RISE WITH RAGE, MONSTER...
...BUT THEY'RE STILL JUST NUMBERS FOR ME TO WORK WITH!
AFTER YOU, I'LL DEAL WITH THE...LEFTOVER FRACTIONS.
?

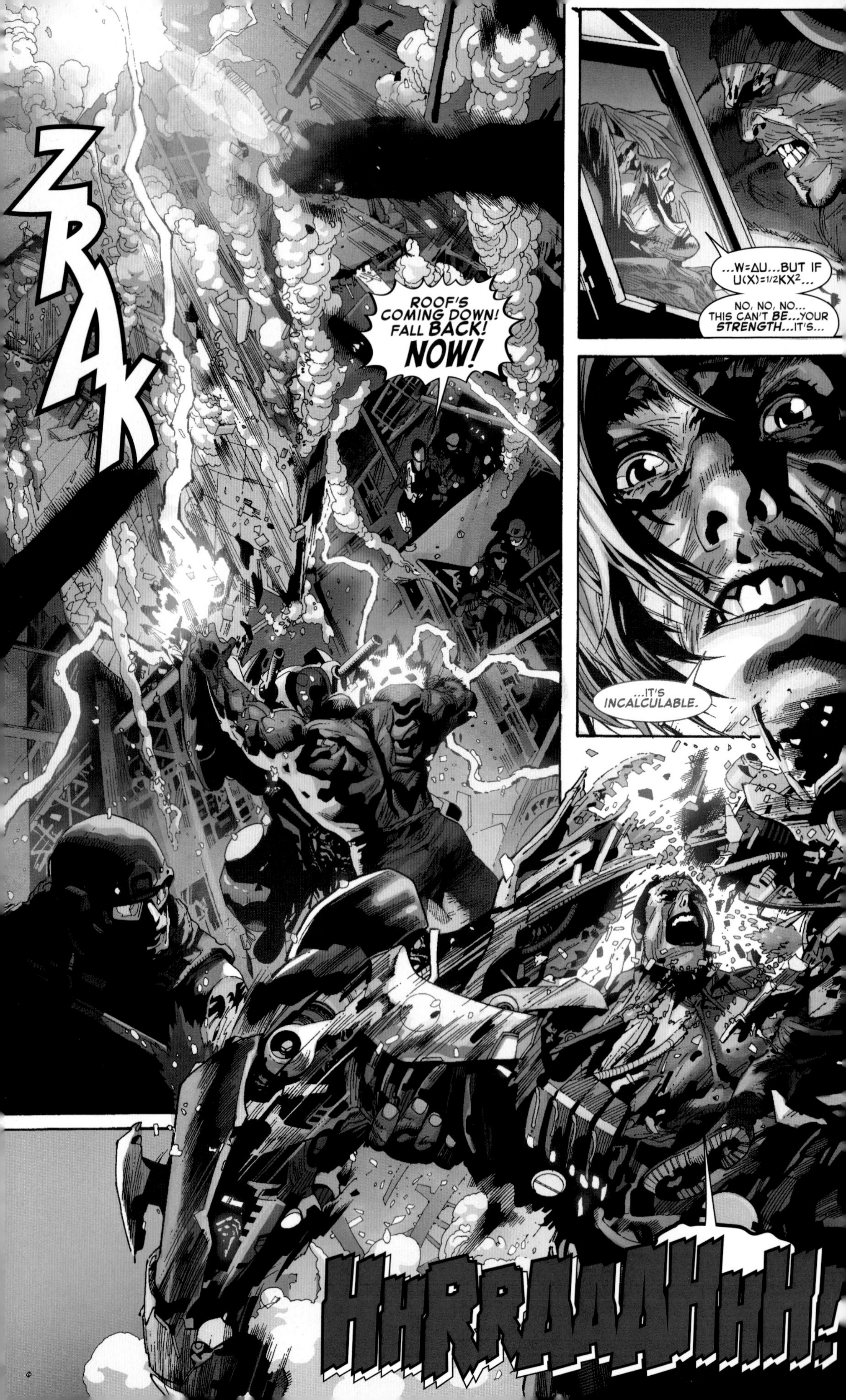
ZRAK
ROOF'S COMING DOWN! FALL BACK! NOW!
...W=ΔU...BUT IF U(X)=1/2KX²...
NO, NO, NO... THIS CAN'T BE...YOUR STRENGTH...IT'S...
...IT'S INCALCULABLE.
HHRRAAAHHH!

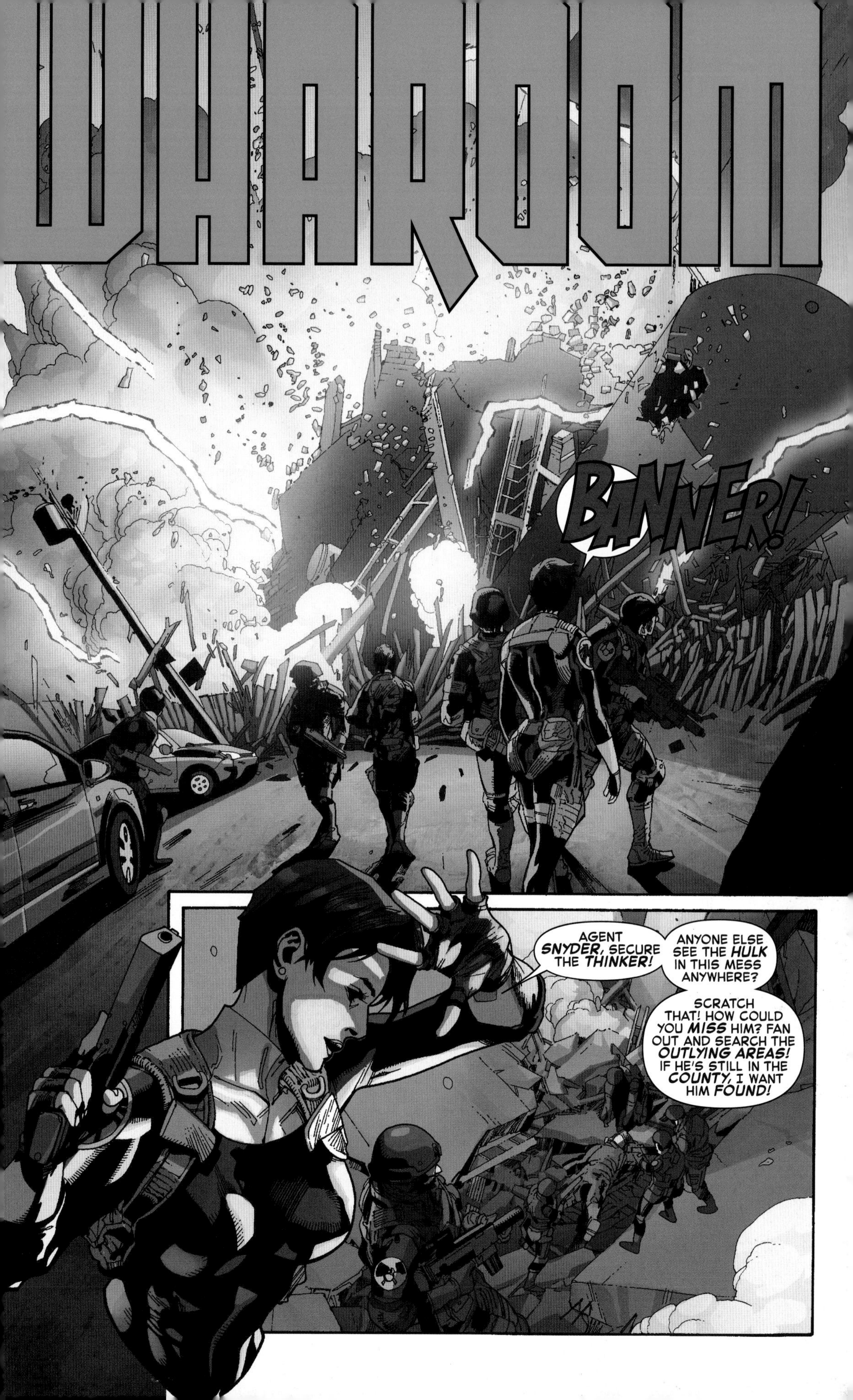
WARROOM
BANNER!
AGENT SNYDER, SECURE THE THINKER!
ANYONE ELSE SEE THE HULK IN THIS MESS ANYWHERE?
SCRATCH THAT! HOW COULD YOU MISS HIM? FAN OUT AND SEARCH THE OUTLYING AREAS! IF HE'S STILL IN THE COUNTY, I WANT HIM FOUND!

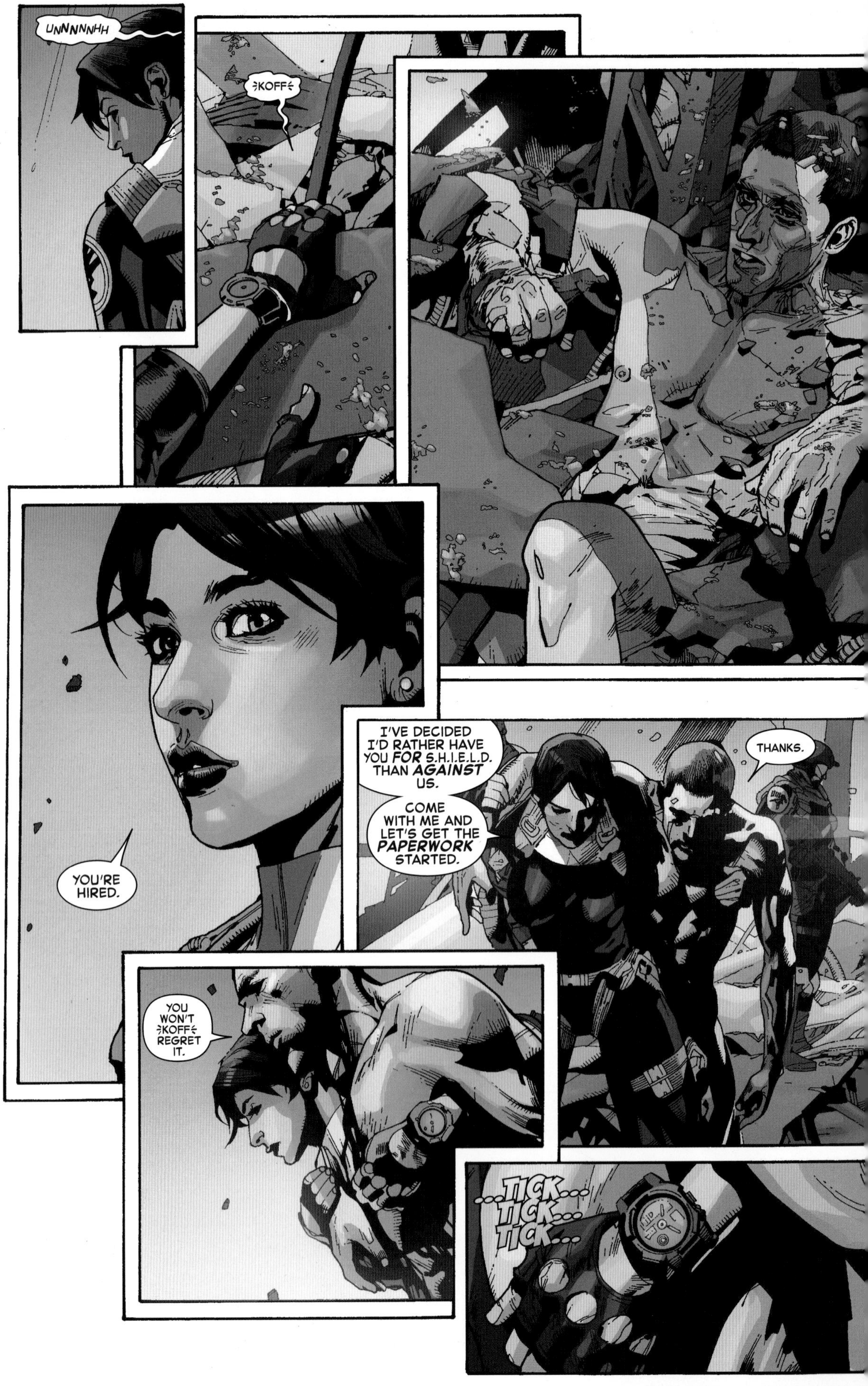
UNNNNNHH
≷KOFF≶
YOU'RE HIRED.
I'VE DECIDED I'D RATHER HAVE YOU FOR S.H.I.E.L.D. THAN AGAINST US.
COME WITH ME AND LET'S GET THE PAPERWORK STARTED.
THANKS.
YOU WON'T ≷KOFF≶ REGRET IT.
...TICK... TICK... TICK...

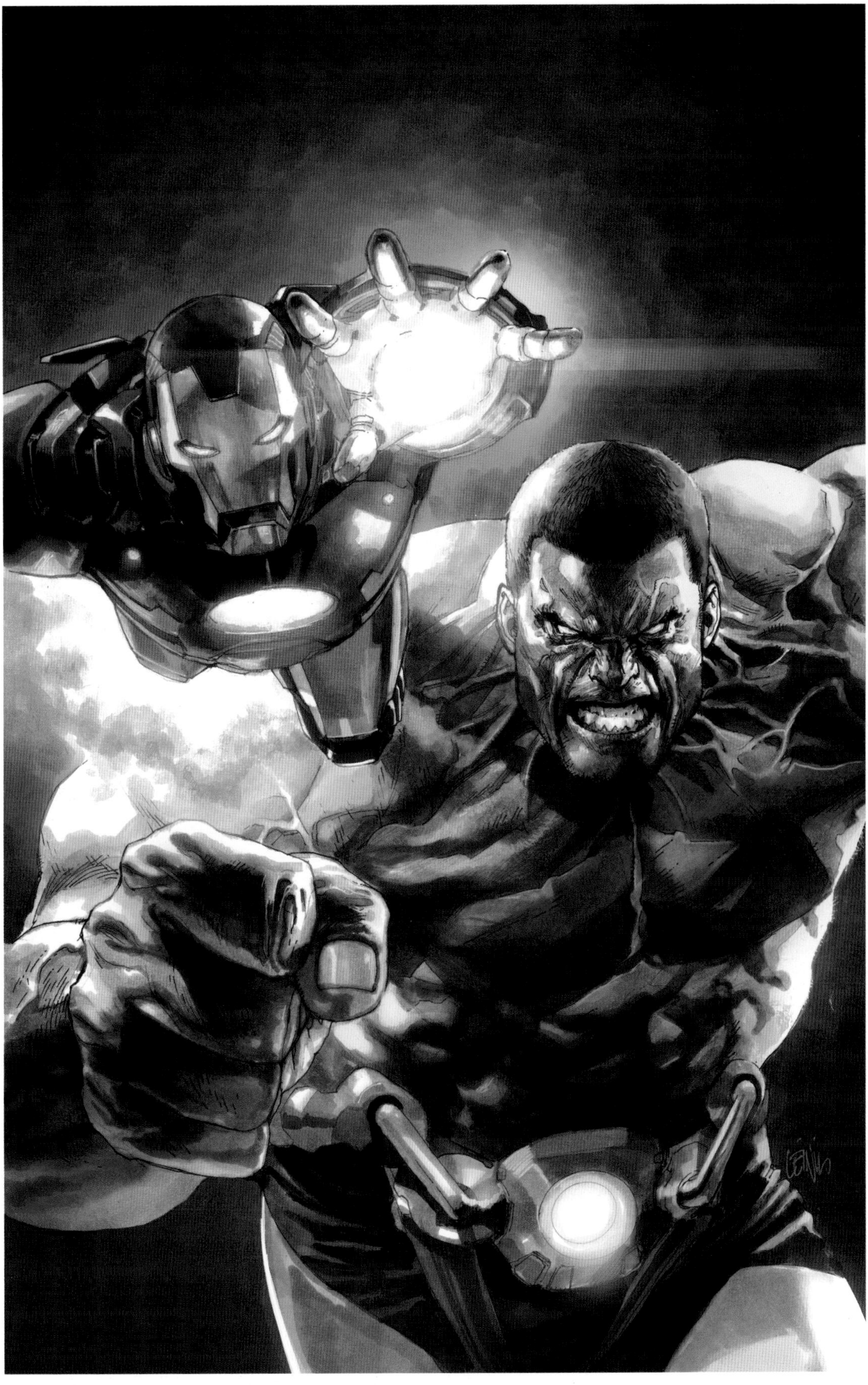

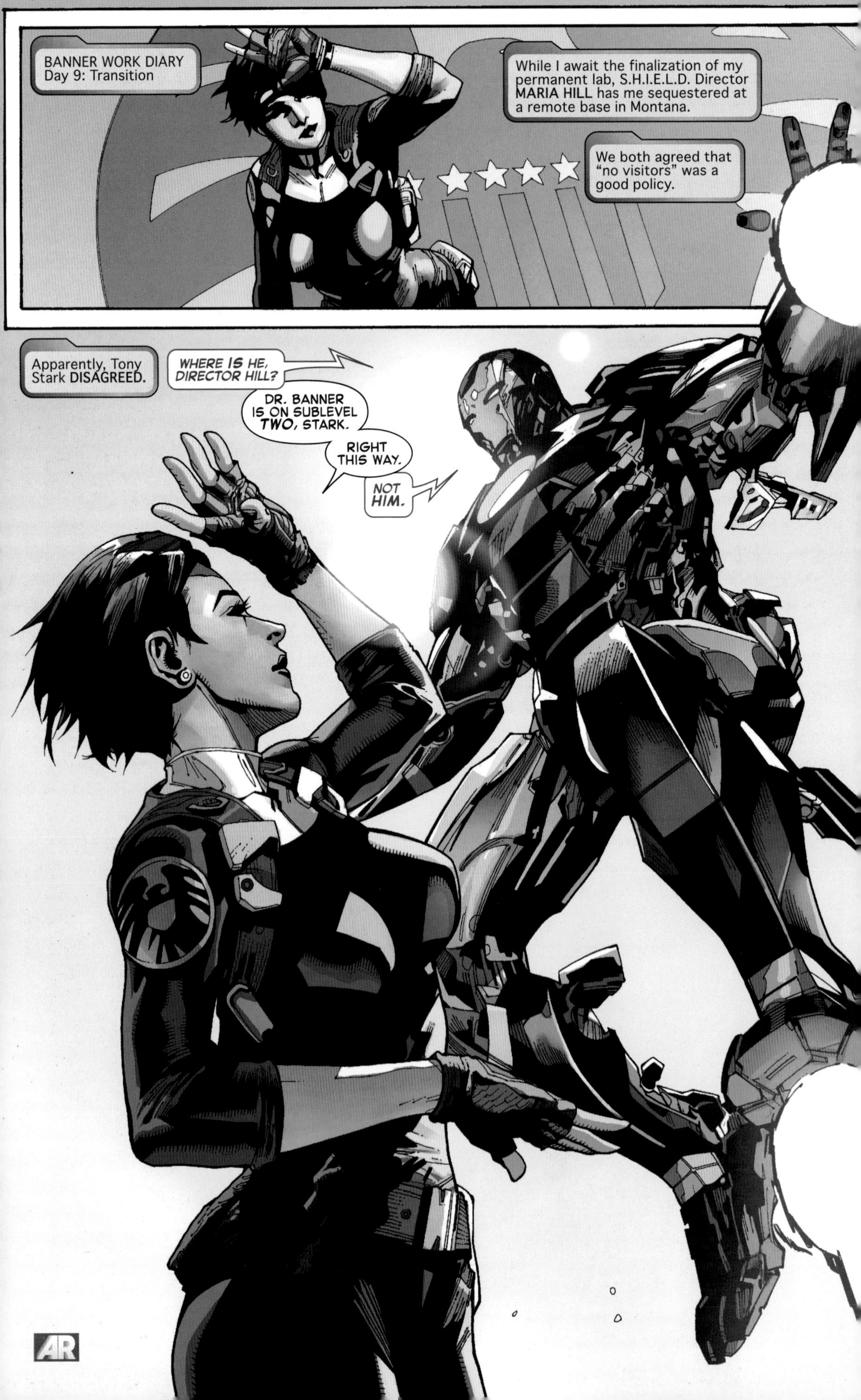
BANNER WORK DIARY
Day 9: Transition
While I await the finalization of my permanent lab, S.H.I.E.L.D. Director MARIA HILL has me sequestered at a remote base in Montana.
We both agreed that "no visitors" was a good policy.
Apparently, Tony Stark DISAGREED.
WHERE IS HE, DIRECTOR HILL?
DR. BANNER IS ON SUBLEVEL TWO, STARK.
RIGHT THIS WAY.
NOT HIM.

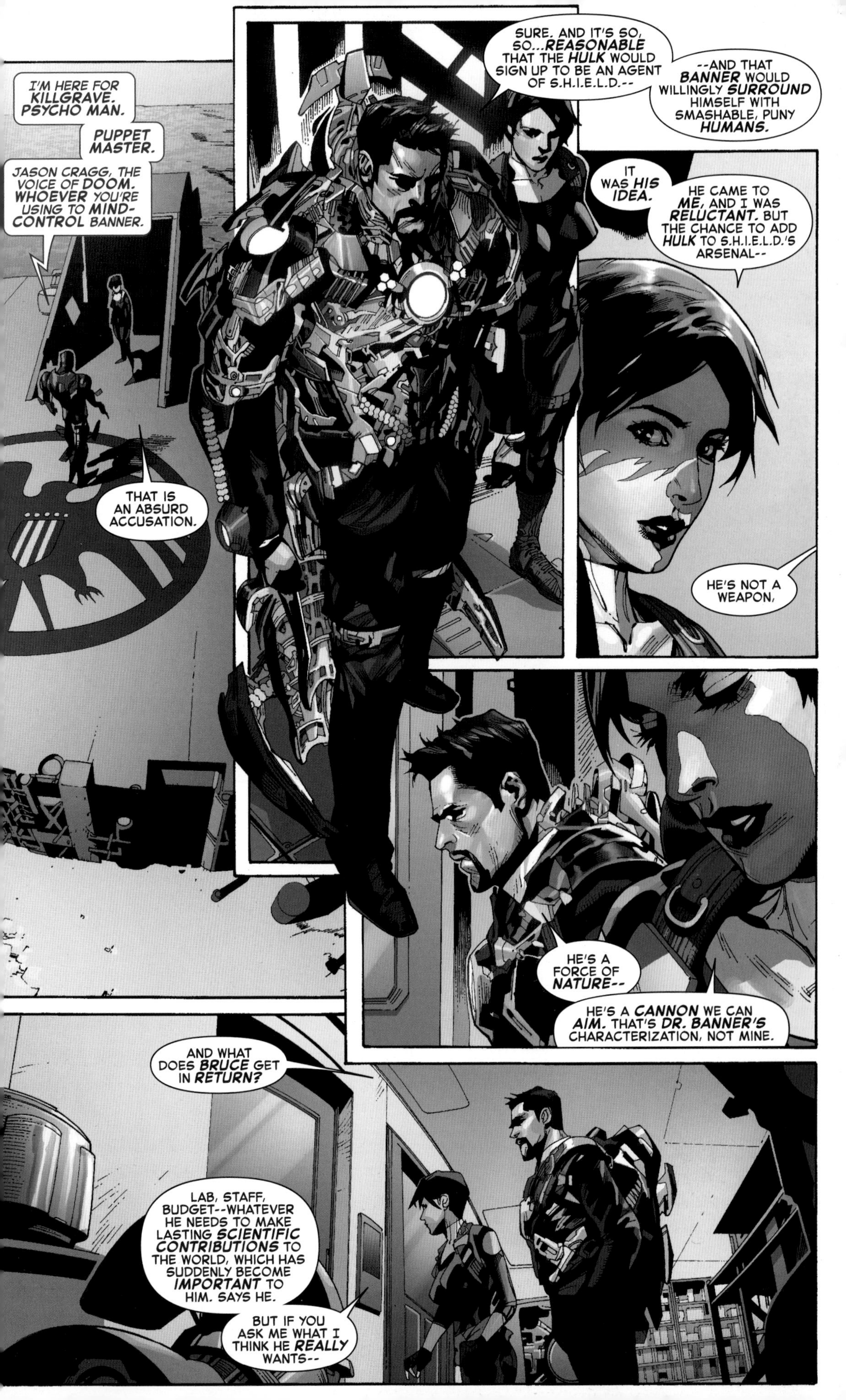

I'M HERE FOR KILLGRAVE. PSYCHO MAN.
PUPPET MASTER.
JASON CRAGG, THE VOICE OF DOOM. WHOEVER YOU'RE USING TO MIND-CONTROL BANNER.
THAT IS AN ABSURD ACCUSATION.
SURE. AND IT'S SO, SO...REASONABLE THAT THE HULK WOULD SIGN UP TO BE AN AGENT OF S.H.I.E.L.D.--
--AND THAT BANNER WOULD WILLINGLY SURROUND HIMSELF WITH SMASHABLE, PUNY HUMANS.
IT WAS HIS IDEA.
HE CAME TO ME, AND I WAS RELUCTANT. BUT THE CHANCE TO ADD HULK TO S.H.I.E.L.D.'S ARSENAL--
HE'S NOT A WEAPON,
HE'S A FORCE OF NATURE--
HE'S A CANNON WE CAN AIM. THAT'S DR. BANNER'S CHARACTERIZATION, NOT MINE.
AND WHAT DOES BRUCE GET IN RETURN?
LAB, STAFF, BUDGET--WHATEVER HE NEEDS TO MAKE LASTING SCIENTIFIC CONTRIBUTIONS TO THE WORLD, WHICH HAS SUDDENLY BECOME IMPORTANT TO HIM. SAYS HE.
BUT IF YOU ASK ME WHAT I THINK HE REALLY WANTS--

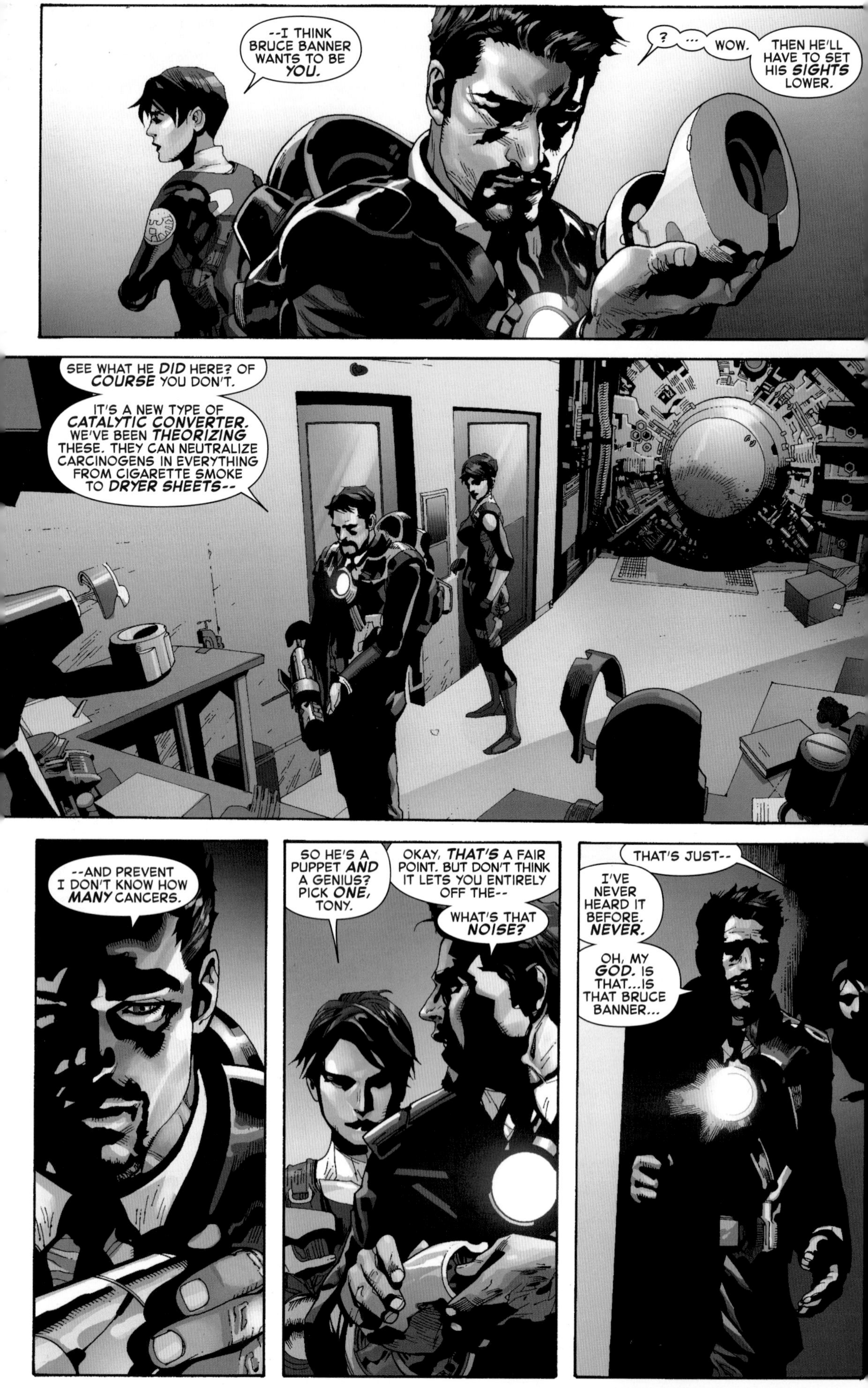
--I THINK BRUCE BANNER WANTS TO BE YOU.
? ...
WOW.
THEN HE'LL HAVE TO SET HIS SIGHTS LOWER.
SEE WHAT HE DID HERE? OF COURSE YOU DON'T.
IT'S A NEW TYPE OF CATALYTIC CONVERTER. WE'VE BEEN THEORIZING THESE. THEY CAN NEUTRALIZE CARCINOGENS IN EVERYTHING FROM CIGARETTE SMOKE TO DRYER SHEETS--
--AND PREVENT I DON'T KNOW HOW MANY CANCERS.
SO HE'S A PUPPET AND A GENIUS? PICK ONE, TONY.
OKAY, THAT'S A FAIR POINT. BUT DON'T THINK IT LETS YOU ENTIRELY OFF THE--
WHAT'S THAT NOISE?
THAT'S JUST--
I'VE NEVER HEARD IT BEFORE. NEVER.
OH, MY GOD. IS THAT...IS THAT BRUCE BANNER...

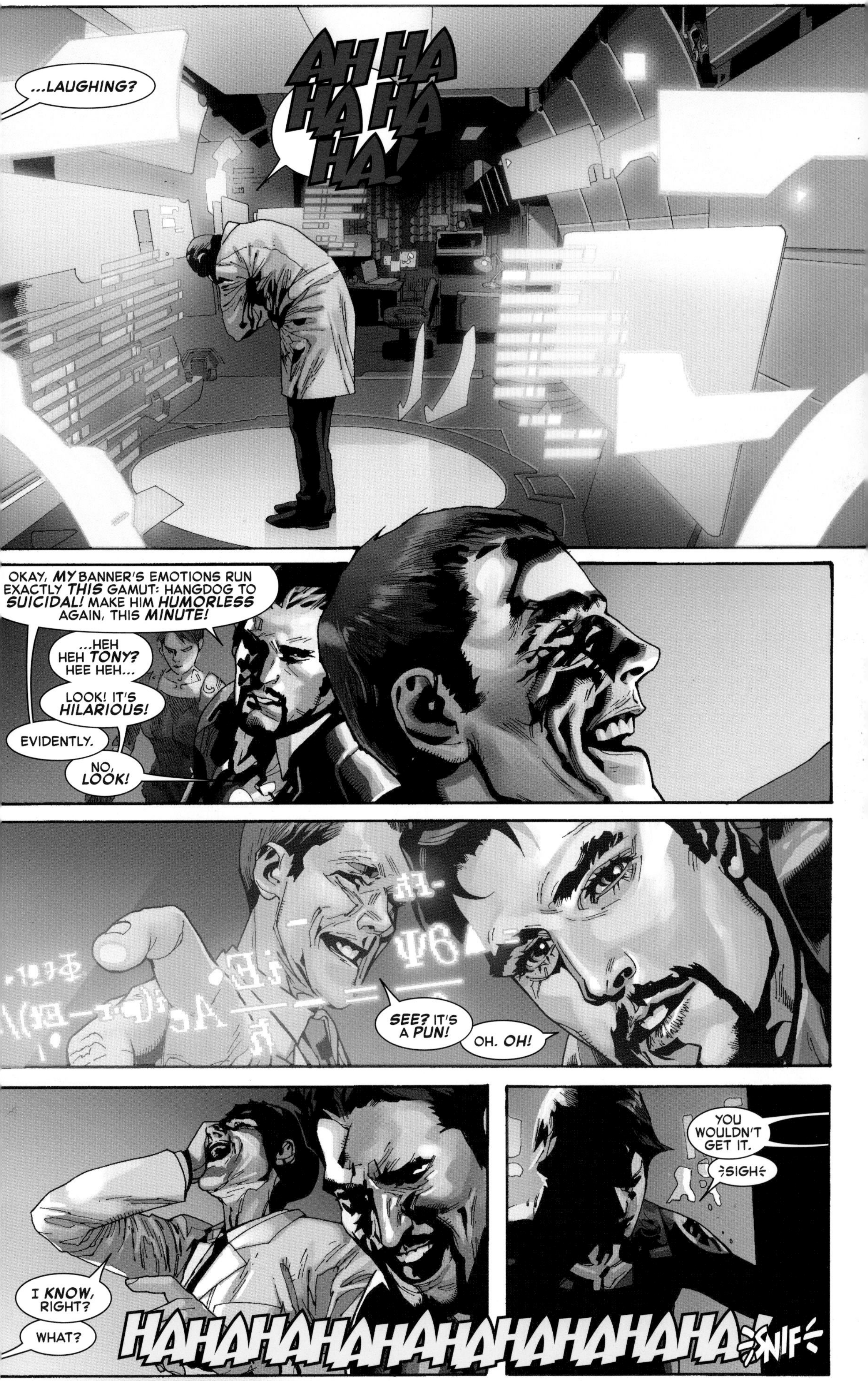
...LAUGHING?
AH HA HA HA HA HA!
OKAY, MY BANNER'S EMOTIONS RUN EXACTLY THIS GAMUT: HANGDOG TO SUICIDAL! MAKE HIM HUMORLESS AGAIN, THIS MINUTE!
...HEH HEH TONY? HEE HEH...
LOOK! IT'S HILARIOUS!
EVIDENTLY.
NO, LOOK!
SEE? IT'S A PUN!
OH. OH!
I KNOW, RIGHT?
WHAT?
HAHAHAHAHAHAHAHAHAHAHAHA!
YOU WOULDN'T GET IT.
SIGH
SNIF

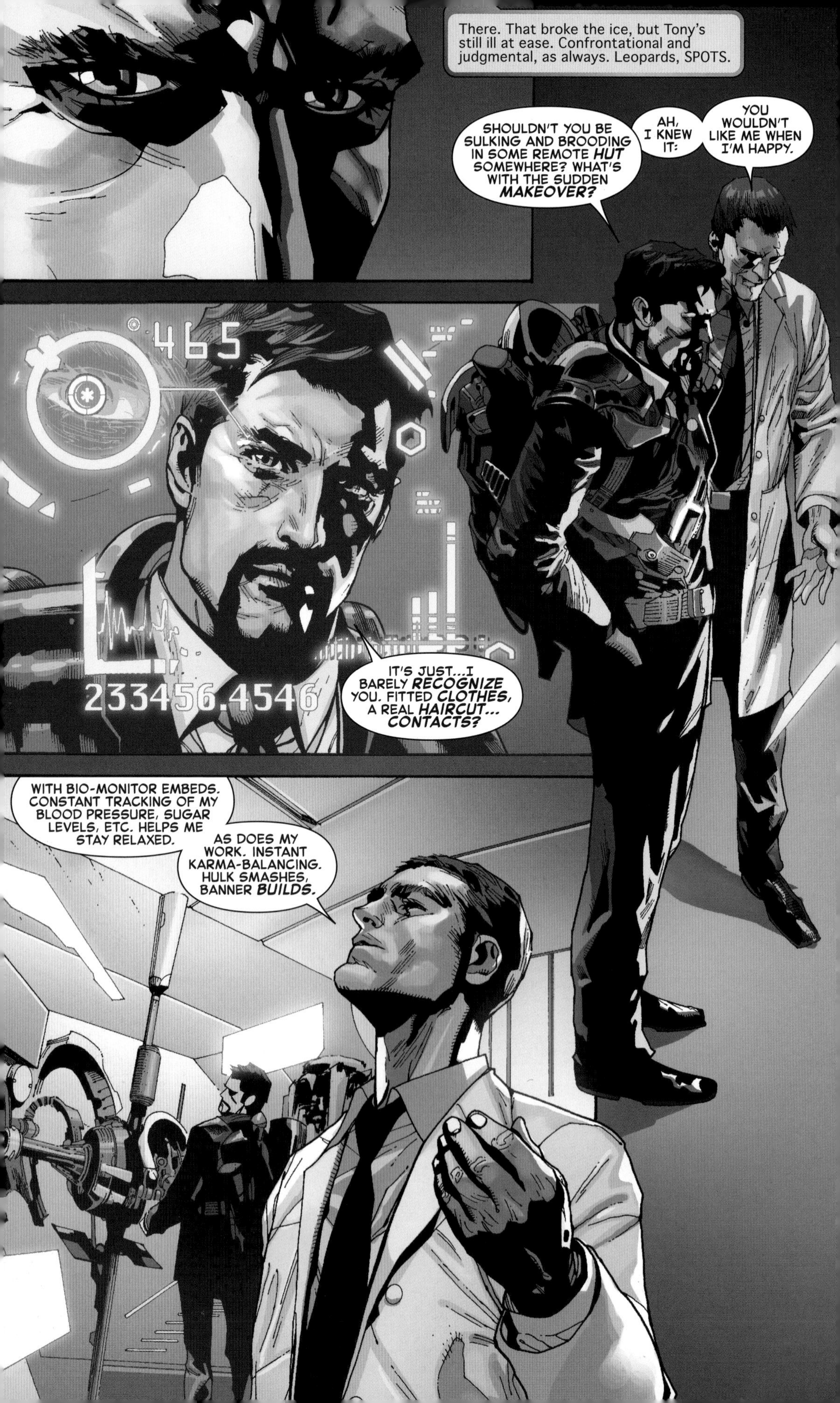
There. That broke the ice, but Tony's still ill at ease. Confrontational and judgmental, as always. Leopards, SPOTS.
SHOULDN'T YOU BE SULKING AND BROODING IN SOME REMOTE HUT SOMEWHERE? WHAT'S WITH THE SUDDEN MAKEOVER?
AH, I KNEW IT:
YOU WOULDN'T LIKE ME WHEN I'M HAPPY.
465
233456.4546
IT'S JUST...I BARELY RECOGNIZE YOU. FITTED CLOTHES, A REAL HAIRCUT... CONTACTS?
WITH BIO-MONITOR EMBEDS. CONSTANT TRACKING OF MY BLOOD PRESSURE, SUGAR LEVELS, ETC. HELPS ME STAY RELAXED.
AS DOES MY WORK. INSTANT KARMA-BALANCING. HULK SMASHES, BANNER BUILDS.

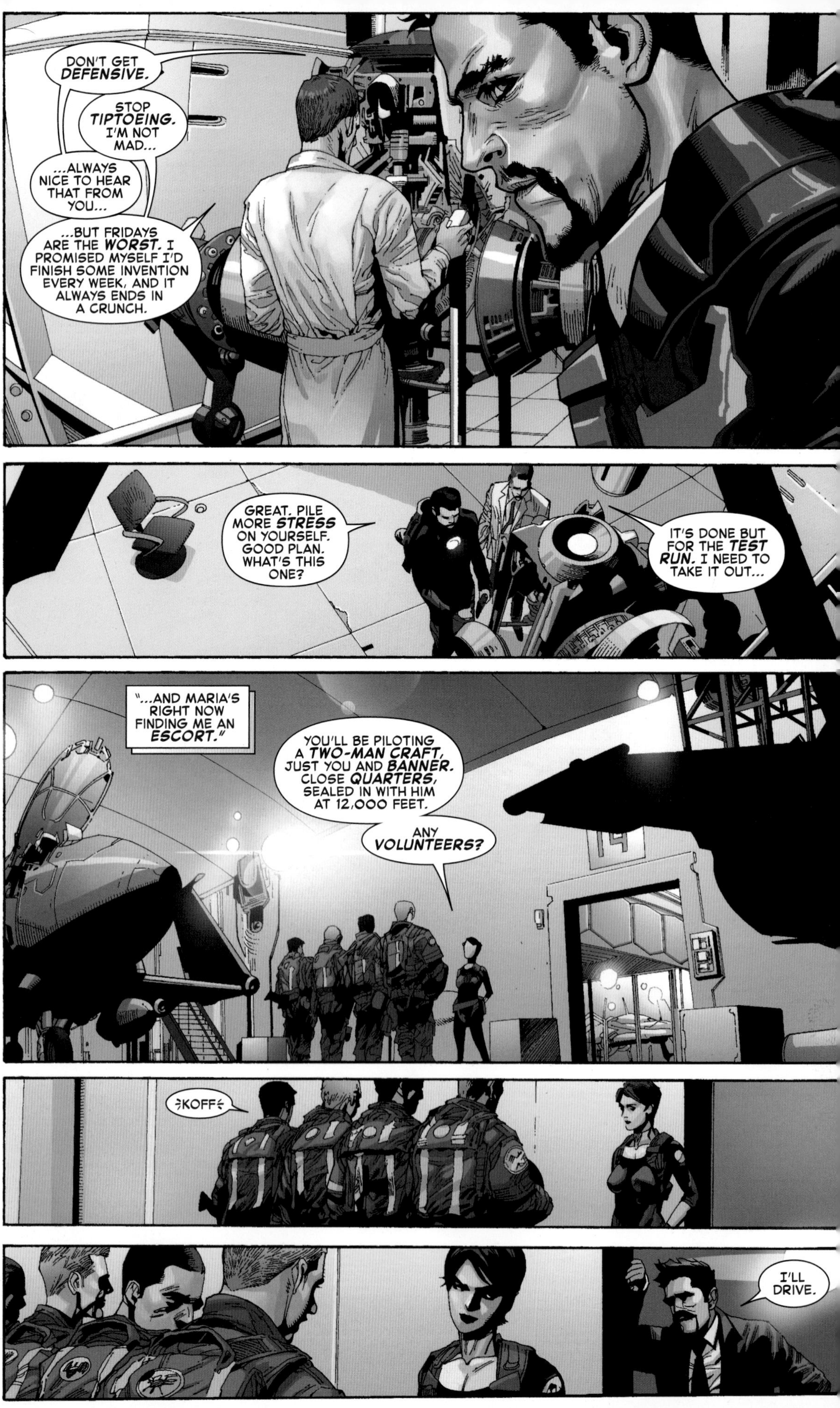
DON'T GET DEFENSIVE.
STOP TIPTOEING. I'M NOT MAD...
...ALWAYS NICE TO HEAR THAT FROM YOU...
...BUT FRIDAYS ARE THE WORST. I PROMISED MYSELF I'D FINISH SOME INVENTION EVERY WEEK, AND IT ALWAYS ENDS IN A CRUNCH.
GREAT. PILE MORE STRESS ON YOURSELF. GOOD PLAN. WHAT'S THIS ONE?
IT'S DONE BUT FOR THE TEST RUN. I NEED TO TAKE IT OUT...
"...AND MARIA'S RIGHT NOW FINDING ME AN ESCORT."
YOU'LL BE PILOTING A TWO-MAN CRAFT, JUST YOU AND BANNER. CLOSE QUARTERS, SEALED IN WITH HIM AT 12,000 FEET.
ANY VOLUNTEERS?
KOFF
I'LL DRIVE.

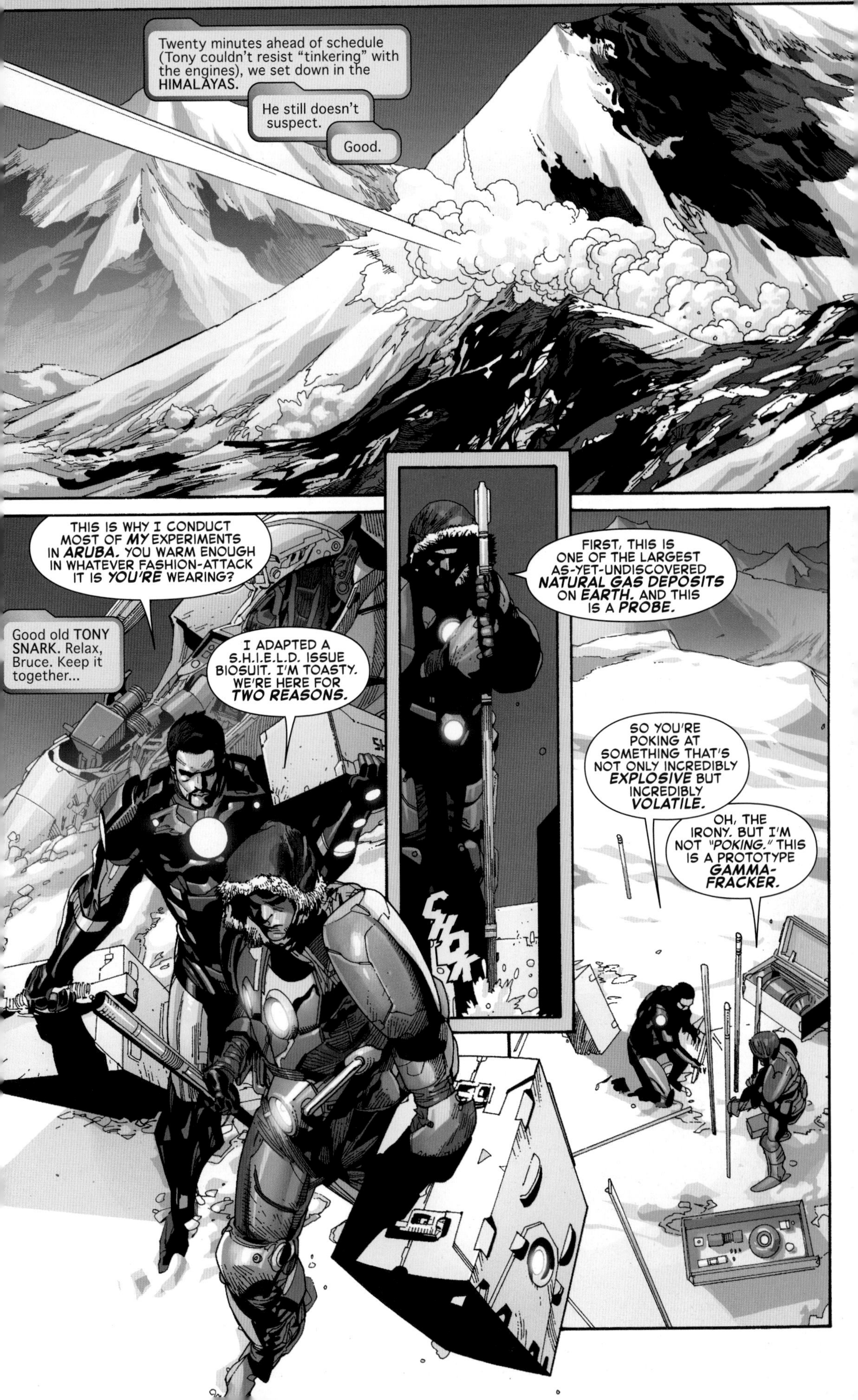
Twenty minutes ahead of schedule (Tony couldn't resist "tinkering" with the engines), we set down in the HIMALAYAS.
He still doesn't suspect.
Good.
THIS IS WHY I CONDUCT MOST OF MY EXPERIMENTS IN ARUBA. YOU WARM ENOUGH IN WHATEVER FASHION-ATTACK IT IS YOU'RE WEARING?
Good old TONY SNARK. Relax, Bruce. Keep it together...
I ADAPTED A S.H.I.E.L.D. ISSUE BIOSUIT. I'M TOASTY. WE'RE HERE FOR TWO REASONS.
FIRST, THIS IS ONE OF THE LARGEST AS-YET-UNDISCOVERED NATURAL GAS DEPOSITS ON EARTH. AND THIS IS A PROBE.
SHOK
SO YOU'RE POKING AT SOMETHING THAT'S NOT ONLY INCREDIBLY EXPLOSIVE BUT INCREDIBLY VOLATILE.
OH, THE IRONY. BUT I'M NOT "POKING." THIS IS A PROTOTYPE GAMMA-FRACKER.

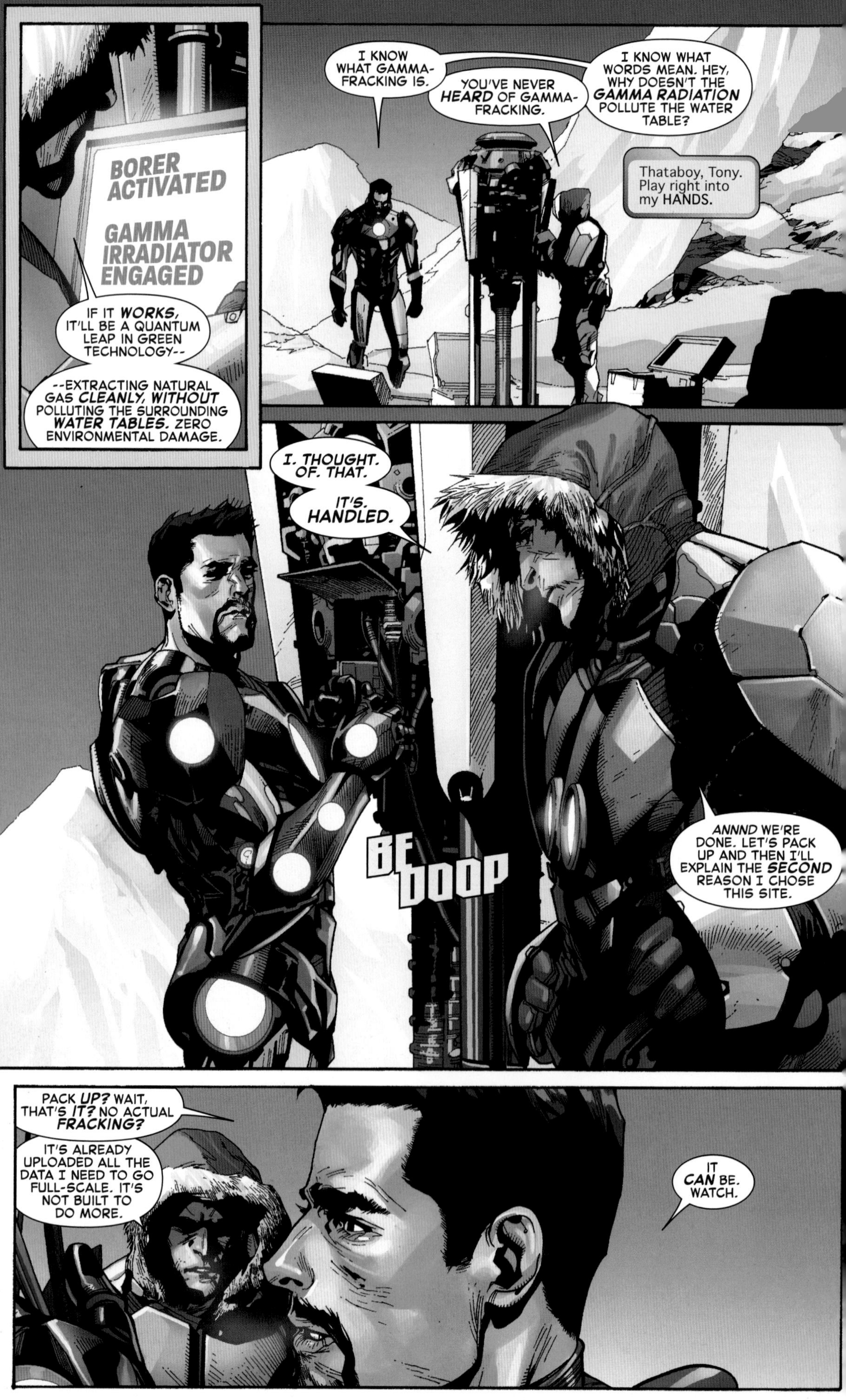
BORER ACTIVATED
GAMMA IRRADIATOR ENGAGED
IF IT WORKS, IT'LL BE A QUANTUM LEAP IN GREEN TECHNOLOGY--
--EXTRACTING NATURAL GAS CLEANLY, WITHOUT POLLUTING THE SURROUNDING WATER TABLES. ZERO ENVIRONMENTAL DAMAGE.
I KNOW WHAT GAMMA-FRACKING IS.
YOU'VE NEVER HEARD OF GAMMA-FRACKING.
I KNOW WHAT WORDS MEAN. HEY, WHY DOESN'T THE GAMMA RADIATION POLLUTE THE WATER TABLE?
Thataboy, Tony. Play right into my HANDS.
I. THOUGHT. OF. THAT.
IT'S. HANDLED.
BE DOOP
ANNND WE'RE DONE. LET'S PACK UP AND THEN I'LL EXPLAIN THE SECOND REASON I CHOSE THIS SITE.
PACK UP? WAIT, THAT'S IT? NO ACTUAL FRACKING?
IT'S ALREADY UPLOADED ALL THE DATA I NEED TO GO FULL-SCALE. IT'S NOT BUILT TO DO MORE.
IT CAN BE. WATCH.

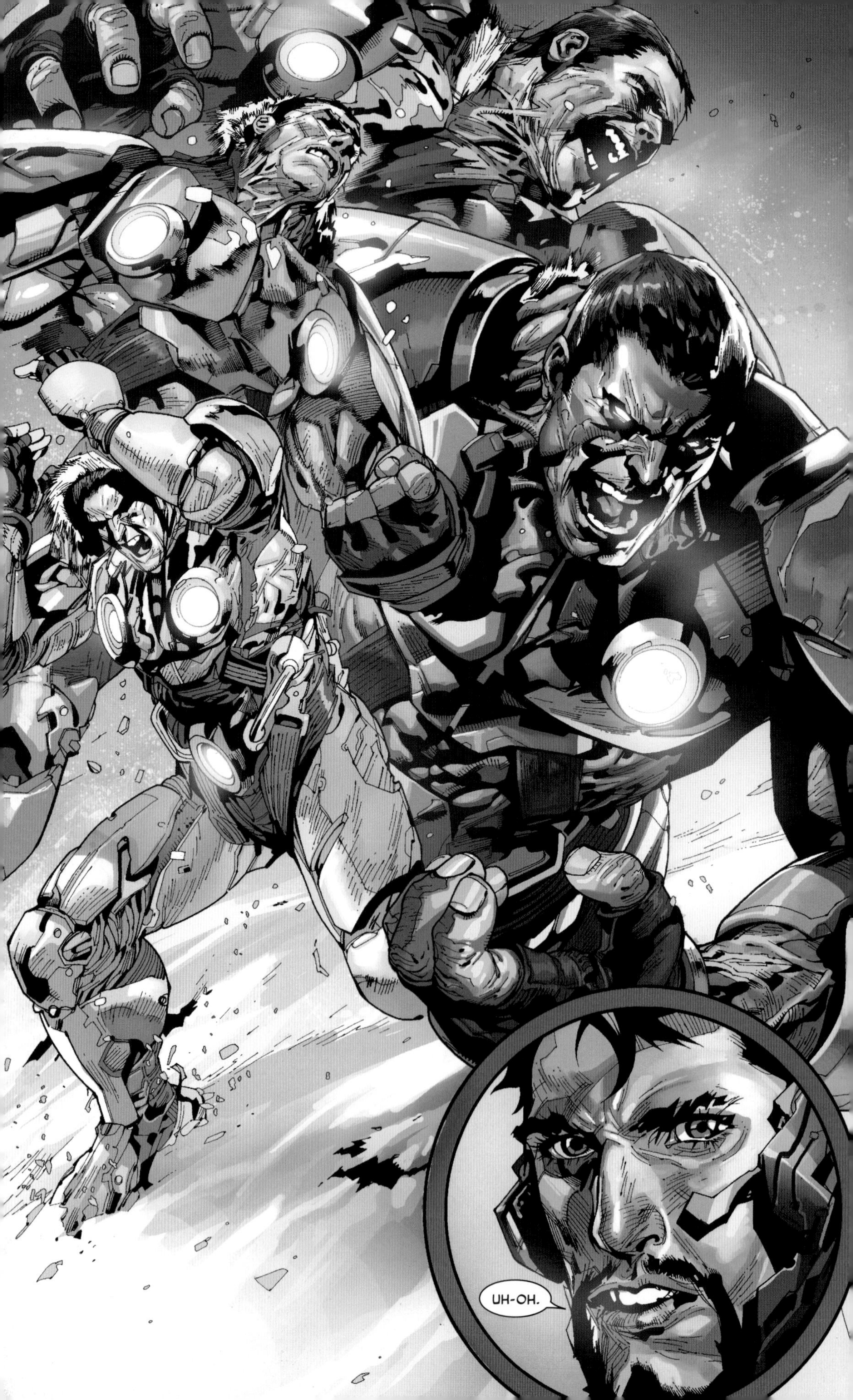
UH-OH.

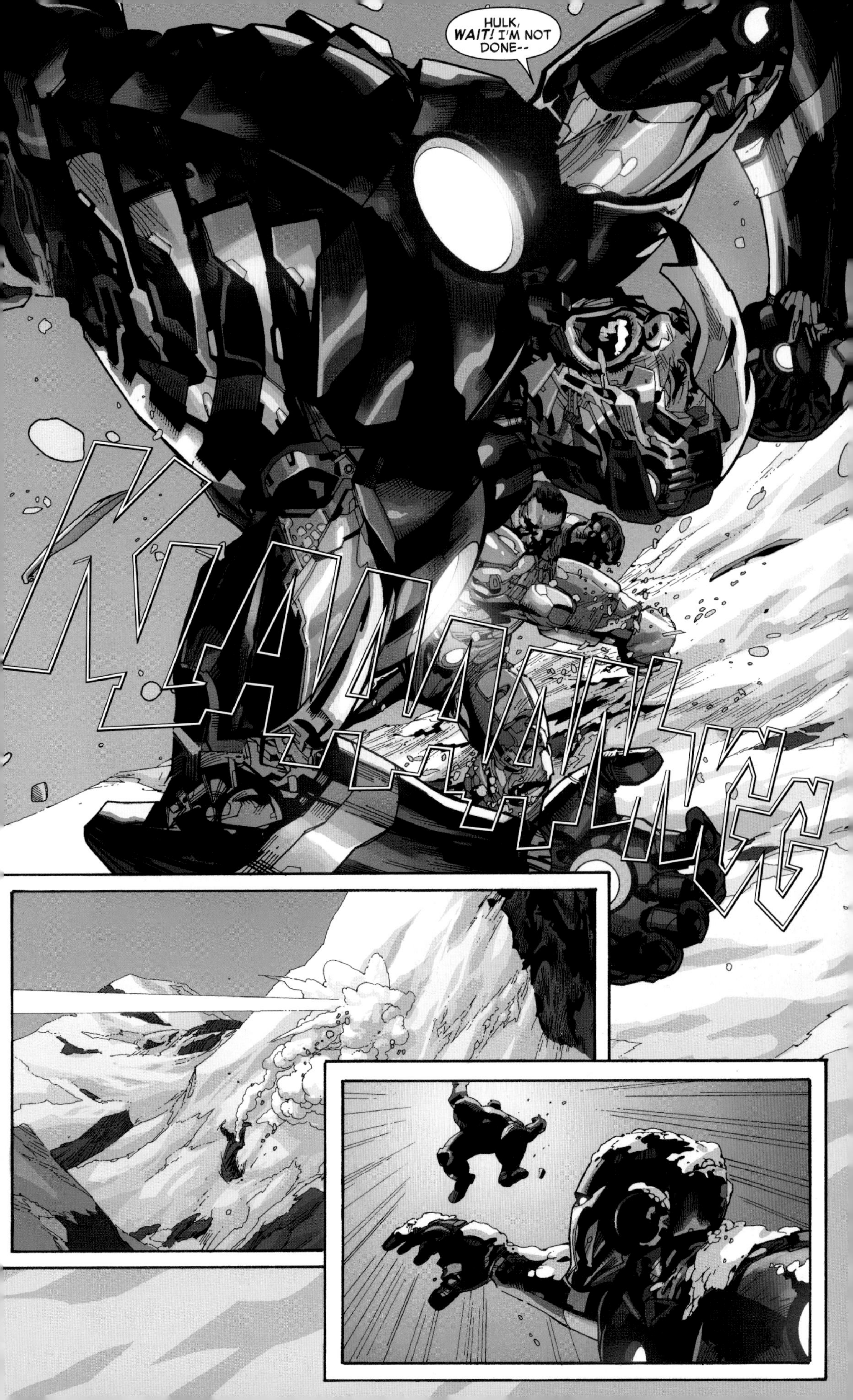
HULK, WAIT! I'M NOT DONE--
KRAAANNNNG

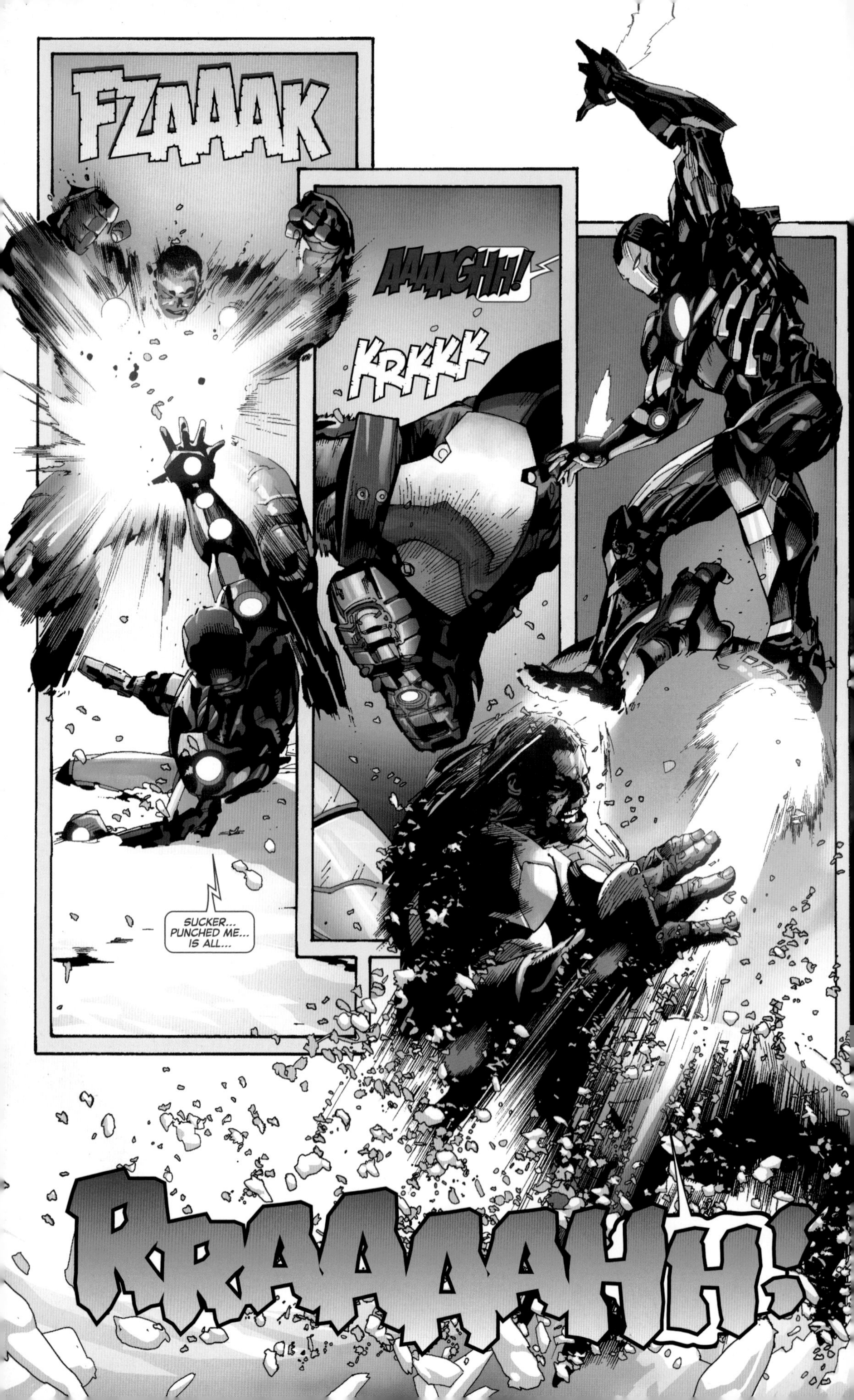
FZAAAK
AAAAGHH!
KRKKK
SUCKER... PUNCHED ME... IS ALL...
RRAAAAHH!

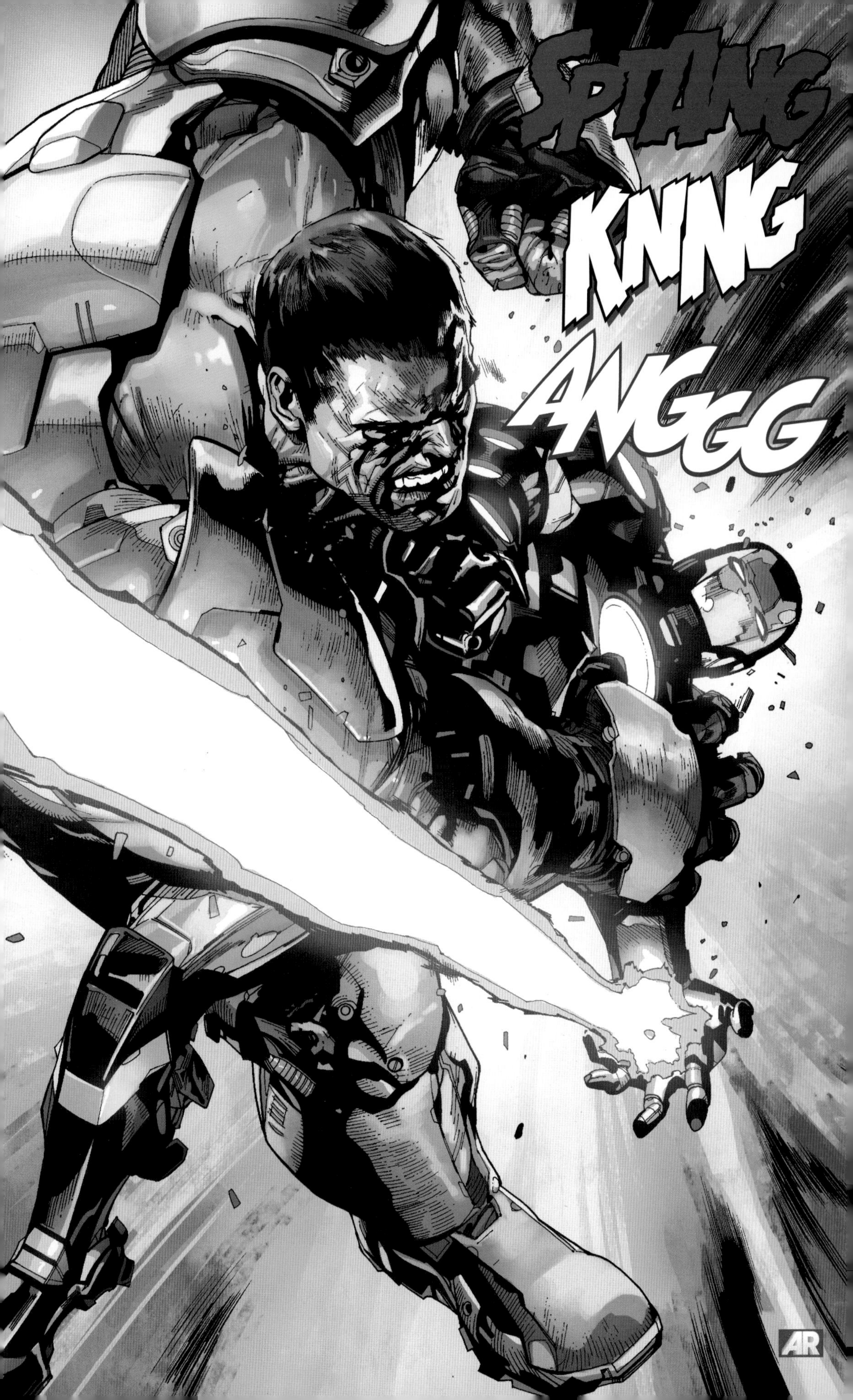
SPTANG
KNNG
ANGGG

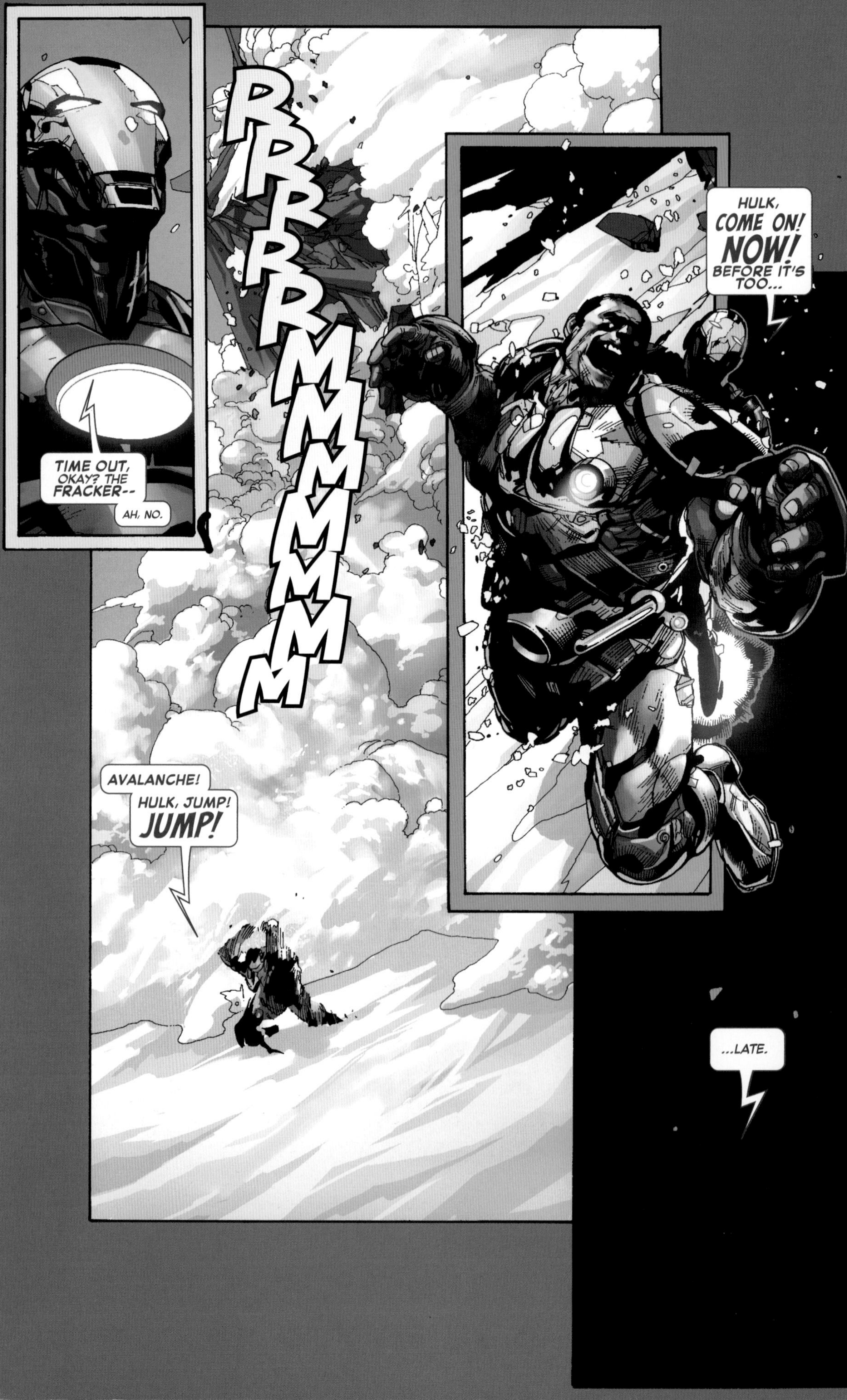
TIME OUT, OKAY? THE FRACKER--
AH, NO.
RRRRRMMMMMMM
HULK, COME ON! NOW! BEFORE IT'S TOO...
AVALANCHE!
HULK, JUMP! JUMP!
...LATE.

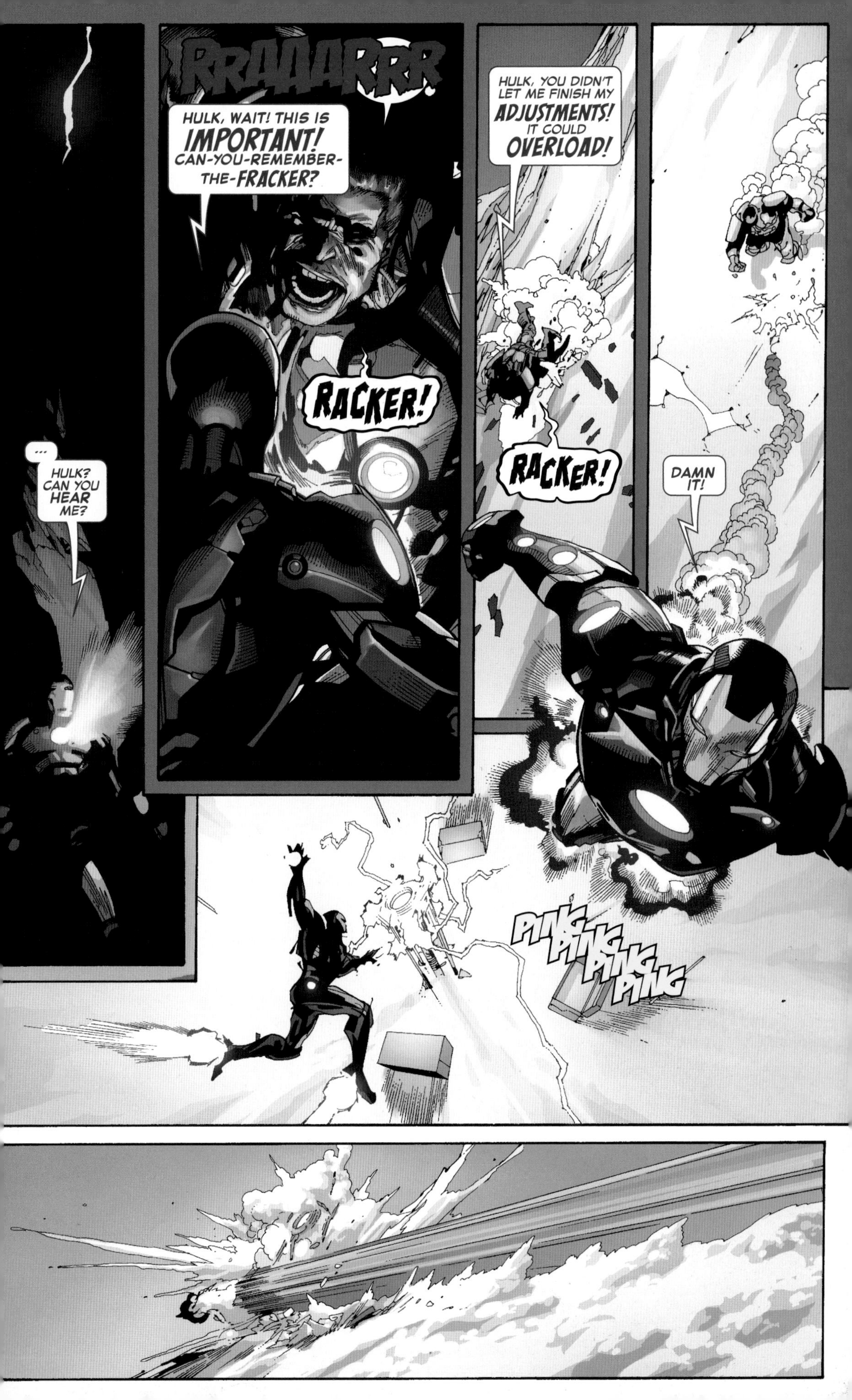
RRAAARRR
HULK, WAIT! THIS IS IMPORTANT! CAN-YOU-REMEMBER-THE-FRACKER?
RACKER!
HULK, YOU DIDN'T LET ME FINISH MY ADJUSTMENTS! IT COULD OVERLOAD!
RACKER!
DAMN IT!
... HULK? CAN YOU HEAR ME?
PING PING PING PING

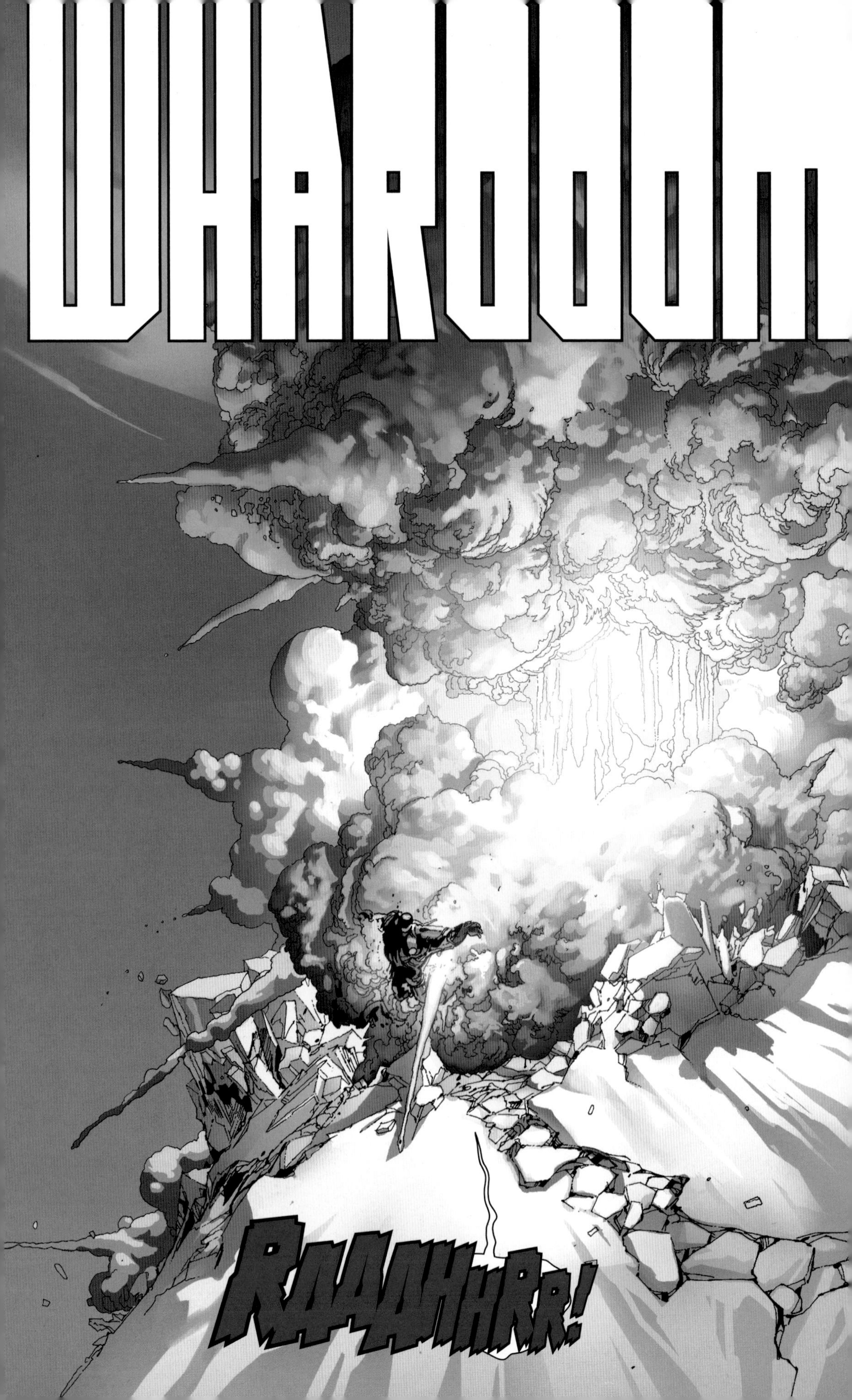
WHAROOOM
RAAAHHRR!

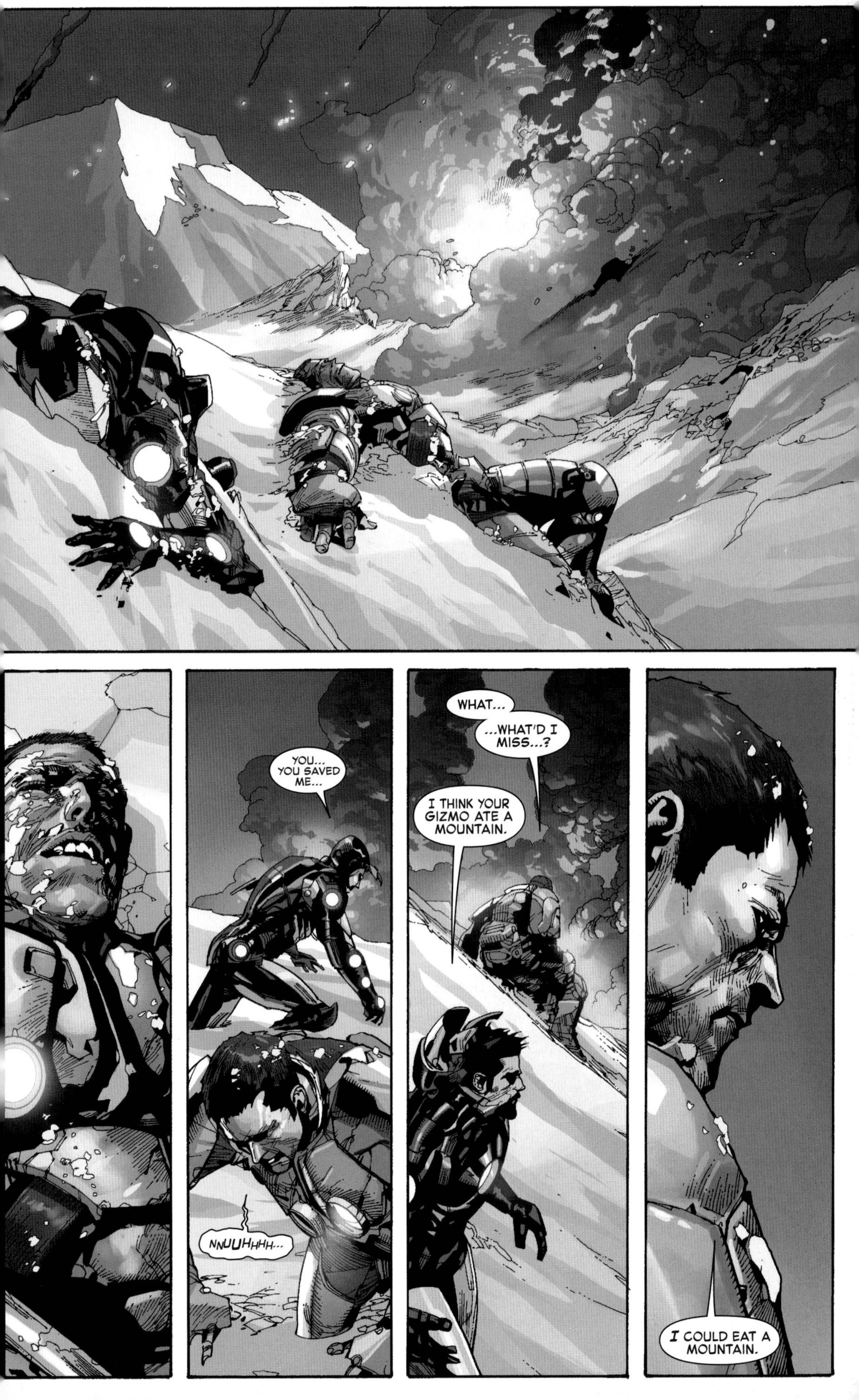

YOU... YOU SAVED ME...
NNUUHHHH...
WHAT...
...WHAT'D I MISS...?
I THINK YOUR GIZMO ATE A MOUNTAIN.
I COULD EAT A MOUNTAIN.

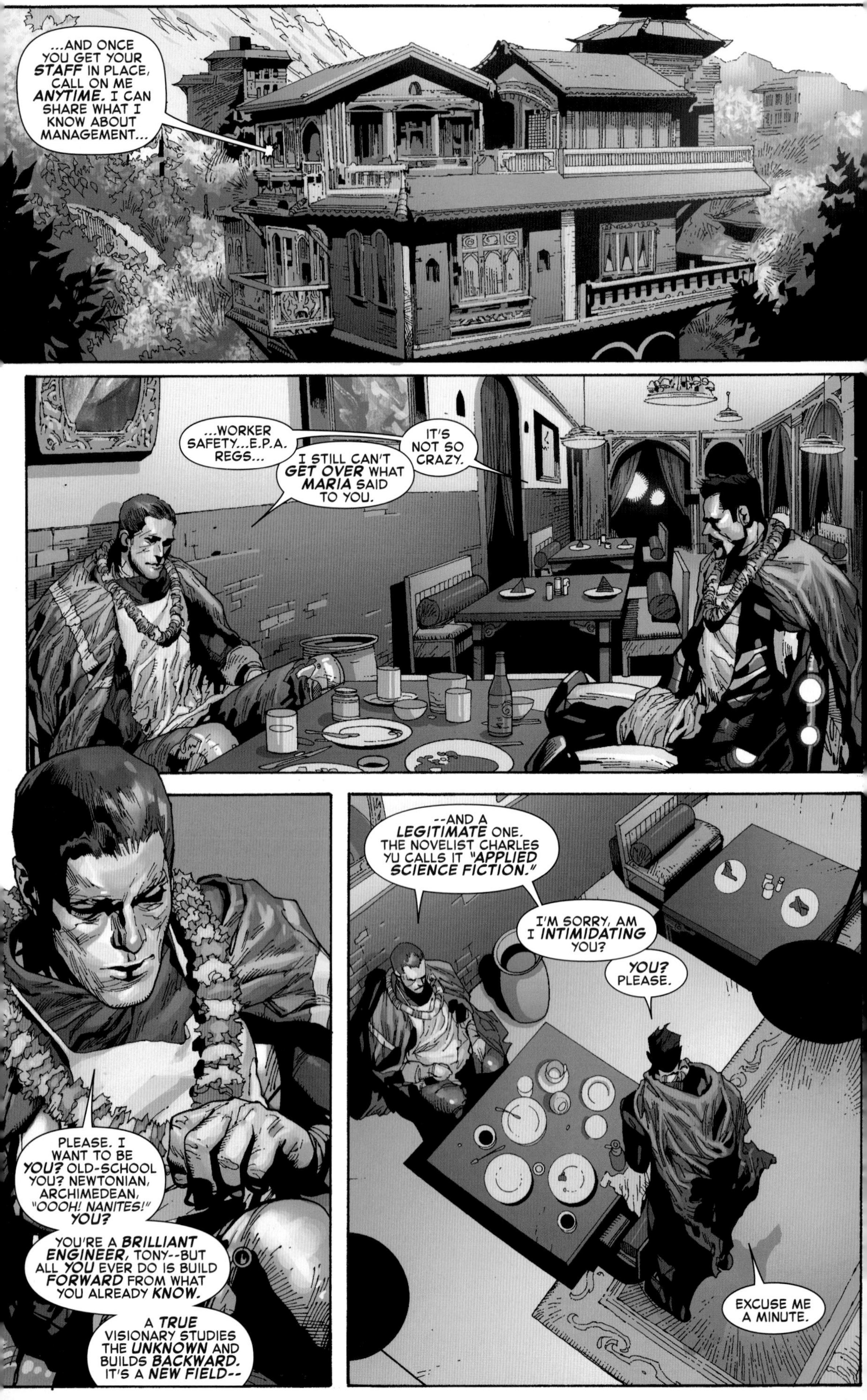
...AND ONCE YOU GET YOUR STAFF IN PLACE, CALL ON ME ANYTIME. I CAN SHARE WHAT I KNOW ABOUT MANAGEMENT...
...WORKER SAFETY...E.P.A. REGS...
I STILL CAN'T GET OVER WHAT MARIA SAID TO YOU.
IT'S NOT SO CRAZY.
PLEASE. I WANT TO BE YOU? OLD-SCHOOL YOU? NEWTONIAN, ARCHIMEDEAN, "OOOH! NANITES!" YOU?
YOU'RE A BRILLIANT ENGINEER, TONY--BUT ALL YOU EVER DO IS BUILD FORWARD FROM WHAT YOU ALREADY KNOW.
A TRUE VISIONARY STUDIES THE UNKNOWN AND BUILDS BACKWARD. IT'S A NEW FIELD--
--AND A LEGITIMATE ONE. THE NOVELIST CHARLES YU CALLS IT "APPLIED SCIENCE FICTION."
I'M SORRY, AM I INTIMIDATING YOU?
YOU? PLEASE.
EXCUSE ME A MINUTE.

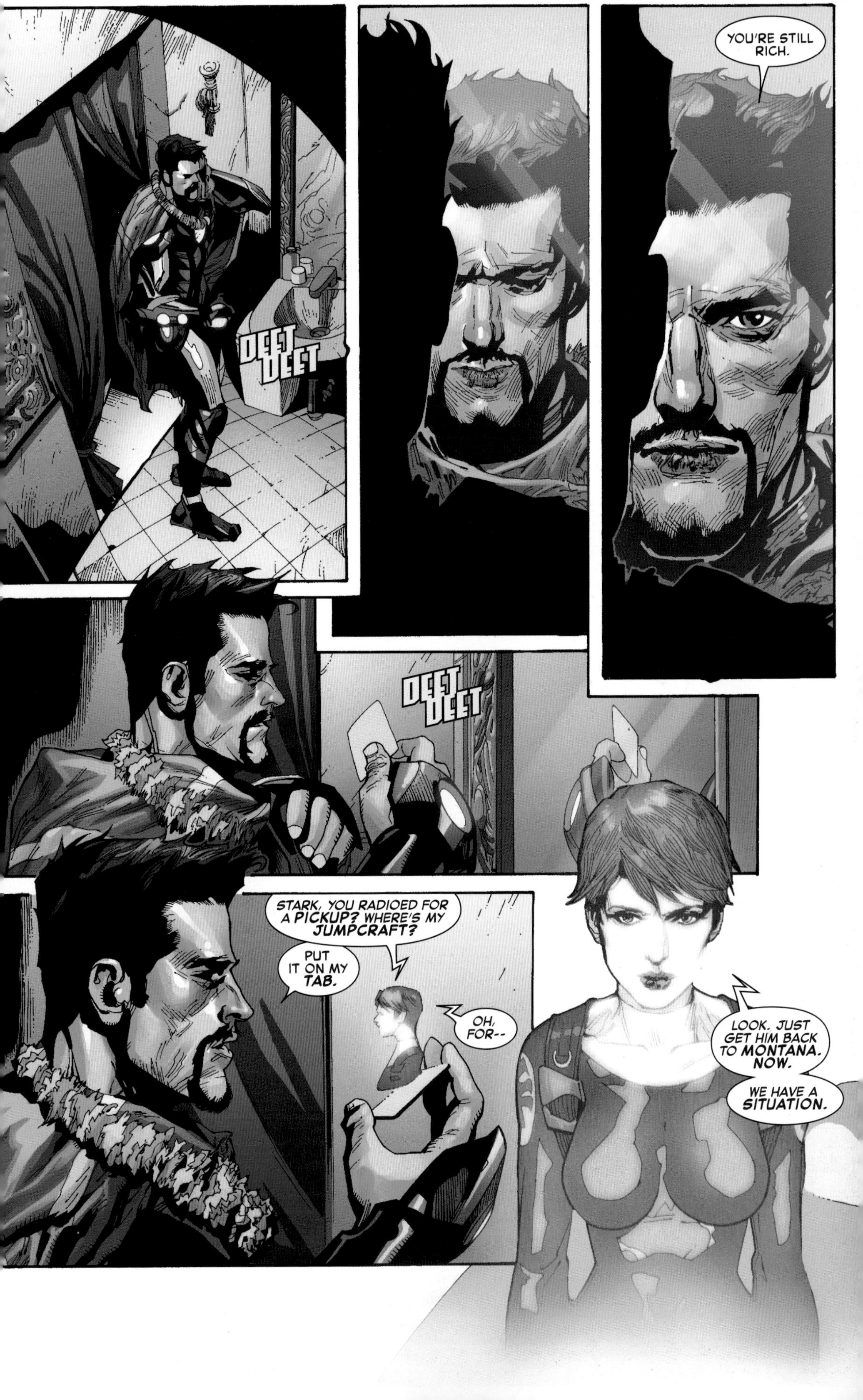

DEET DEET
YOU'RE STILL RICH.
DEET DEET
STARK, YOU RADIOED FOR A PICKUP? WHERE'S MY JUMPCRAFT?
PUT IT ON MY TAB.
OH, FOR--
LOOK. JUST GET HIM BACK TO MONTANA. NOW.
WE HAVE A SITUATION.

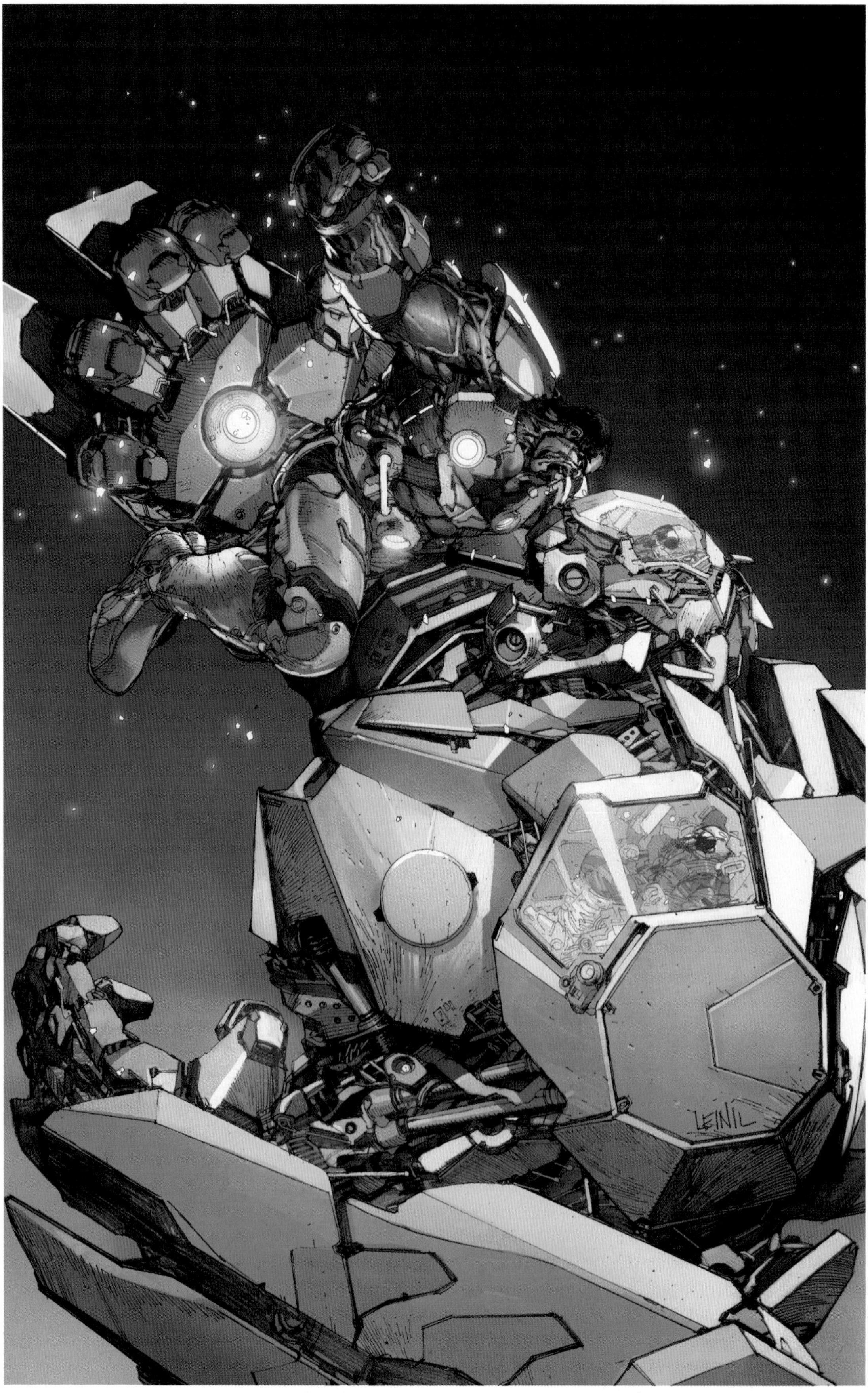
LEINIL

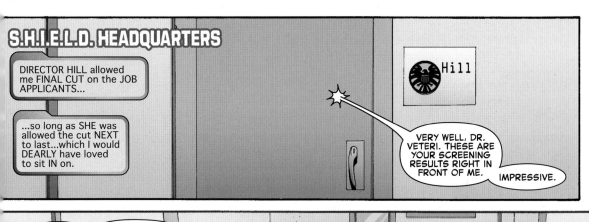

DIRECTOR HILL allowed me FINAL CUT on the JOB APPLICANTS...

...so long as SHE was allowed the cut NEXT to last...which I would DEARLY have loved to sit IN on.

Hill

VERY WELL, DR. VETERI. THESE ARE YOUR SCREENING RESULTS RIGHT IN FRONT OF ME. IMPRESSIVE.

JUST ONE FINAL GRILLING.

I HAVE A SERIES OF IMAGES TO SHOW YOU, AND I WANT TO GAUGE YOUR IMMEDIATE REACTIONS.

A RORSCHACH TEST?

IT'S...LIKE A RORSCHACH TEST. READY?

THAT'S-- THAT'S THE HULK, ISN'T IT--? MY GOD...!

SO NOTED. NEXT:

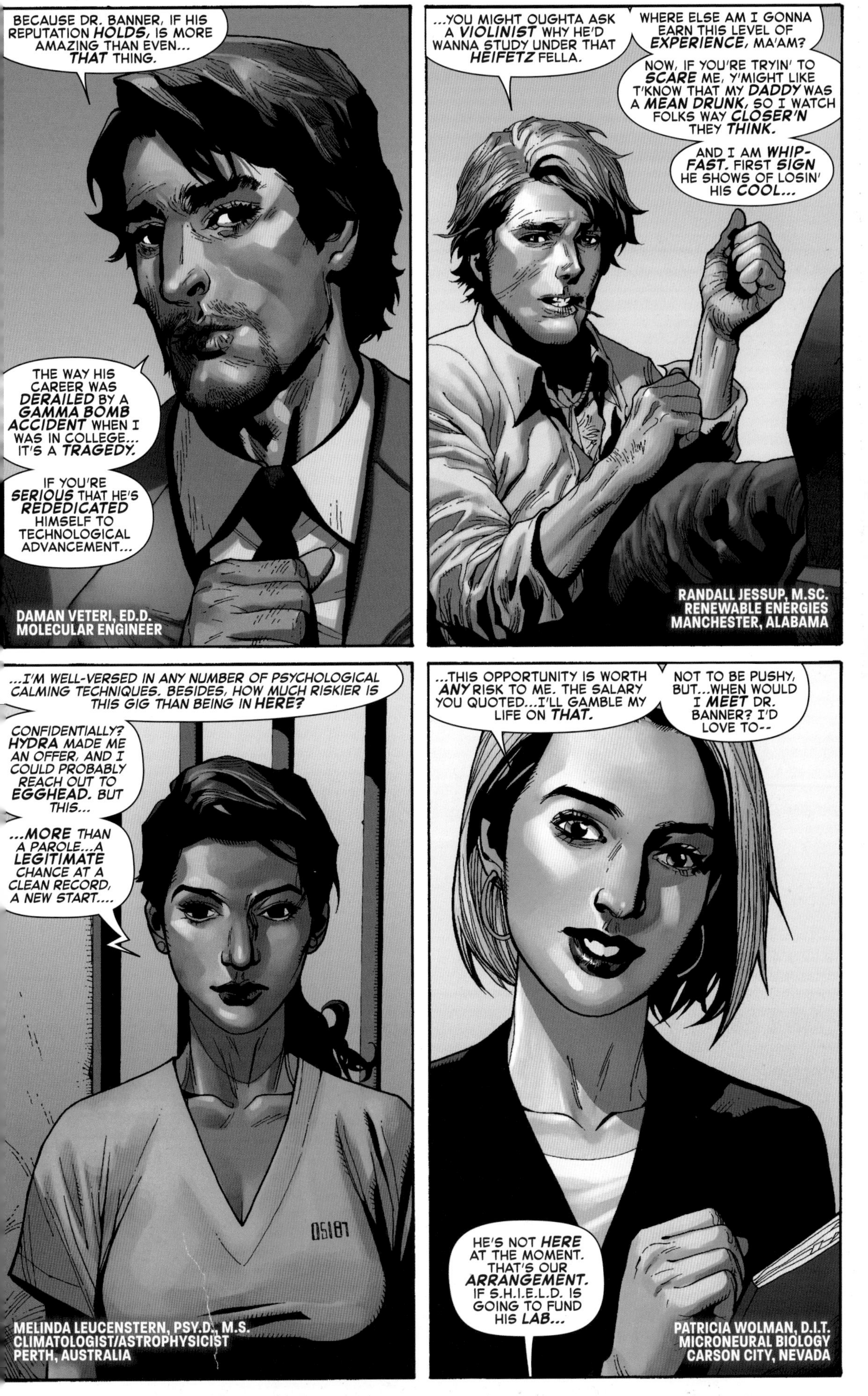
BECAUSE DR. BANNER, IF HIS REPUTATION HOLDS, IS MORE AMAZING THAN EVEN... THAT THING.
THE WAY HIS CAREER WAS DERAILED BY A GAMMA BOMB ACCIDENT WHEN I WAS IN COLLEGE... IT'S A TRAGEDY.
IF YOU'RE SERIOUS THAT HE'S REDEDICATED HIMSELF TO TECHNOLOGICAL ADVANCEMENT...
DAMAN VETERI, ED.D.
MOLECULAR ENGINEER
...YOU MIGHT OUGHTA ASK A VIOLINIST WHY HE'D WANNA STUDY UNDER THAT HEIFETZ FELLA.
WHERE ELSE AM I GONNA EARN THIS LEVEL OF EXPERIENCE, MA'AM?
NOW, IF YOU'RE TRYIN' TO SCARE ME, Y'MIGHT LIKE T'KNOW THAT MY DADDY WAS A MEAN DRUNK, SO I WATCH FOLKS WAY CLOSER'N THEY THINK.
AND I AM WHIP-FAST. FIRST SIGN HE SHOWS OF LOSIN' HIS COOL...
RANDALL JESSUP, M.SC.
RENEWABLE ENERGIES
MANCHESTER, ALABAMA
...I'M WELL-VERSED IN ANY NUMBER OF PSYCHOLOGICAL CALMING TECHNIQUES. BESIDES, HOW MUCH RISKIER IS THIS GIG THAN BEING IN HERE?
CONFIDENTIALLY? HYDRA MADE ME AN OFFER, AND I COULD PROBABLY REACH OUT TO EGGHEAD. BUT THIS...
...MORE THAN A PAROLE...A LEGITIMATE CHANCE AT A CLEAN RECORD, A NEW START....
05187
MELINDA LEUCENSTERN, PSY.D., M.S.
CLIMATOLOGIST/ASTROPHYSICIST
PERTH, AUSTRALIA
...THIS OPPORTUNITY IS WORTH ANY RISK TO ME. THE SALARY YOU QUOTED...I'LL GAMBLE MY LIFE ON THAT.
NOT TO BE PUSHY, BUT...WHEN WOULD I MEET DR. BANNER? I'D LOVE TO--
HE'S NOT HERE AT THE MOMENT. THAT'S OUR ARRANGEMENT. IF S.H.I.E.L.D. IS GOING TO FUND HIS LAB...
PATRICIA WOLMAN, D.I.T.
MICRONEURAL BIOLOGY
CARSON CITY, NEVADA

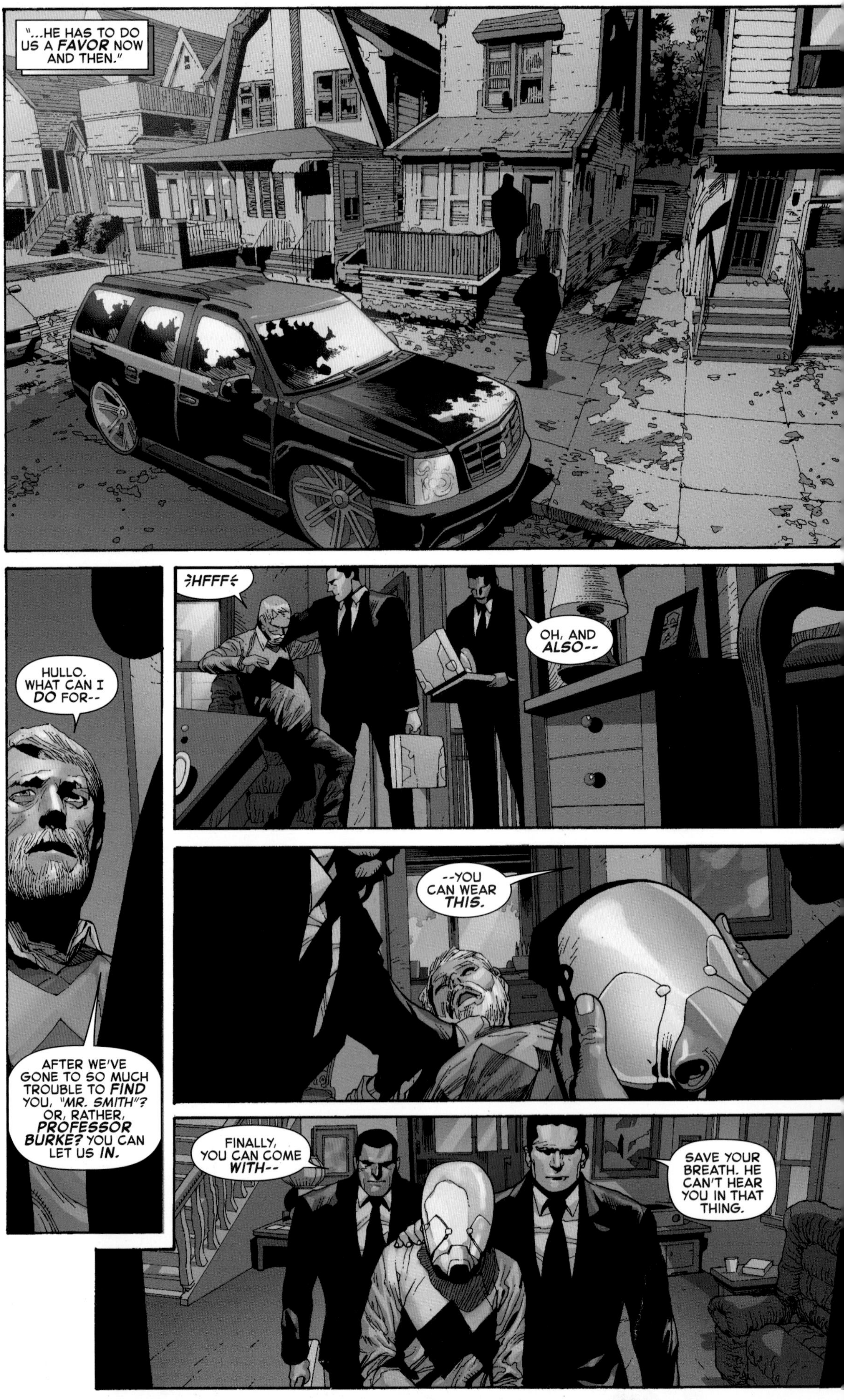
"...HE HAS TO DO US A FAVOR NOW AND THEN."
HULLO. WHAT CAN I DO FOR--
AFTER WE'VE GONE TO SO MUCH TROUBLE TO FIND YOU, "MR. SMITH"? OR, RATHER, PROFESSOR BURKE? YOU CAN LET US IN.
HFFF
OH, AND ALSO--
--YOU CAN WEAR THIS.
FINALLY, YOU CAN COME WITH--
SAVE YOUR BREATH. HE CAN'T HEAR YOU IN THAT THING.

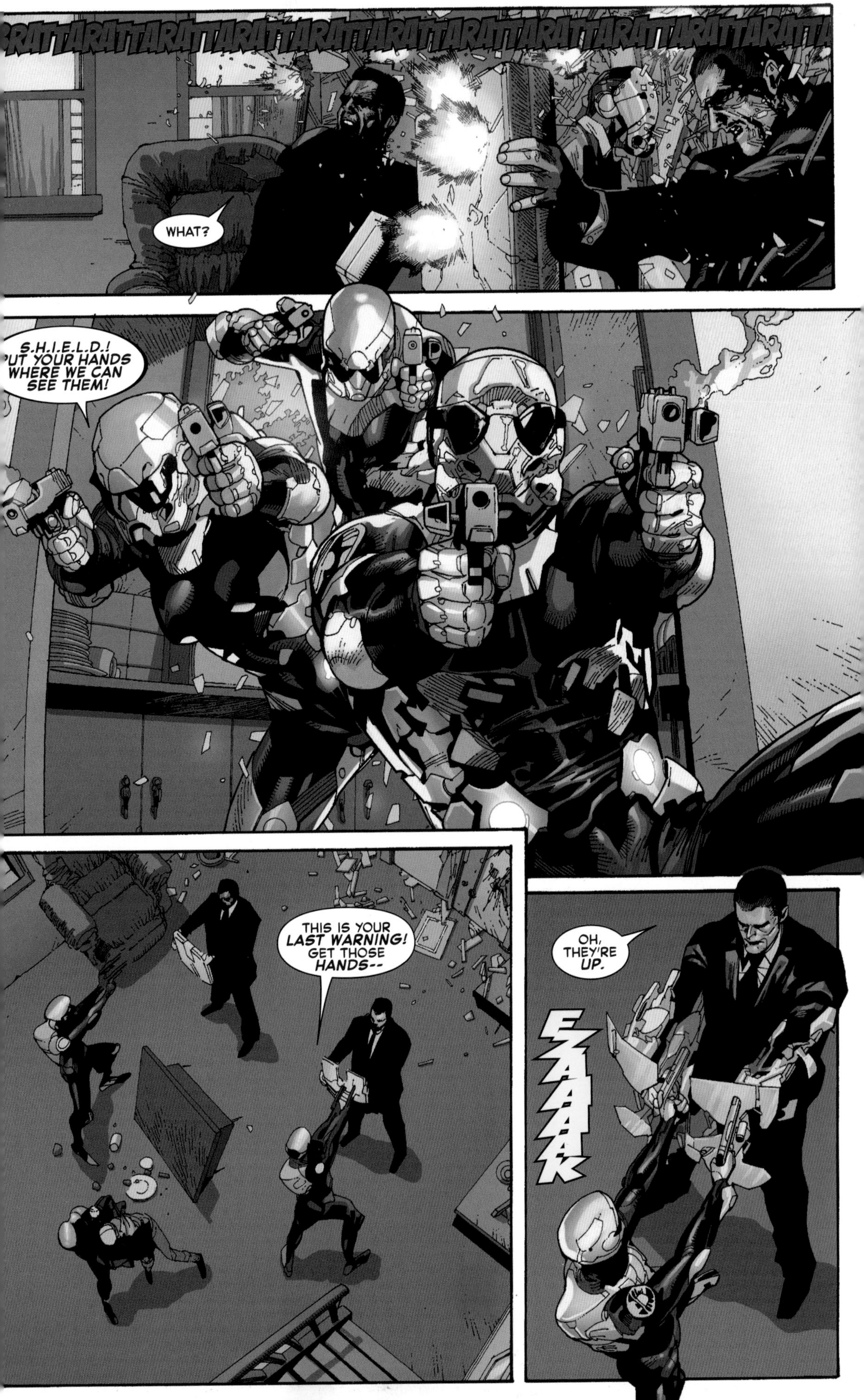
BRATTARATTARATTARATTARATTARATTARATTARATTA
WHAT?
S.H.I.E.L.D.! PUT YOUR HANDS WHERE WE CAN SEE THEM!
THIS IS YOUR LAST WARNING! GET THOSE HANDS--
OH, THEY'RE UP.
ZZAAAAK

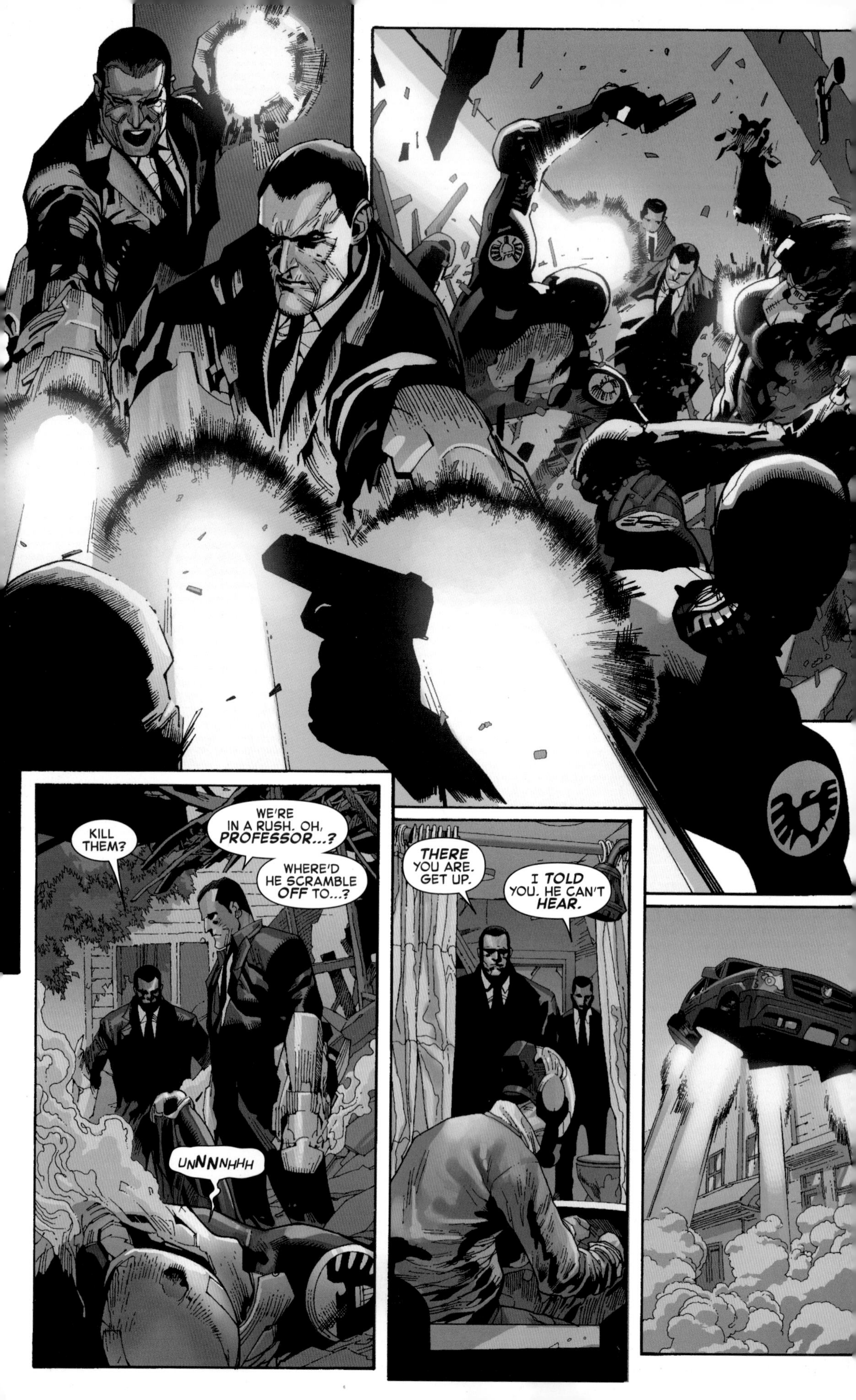
KILL THEM?
WE'RE IN A RUSH. OH, PROFESSOR...?
WHERE'D HE SCRAMBLE OFF TO...?
UNNNHHH
THERE YOU ARE. GET UP.
I TOLD YOU. HE CAN'T HEAR.

DEVIL'S MOUTH, SOUTH PACIFIC

RESEARCH AND DEVELOPMENT SITE FOR
TECHNOLOGICAL TERRORIST GROUP A.I.M.

I WAS APPRISED AS TO YOUR LITTLE ACTION SCENE. WE'LL BE LUCKY IF YOU WEREN'T TAILED.

SHUT UP. HOW HAS THIS PROFESSION BECOME SO DEBASED?

WHAT YOU CALL ESPIONAGE, WE USED TO CALL FAILURE. NOW IT'S ALL CONSPICUOUS VIOLENCE, EXPENSIVE WEAPONRY--

MR. THIRTY-THREE, SIR, THAT'S IMPOSSI--

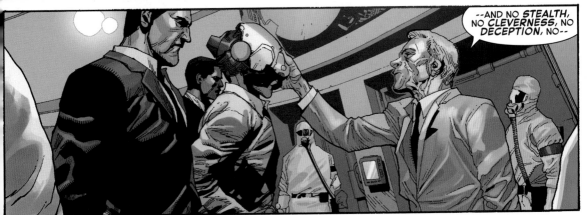

--AND NO STEALTH, NO CLEVERNESS, NO DECEPTION, NO--

WELL.

I STAND CORRECTED. THEY CALL ME COLIN THIRTY-THREE, SIR. AND WHO MIGHT YOU BE?

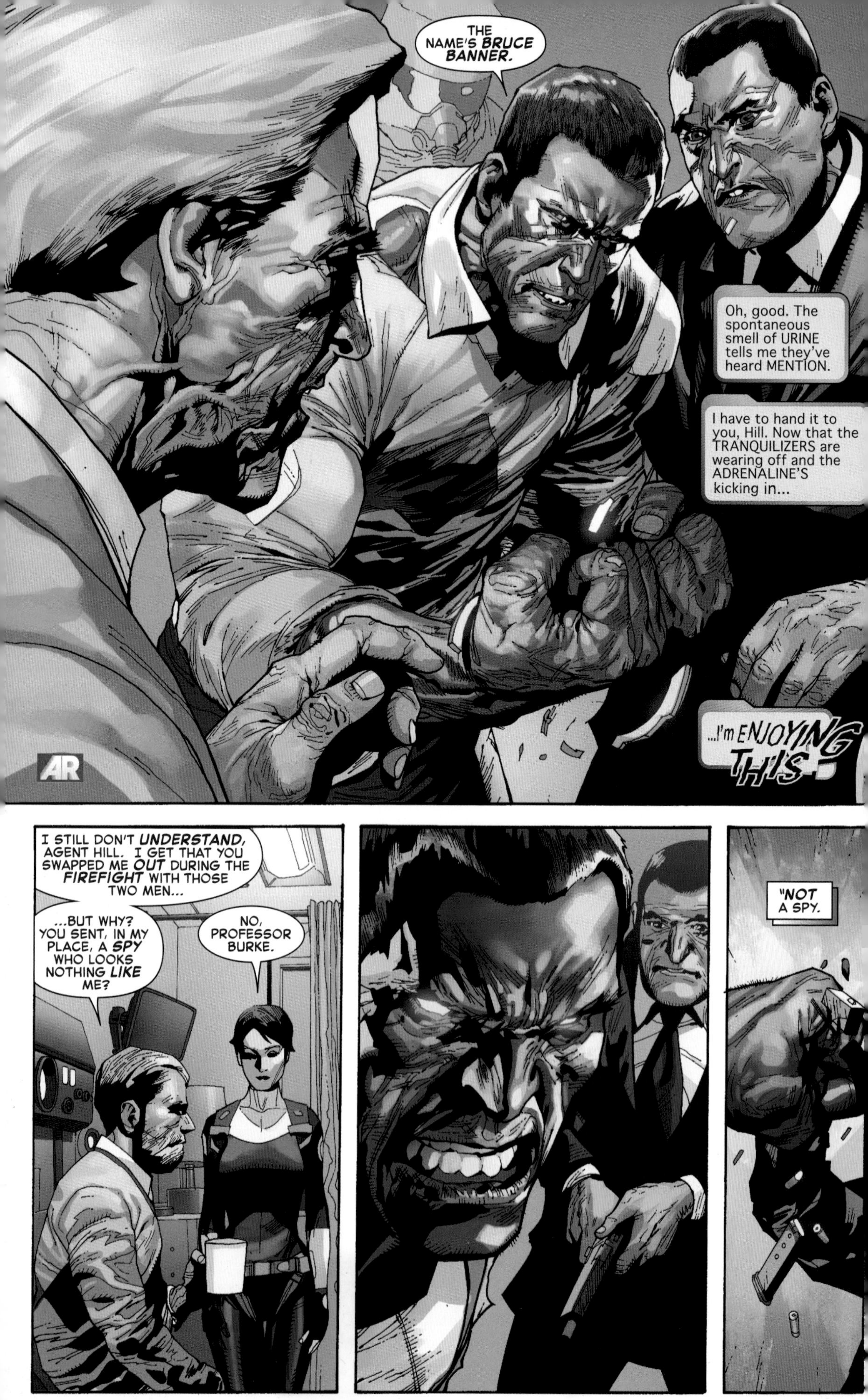
THE NAME'S BRUCE BANNER.
Oh, good. The spontaneous smell of URINE tells me they've heard MENTION.
I have to hand it to you, Hill. Now that the TRANQUILIZERS are wearing off and the ADRENALINE'S kicking in...
...I'm ENJOYING THIS.
I STILL DON'T UNDERSTAND, AGENT HILL. I GET THAT YOU SWAPPED ME OUT DURING THE FIREFIGHT WITH THOSE TWO MEN...
...BUT WHY? YOU SENT, IN MY PLACE, A SPY WHO LOOKS NOTHING LIKE ME?
NO, PROFESSOR BURKE.
"NOT A SPY.

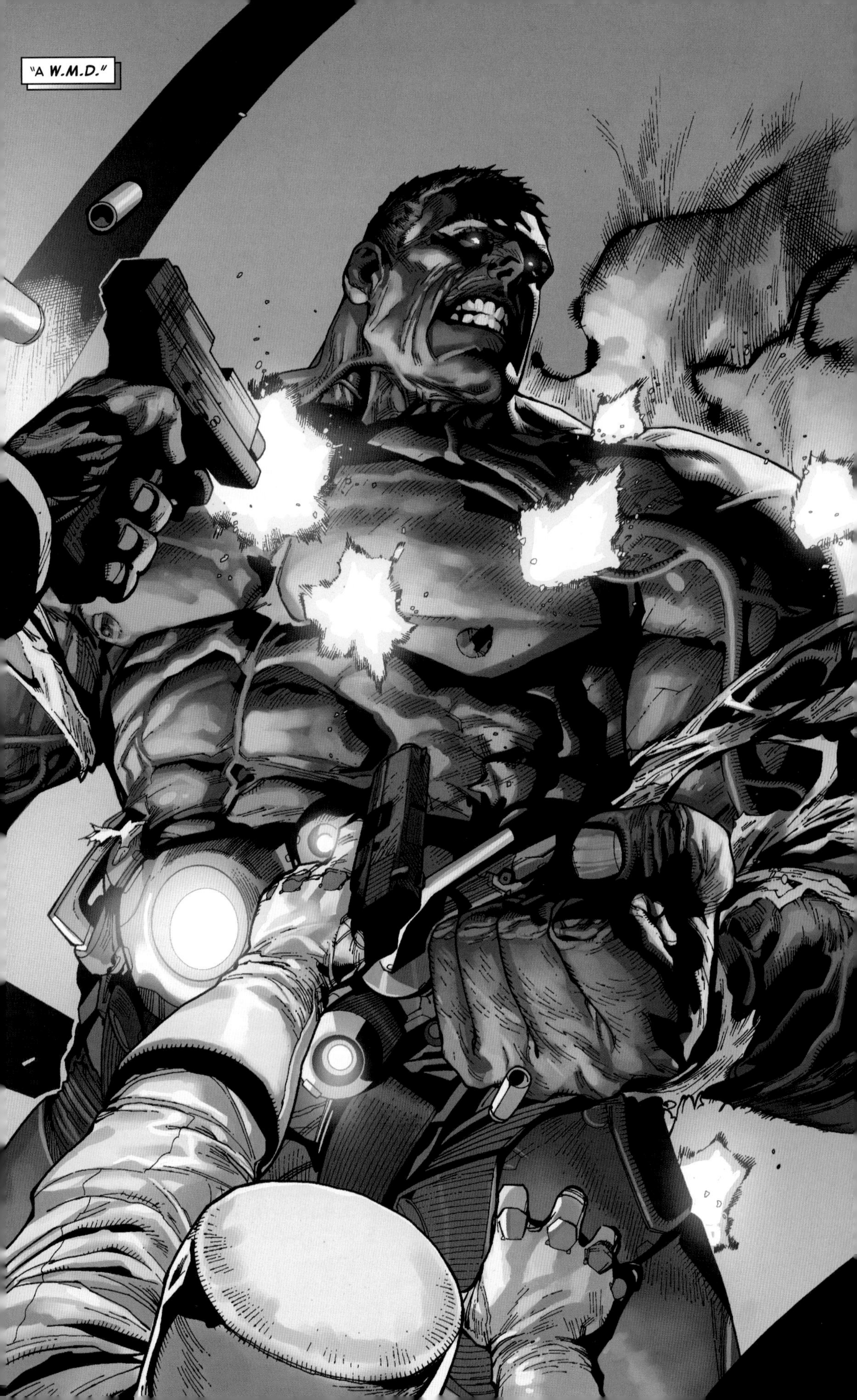
"A W.M.D."

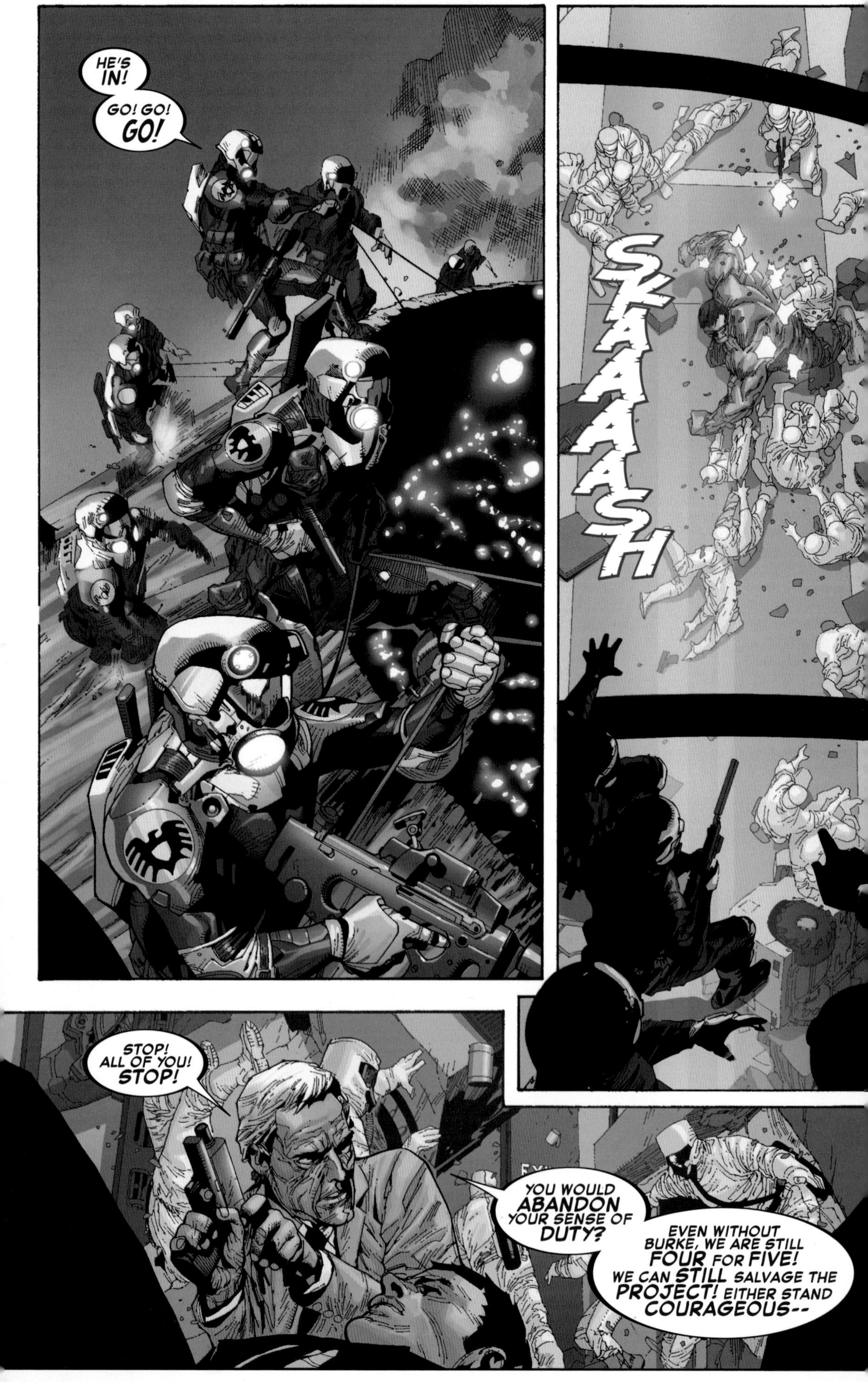
HE'S IN!
GO! GO! GO!
SKAAAAASH
STOP! ALL OF YOU! STOP!
YOU WOULD ABANDON YOUR SENSE OF DUTY?
EVEN WITHOUT BURKE, WE ARE STILL FOUR FOR FIVE! WE CAN STILL SALVAGE THE PROJECT! EITHER STAND COURAGEOUS--

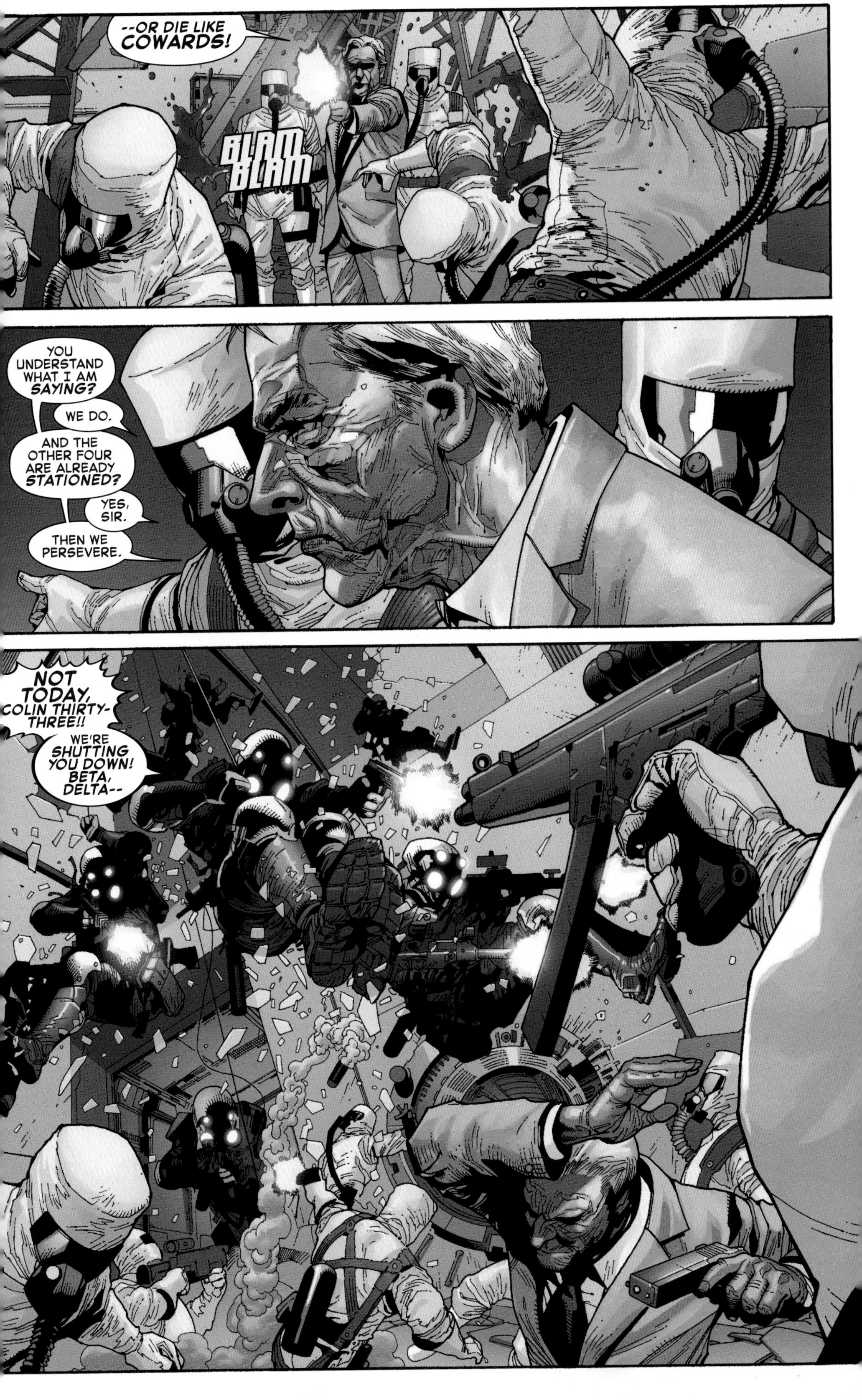
--OR DIE LIKE COWARDS!
BLAM BLAM
YOU UNDERSTAND WHAT I AM SAYING?
WE DO.
AND THE OTHER FOUR ARE ALREADY STATIONED?
YES, SIR.
THEN WE PERSEVERE.
NOT TODAY, COLIN THIRTY-THREE!!
WE'RE SHUTTING YOU DOWN! BETA, DELTA--

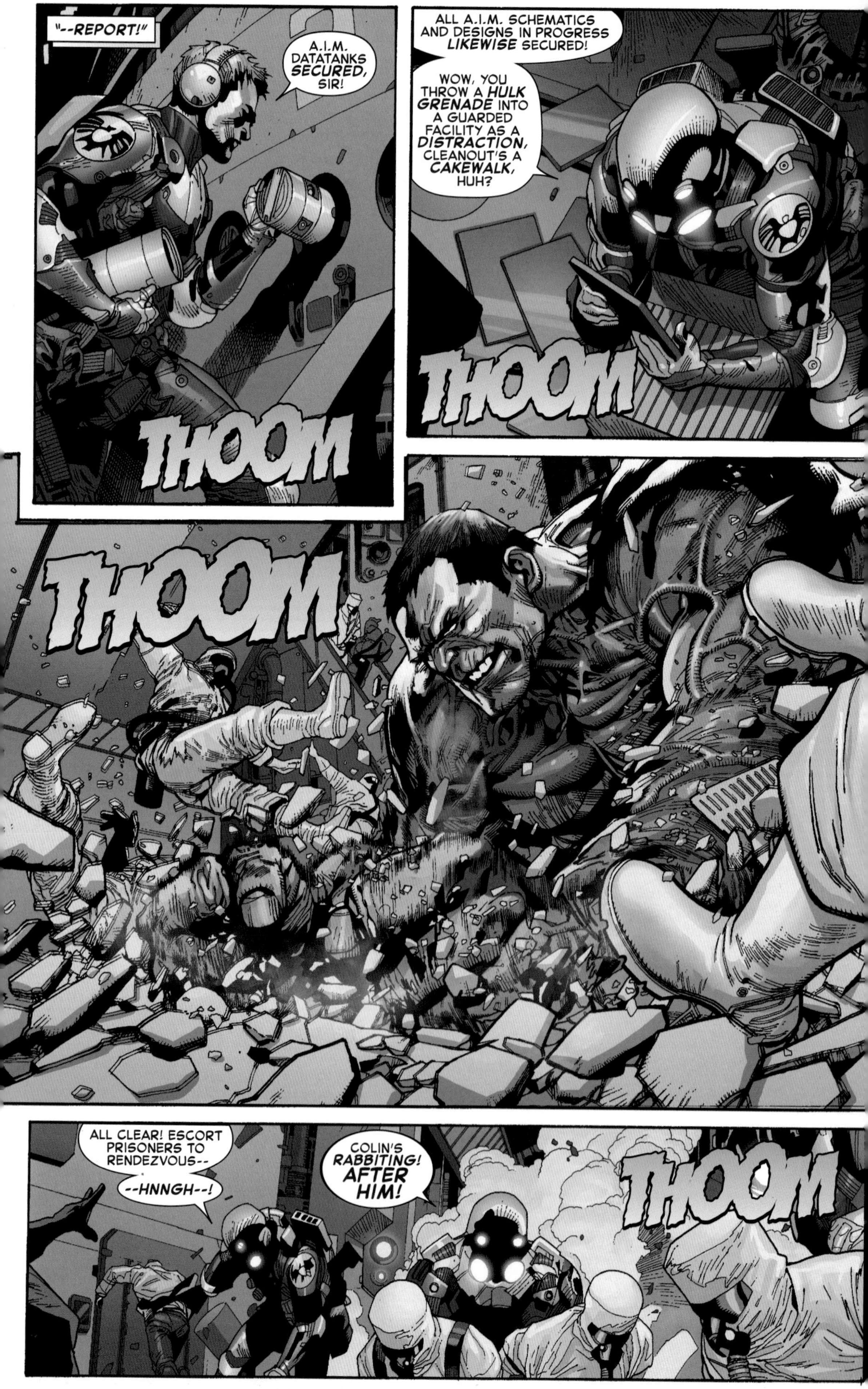
"--REPORT!"
A.I.M. DATATANKS SECURED, SIR!
THOOM
ALL A.I.M. SCHEMATICS AND DESIGNS IN PROGRESS LIKEWISE SECURED!
WOW, YOU THROW A HULK GRENADE INTO A GUARDED FACILITY AS A DISTRACTION, CLEANOUT'S A CAKEWALK, HUH?
THOOM
THOOM
ALL CLEAR! ESCORT PRISONERS TO RENDEZVOUS--
--HNNGH--!
COLIN'S RABBITING! AFTER HIM!
THOOM

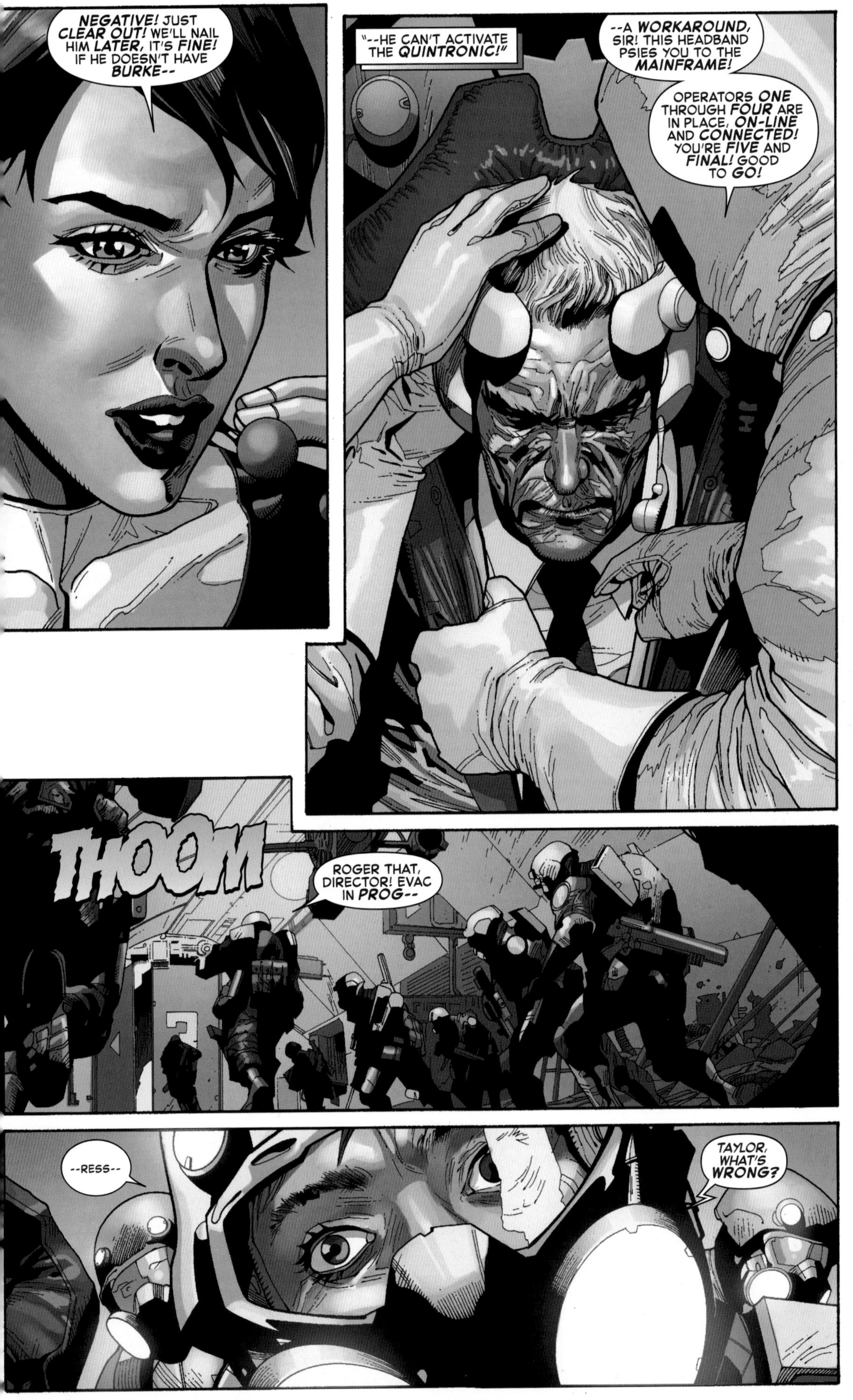
NEGATIVE! JUST CLEAR OUT! WE'LL NAIL HIM LATER, IT'S FINE! IF HE DOESN'T HAVE BURKE--
"--HE CAN'T ACTIVATE THE QUINTRONIC!"
--A WORKAROUND, SIR! THIS HEADBAND PSIES YOU TO THE MAINFRAME!
OPERATORS ONE THROUGH FOUR ARE IN PLACE, ON-LINE AND CONNECTED! YOU'RE FIVE AND FINAL! GOOD TO GO!
THOOM
ROGER THAT, DIRECTOR! EVAC IN PROG--
--RESS--
TAYLOR, WHAT'S WRONG?

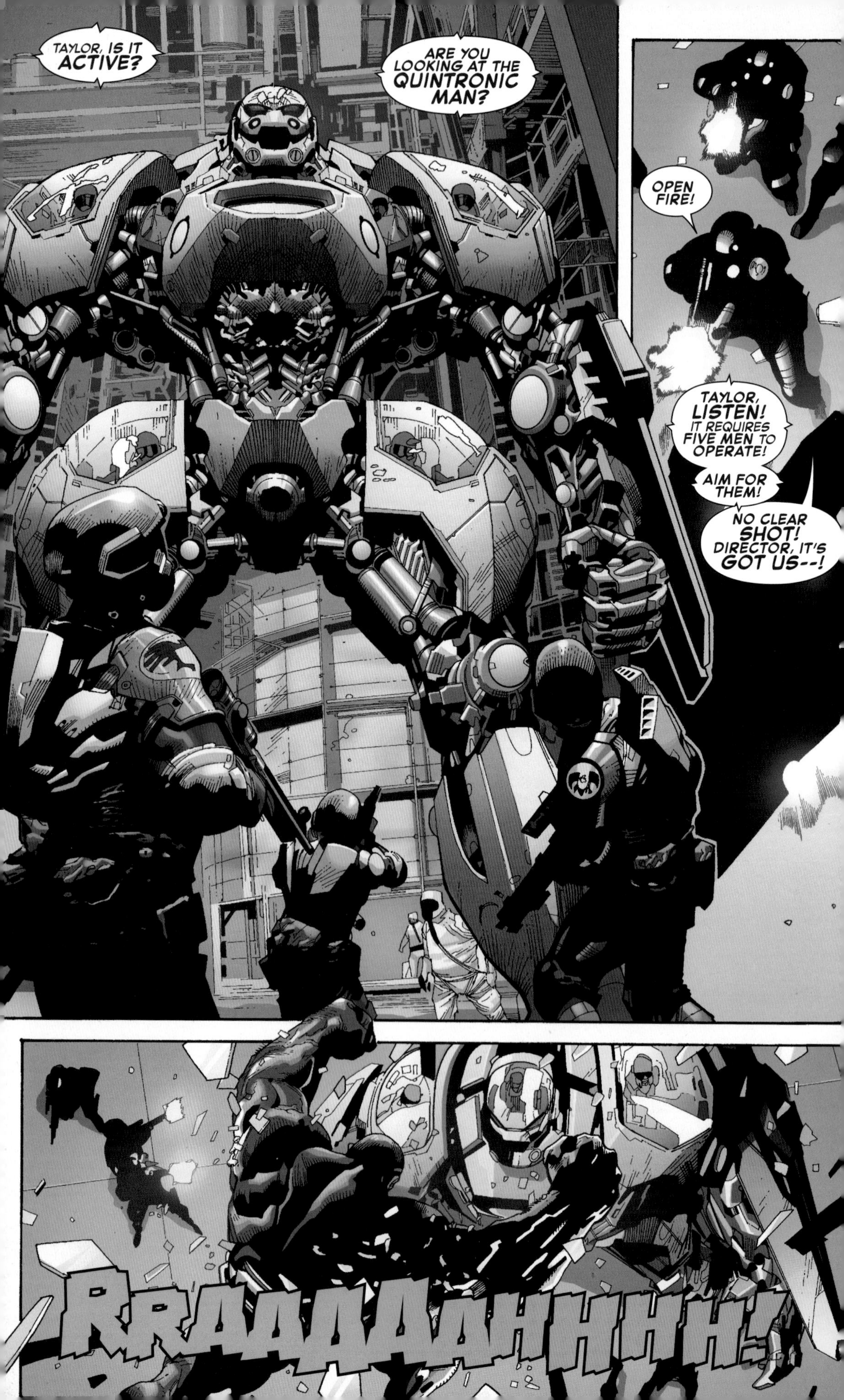
TAYLOR, IS IT ACTIVE?
ARE YOU LOOKING AT THE QUINTRONIC MAN?
OPEN FIRE!
TAYLOR, LISTEN! IT REQUIRES FIVE MEN TO OPERATE!
AIM FOR THEM!
NO CLEAR SHOT! DIRECTOR, IT'S GOT US--!
RRAAAAAHHHH!

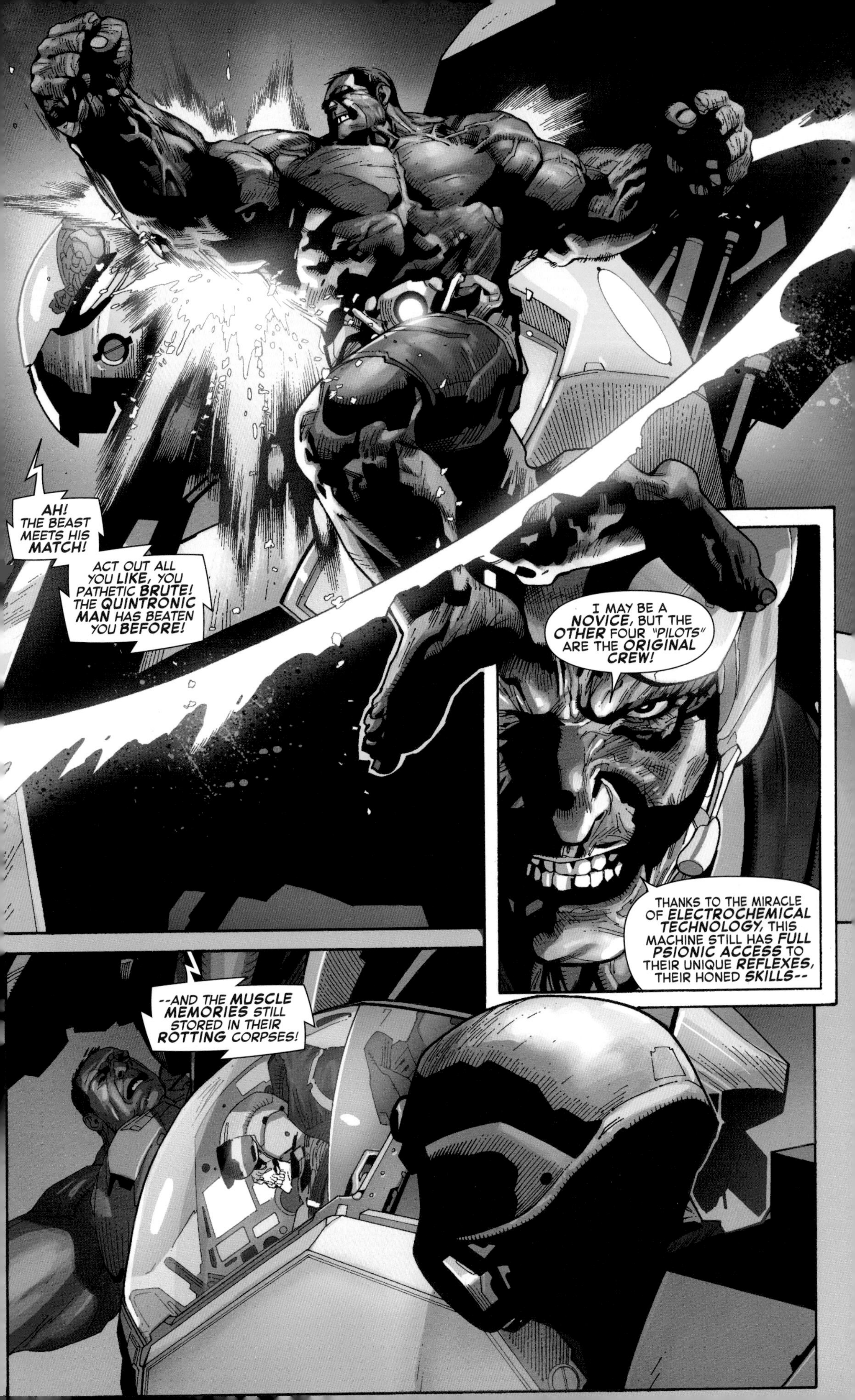
AH! THE BEAST MEETS HIS MATCH!
ACT OUT ALL YOU LIKE, YOU PATHETIC BRUTE! THE QUINTRONIC MAN HAS BEATEN YOU BEFORE!
I MAY BE A NOVICE, BUT THE OTHER FOUR "PILOTS" ARE THE ORIGINAL CREW!
THANKS TO THE MIRACLE OF ELECTROCHEMICAL TECHNOLOGY, THIS MACHINE STILL HAS FULL PSIONIC ACCESS TO THEIR UNIQUE REFLEXES, THEIR HONED SKILLS--
--AND THE MUSCLE MEMORIES STILL STORED IN THEIR ROTTING CORPSES!

THIS MACHINE WAS ENGINEERED FOR **SPACE** EXPLORATION!

IT CAN WITHSTAND ANY **TEMPERATURE**! ANY **PRESSURE**!

CAN **YOU**?

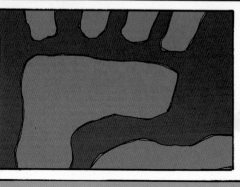

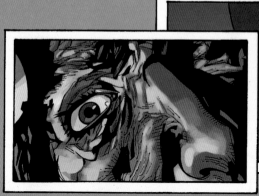

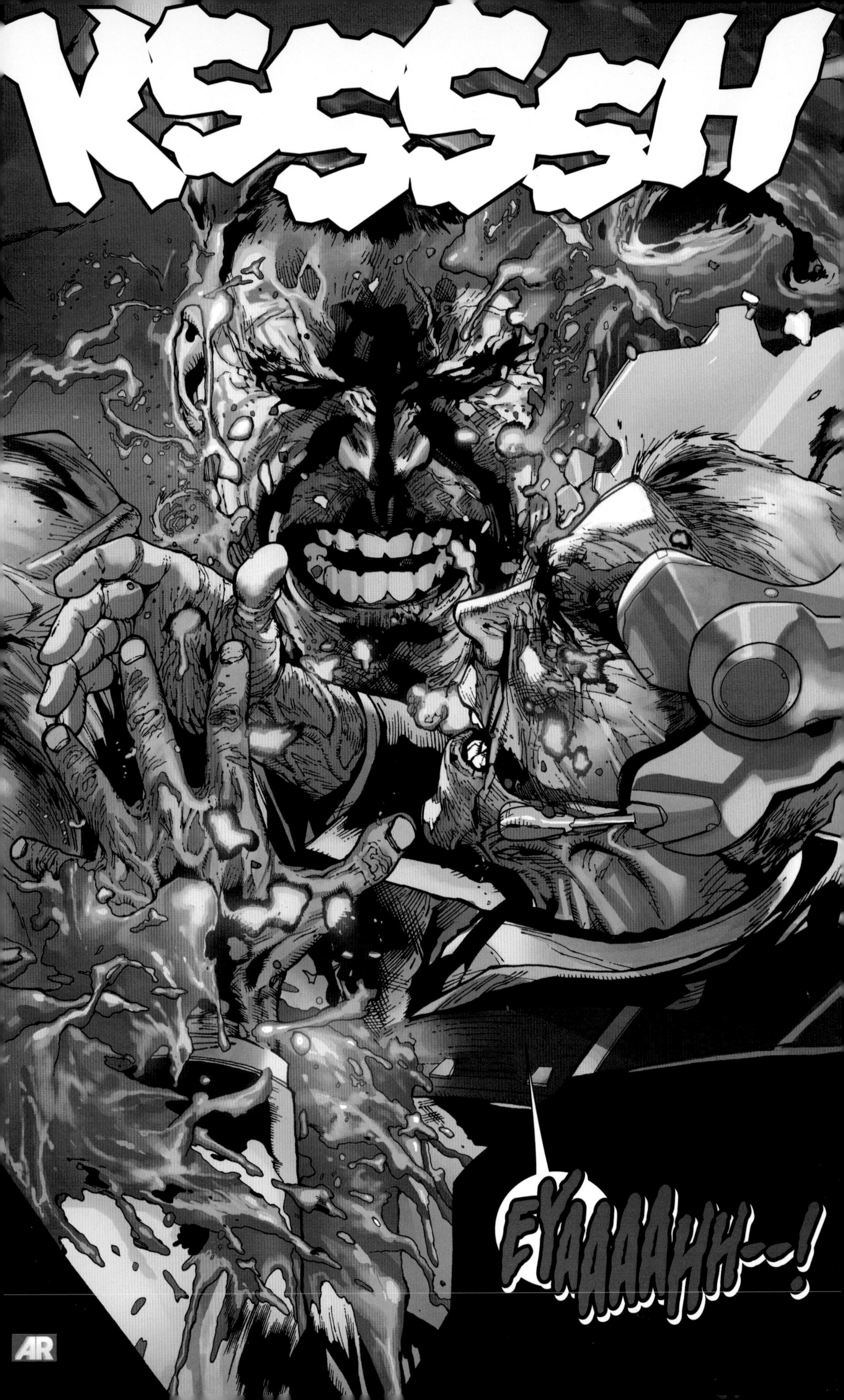
KSSSSH
EYAAAAHH--!

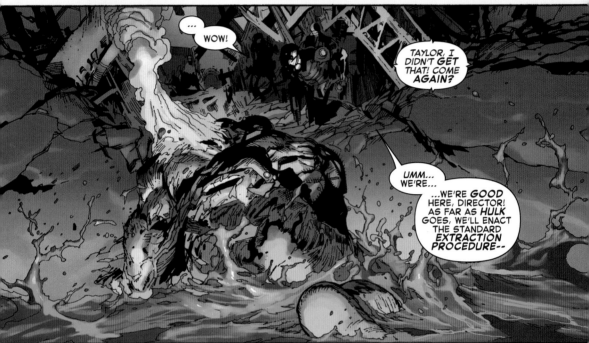

STRATEGIC HAZARD INTERVENTION ESPIONAGE LOGISTICS DIRECTORATE

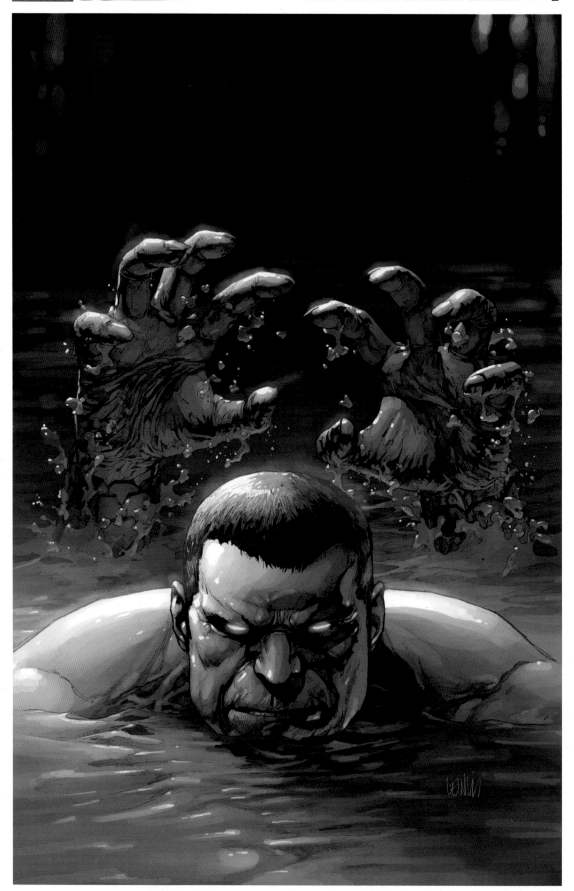

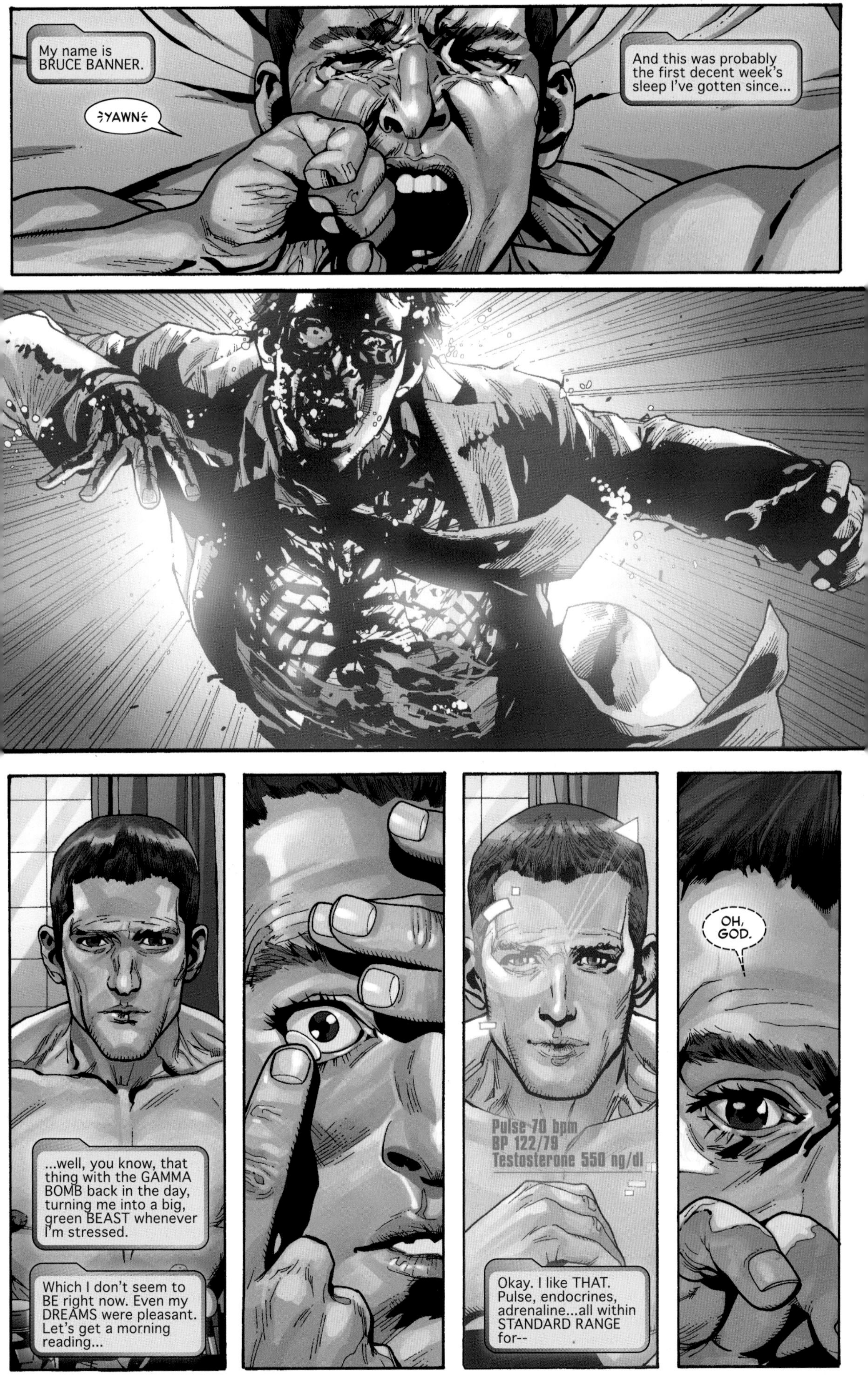
My name is BRUCE BANNER.
YAWN
And this was probably the first decent week's sleep I've gotten since...
...well, you know, that thing with the GAMMA BOMB back in the day, turning me into a big, green BEAST whenever I'm stressed.
Which I don't seem to BE right now. Even my DREAMS were pleasant. Let's get a morning reading...
Pulse 70 bpm
BP 122/79
Testosterone 550 ng/dl
Okay. I like THAT. Pulse, endocrines, adrenaline...all within STANDARD RANGE for--
OH, GOD.

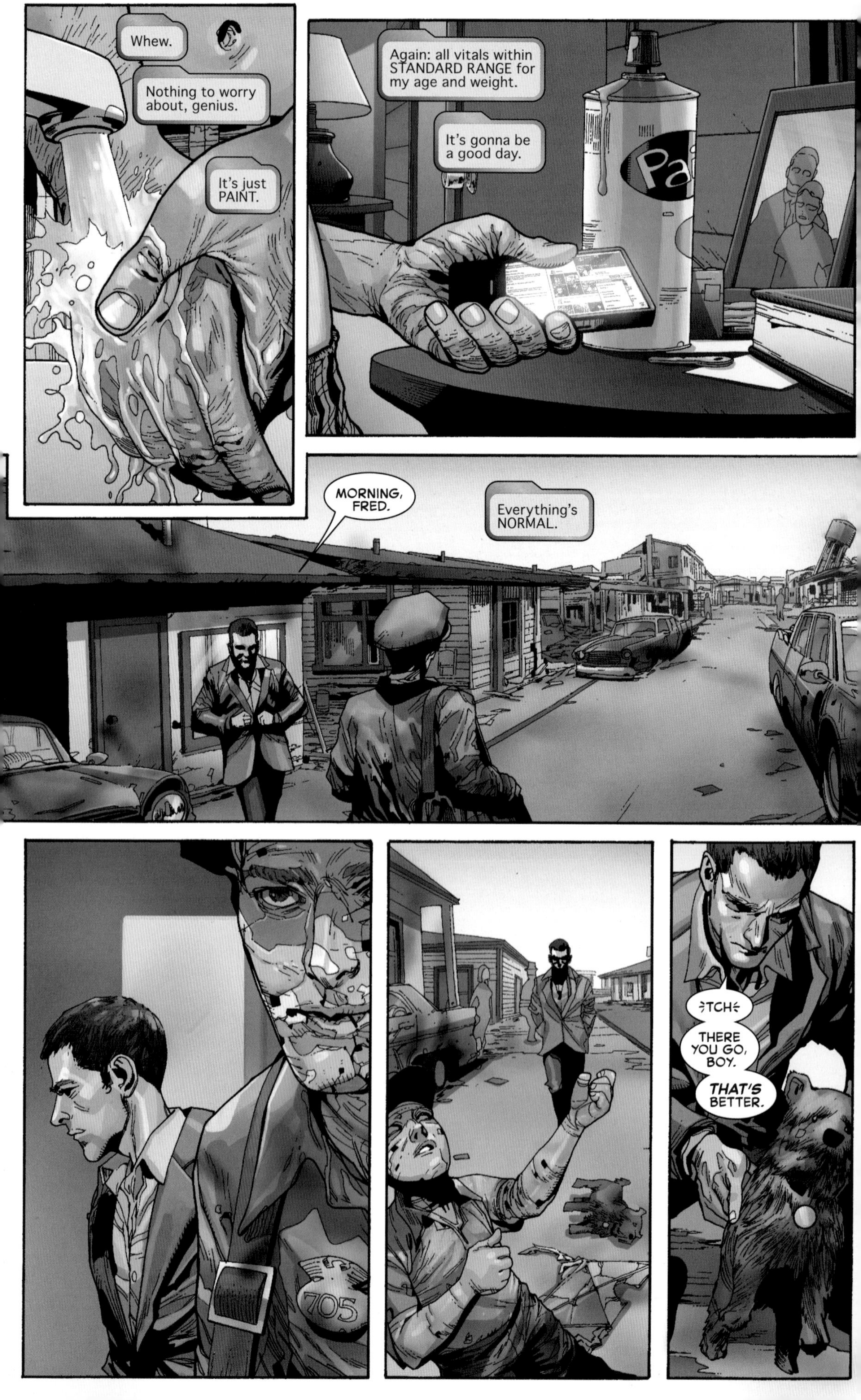

Whew.
Nothing to worry about, genius.
It's just PAINT.
Again: all vitals within STANDARD RANGE for my age and weight.
It's gonna be a good day.
MORNING, FRED.
Everything's NORMAL.
705
⚡TCH⚡
THERE YOU GO, BOY.
THAT'S BETTER.

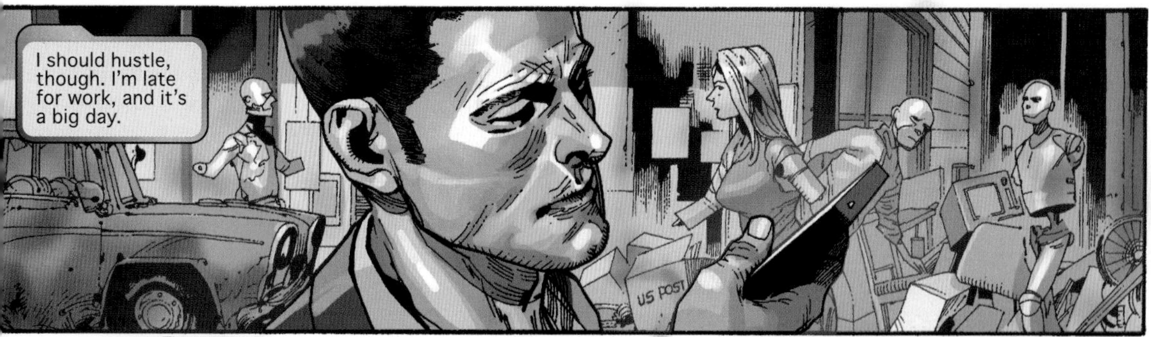
I should hustle, though. I'm late for work, and it's a big day.
US POST

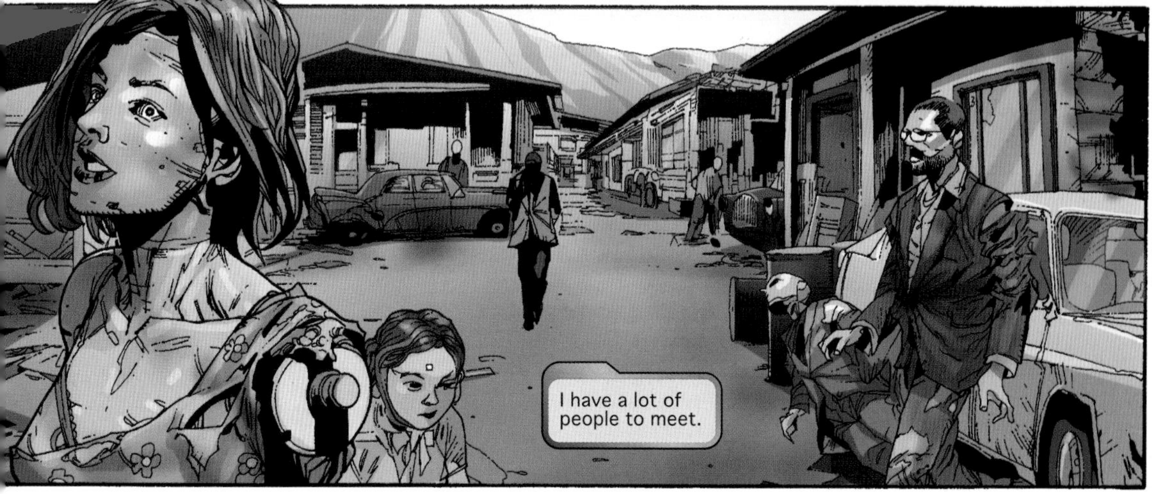
I have a lot of people to meet.

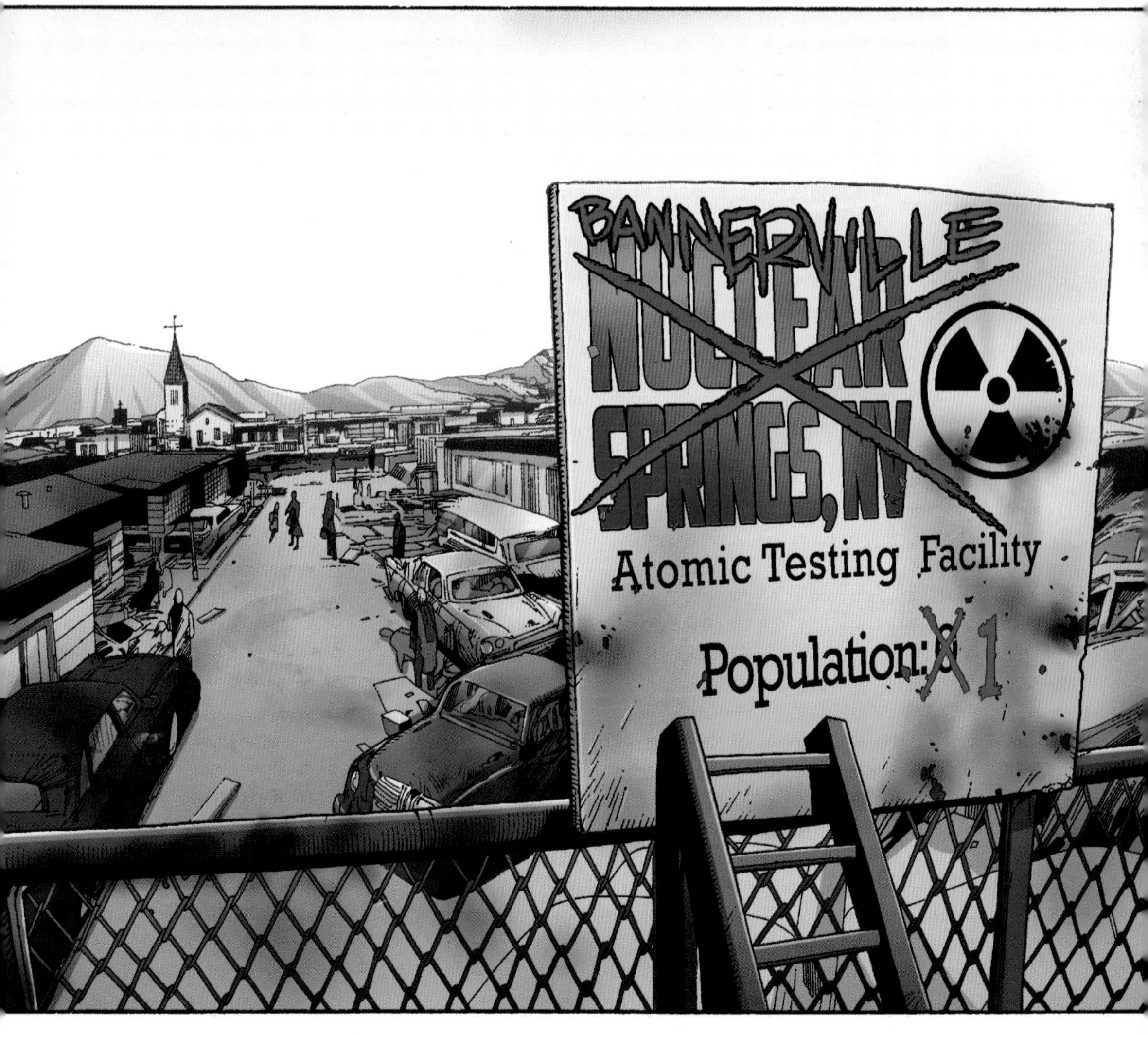
BANNERVILLE
NUCLEAR SPRINGS, NV
Atomic Testing Facility
Population: 0 1

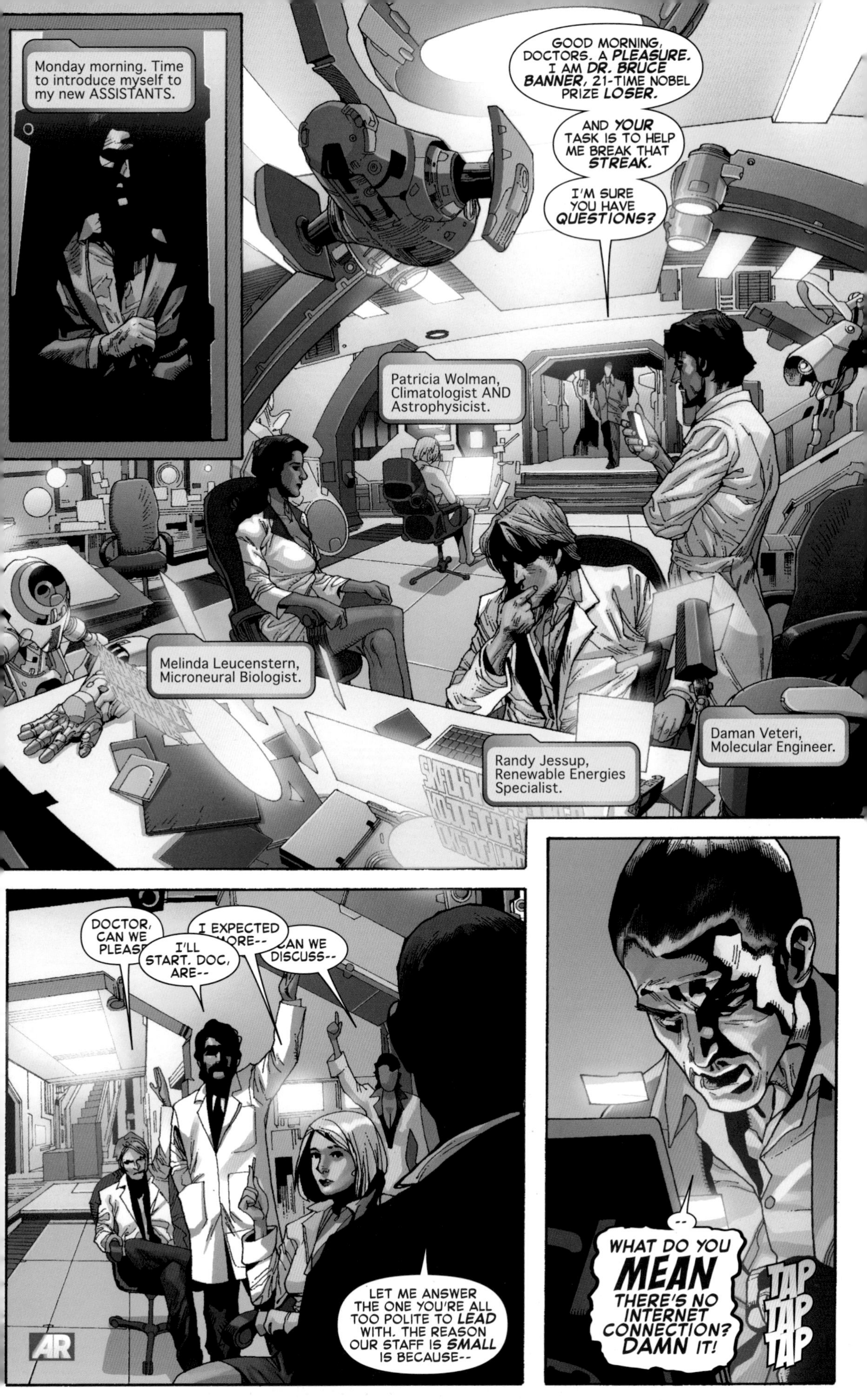

Monday morning. Time to introduce myself to my new ASSISTANTS.
GOOD MORNING, DOCTORS. A PLEASURE. I AM DR. BRUCE BANNER, 21-TIME NOBEL PRIZE LOSER.
AND YOUR TASK IS TO HELP ME BREAK THAT STREAK.
I'M SURE YOU HAVE QUESTIONS?
Patricia Wolman, Climatologist AND Astrophysicist.
Melinda Leucenstern, Microneural Biologist.
Randy Jessup, Renewable Energies Specialist.
Daman Veteri, Molecular Engineer.
DOCTOR, CAN WE PLEAS
I EXPECTED
I'LL START. DOC, ARE--
CAN WE DISCUSS--
LET ME ANSWER THE ONE YOU'RE ALL TOO POLITE TO LEAD WITH. THE REASON OUR STAFF IS SMALL IS BECAUSE--
--
WHAT DO YOU MEAN THERE'S NO INTERNET CONNECTION? DAMN IT!
TAP TAP TAP
AR

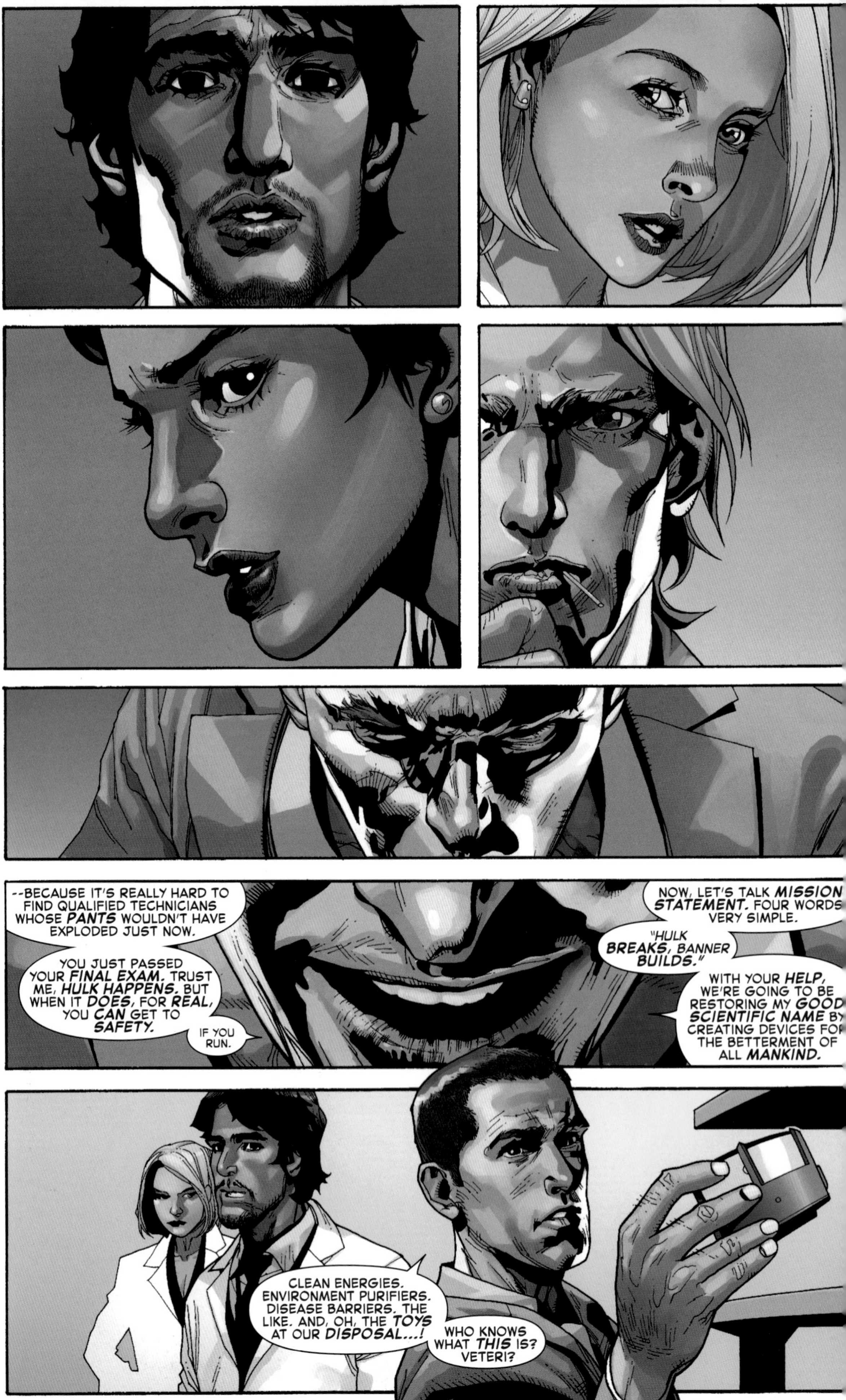
--BECAUSE IT'S REALLY HARD TO FIND QUALIFIED TECHNICIANS WHOSE PANTS WOULDN'T HAVE EXPLODED JUST NOW.
YOU JUST PASSED YOUR FINAL EXAM. TRUST ME, HULK HAPPENS. BUT WHEN IT DOES, FOR REAL, YOU CAN GET TO SAFETY.
IF YOU RUN.
NOW, LET'S TALK MISSION STATEMENT. FOUR WORDS VERY SIMPLE.
"HULK BREAKS, BANNER BUILDS."
WITH YOUR HELP, WE'RE GOING TO BE RESTORING MY GOOD SCIENTIFIC NAME BY CREATING DEVICES FOR THE BETTERMENT OF ALL MANKIND.
CLEAN ENERGIES. ENVIRONMENT PURIFIERS. DISEASE BARRIERS. THE LIKE. AND, OH, THE TOYS AT OUR DISPOSAL...!
WHO KNOWS WHAT THIS IS? VETERI?

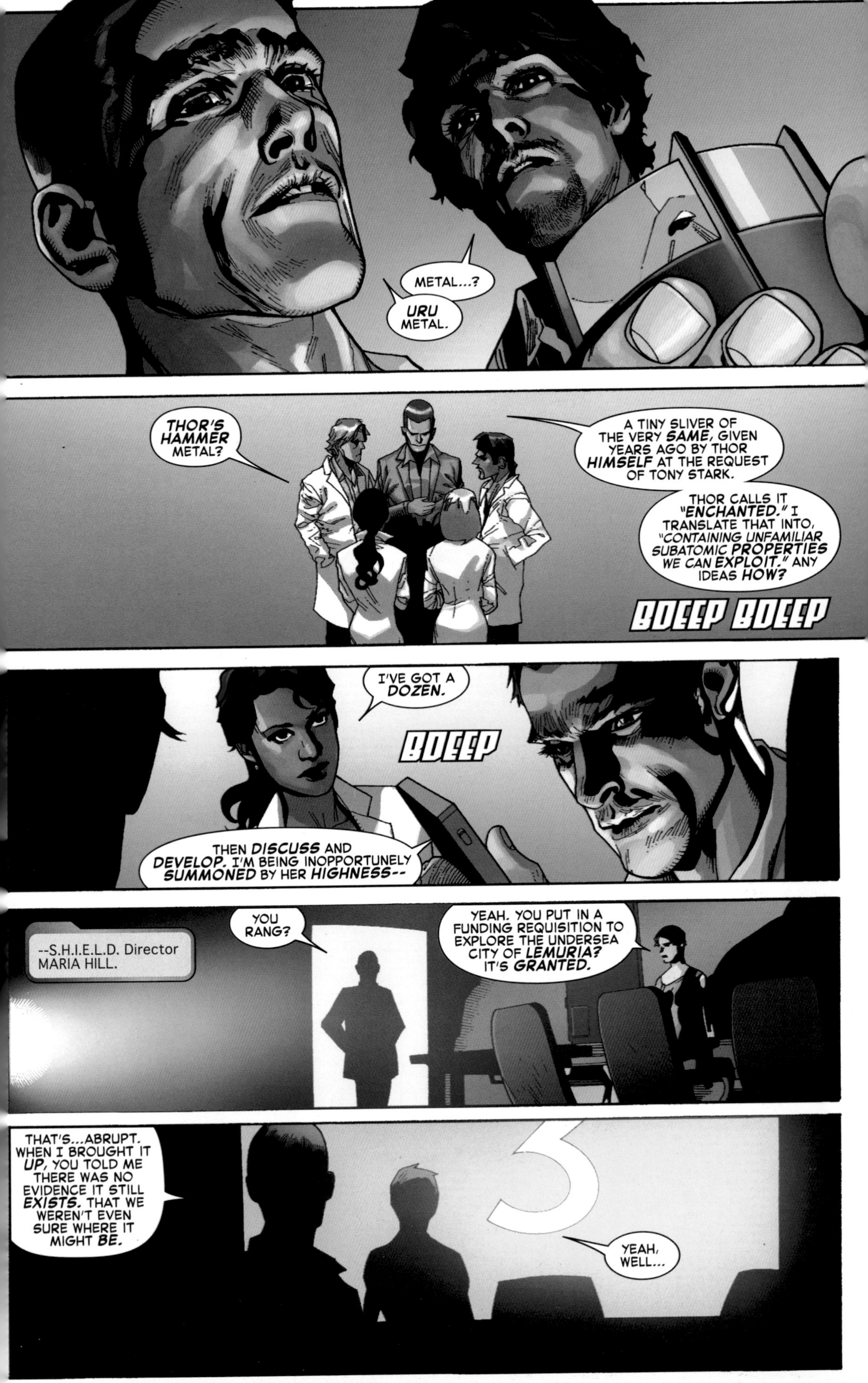
METAL...?
URU METAL.
THOR'S HAMMER METAL?
A TINY SLIVER OF THE VERY SAME, GIVEN YEARS AGO BY THOR HIMSELF AT THE REQUEST OF TONY STARK.
THOR CALLS IT "ENCHANTED." I TRANSLATE THAT INTO, "CONTAINING UNFAMILIAR SUBATOMIC PROPERTIES WE CAN EXPLOIT." ANY IDEAS HOW?
BDEEP BDEEP
I'VE GOT A DOZEN.
BDEEP
THEN DISCUSS AND DEVELOP. I'M BEING INOPPORTUNELY SUMMONED BY HER HIGHNESS--
--S.H.I.E.L.D. Director MARIA HILL.
YOU RANG?
YEAH. YOU PUT IN A FUNDING REQUISITION TO EXPLORE THE UNDERSEA CITY OF LEMURIA? IT'S GRANTED.
THAT'S...ABRUPT. WHEN I BROUGHT IT UP, YOU TOLD ME THERE WAS NO EVIDENCE IT STILL EXISTS. THAT WE WEREN'T EVEN SURE WHERE IT MIGHT BE.
YEAH, WELL...

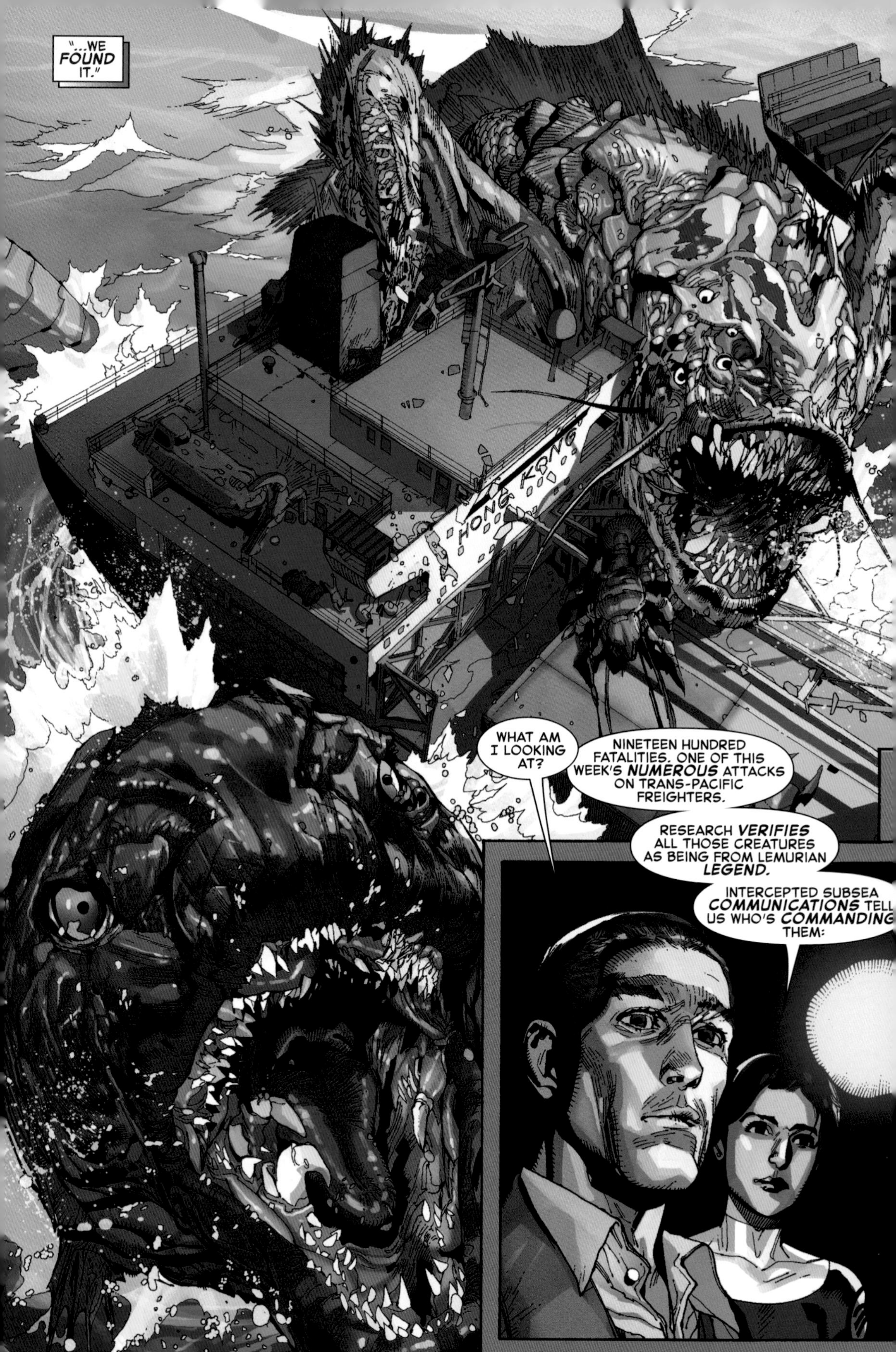
"...WE FOUND IT."
WHAT AM I LOOKING AT?
NINETEEN HUNDRED FATALITIES. ONE OF THIS WEEK'S NUMEROUS ATTACKS ON TRANS-PACIFIC FREIGHTERS.
RESEARCH VERIFIES ALL THOSE CREATURES AS BEING FROM LEMURIAN LEGEND.
INTERCEPTED SUBSEA COMMUNICATIONS TELL US WHO'S COMMANDING THEM:
HONG KONG

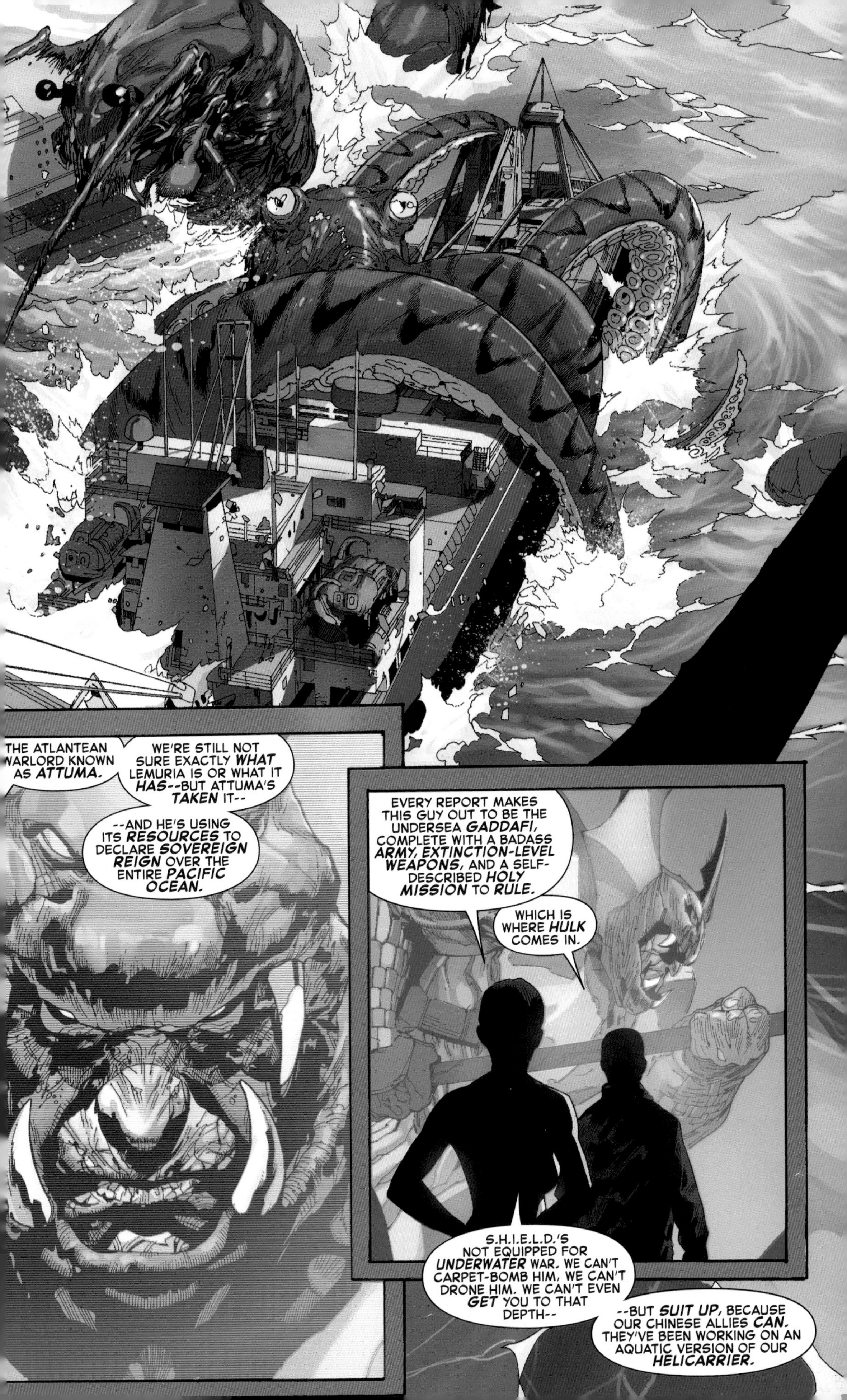
THE ATLANTEAN WARLORD KNOWN AS ATTUMA.
WE'RE STILL NOT SURE EXACTLY WHAT LEMURIA IS OR WHAT IT HAS--BUT ATTUMA'S TAKEN IT--
--AND HE'S USING ITS RESOURCES TO DECLARE SOVEREIGN REIGN OVER THE ENTIRE PACIFIC OCEAN.
EVERY REPORT MAKES THIS GUY OUT TO BE THE UNDERSEA GADDAFI, COMPLETE WITH A BADASS ARMY, EXTINCTION-LEVEL WEAPONS, AND A SELF-DESCRIBED HOLY MISSION TO RULE.
WHICH IS WHERE HULK COMES IN.
S.H.I.E.L.D.'S NOT EQUIPPED FOR UNDERWATER WAR. WE CAN'T CARPET-BOMB HIM, WE CAN'T DRONE HIM. WE CAN'T EVEN GET YOU TO THAT DEPTH--
--BUT SUIT UP, BECAUSE OUR CHINESE ALLIES CAN. THEY'VE BEEN WORKING ON AN AQUATIC VERSION OF OUR HELICARRIER.

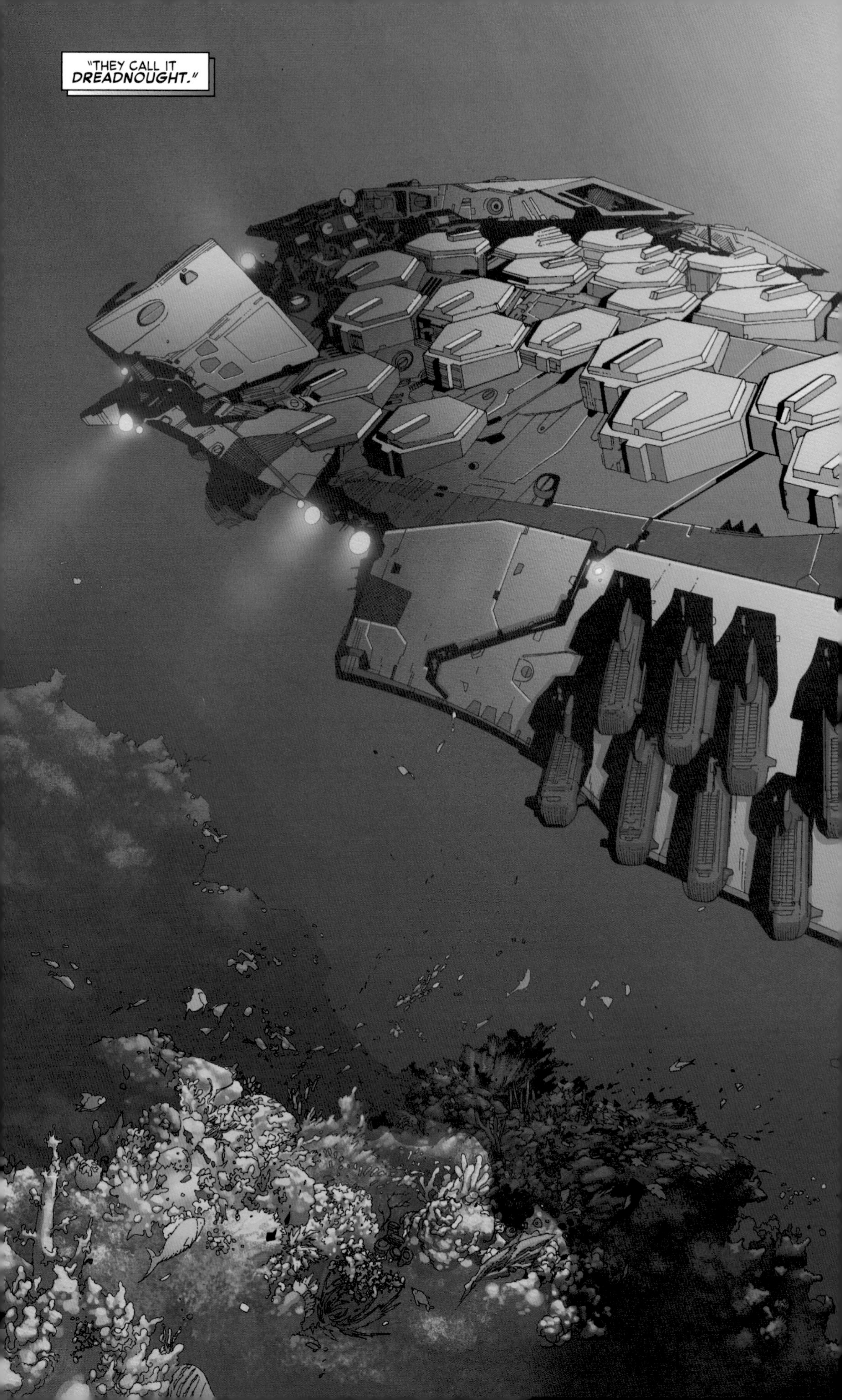
"THEY CALL IT DREADNOUGHT."

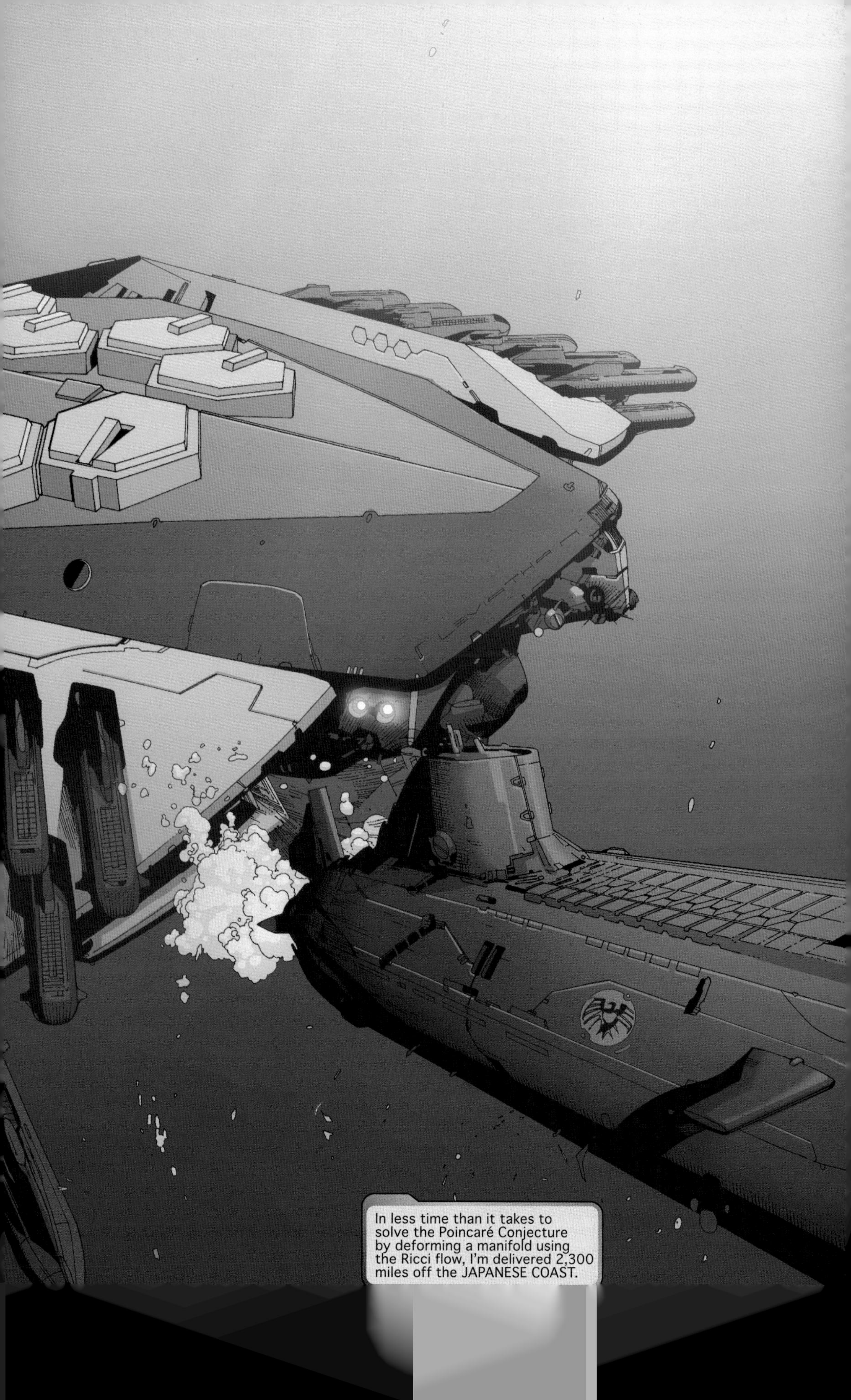
In less time than it takes to solve the Poincaré Conjecture by deforming a manifold using the Ricci flow, I'm delivered 2,300 miles off the JAPANESE COAST.

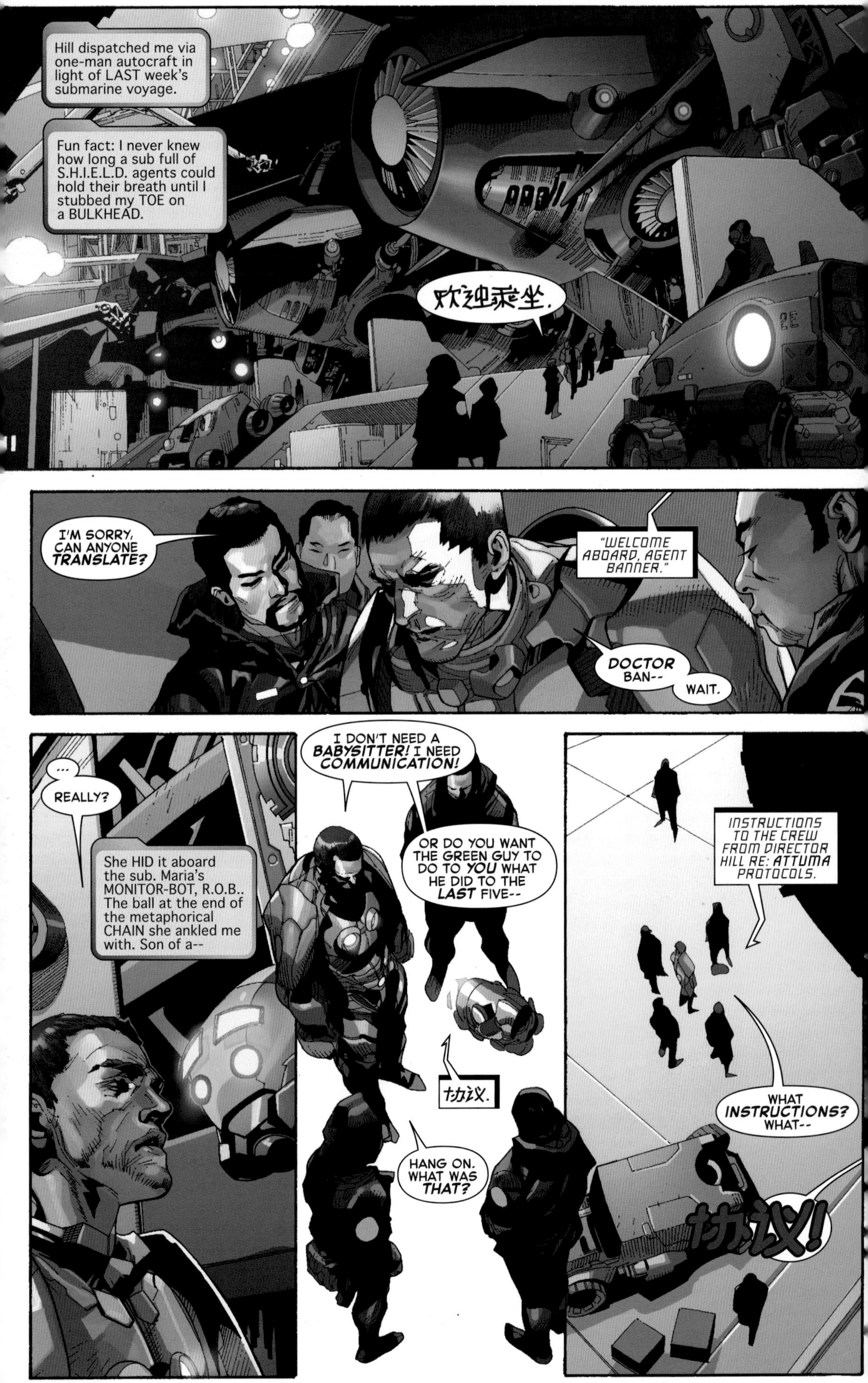
Hill dispatched me via one-man autocraft in light of LAST week's submarine voyage.
Fun fact: I never knew how long a sub full of S.H.I.E.L.D. agents could hold their breath until I stubbed my TOE on a BULKHEAD.
欢迎乘坐.
I'M SORRY, CAN ANYONE TRANSLATE?
"WELCOME ABOARD, AGENT BANNER."
DOCTOR BAN--
WAIT.
...
REALLY?
She HID it aboard the sub. Maria's MONITOR-BOT, R.O.B.. The ball at the end of the metaphorical CHAIN she ankled me with. Son of a--
I DON'T NEED A BABYSITTER! I NEED COMMUNICATION!
OR DO YOU WANT THE GREEN GUY TO DO TO YOU WHAT HE DID TO THE LAST FIVE--
协议.
HANG ON. WHAT WAS THAT?
INSTRUCTIONS TO THE CREW FROM DIRECTOR HILL RE: ATTUMA PROTOCOLS.
WHAT INSTRUCTIONS? WHAT--
协议!

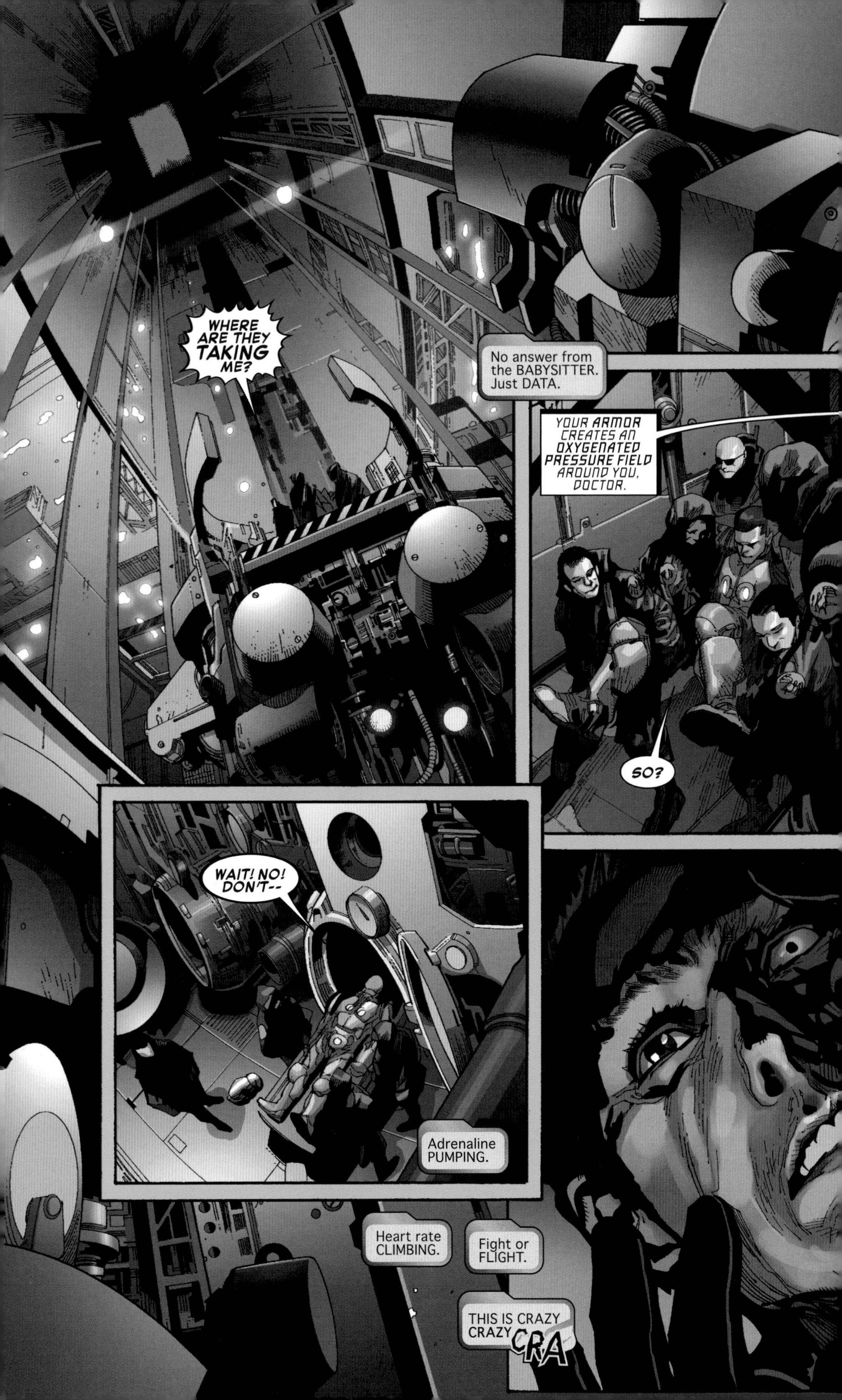
WHERE ARE THEY TAKING ME?
No answer from the BABYSITTER. Just DATA.
YOUR ARMOR CREATES AN OXYGENATED PRESSURE FIELD AROUND YOU, DOCTOR.
SO?
WAIT! NO! DON'T--
Adrenaline PUMPING.
Heart rate CLIMBING.
Fight or FLIGHT.
THIS IS CRAZY CRAZY CRA

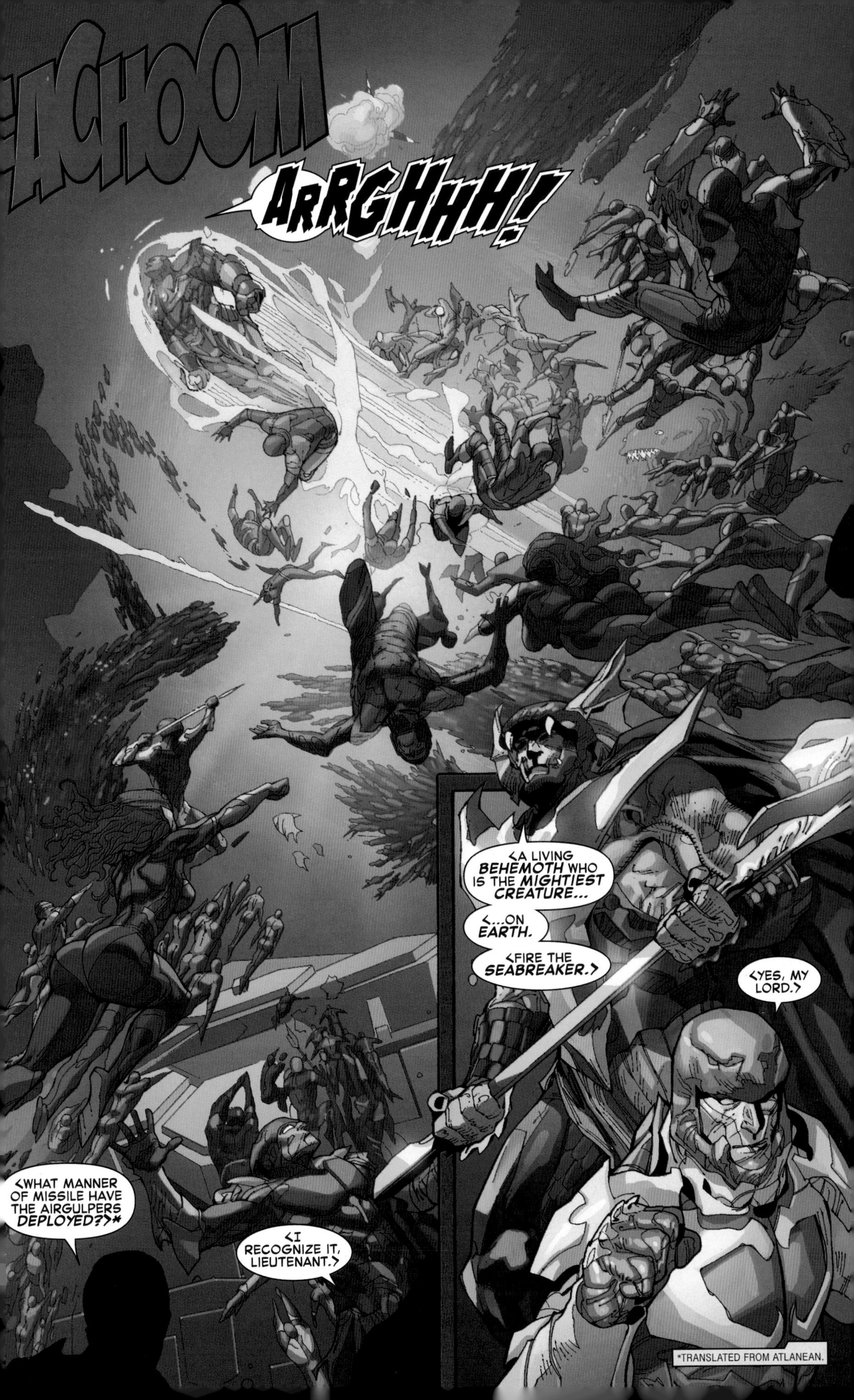

ACHOOM
ARRGHHH!
<A LIVING BEHEMOTH WHO IS THE MIGHTIEST CREATURE...
<...ON EARTH.
<FIRE THE SEABREAKER.>
<YES, MY LORD.>
<WHAT MANNER OF MISSILE HAVE THE AIRGULPERS DEPLOYED?>*
<I RECOGNIZE IT, LIEUTENANT.>
*TRANSLATED FROM ATLANEAN.

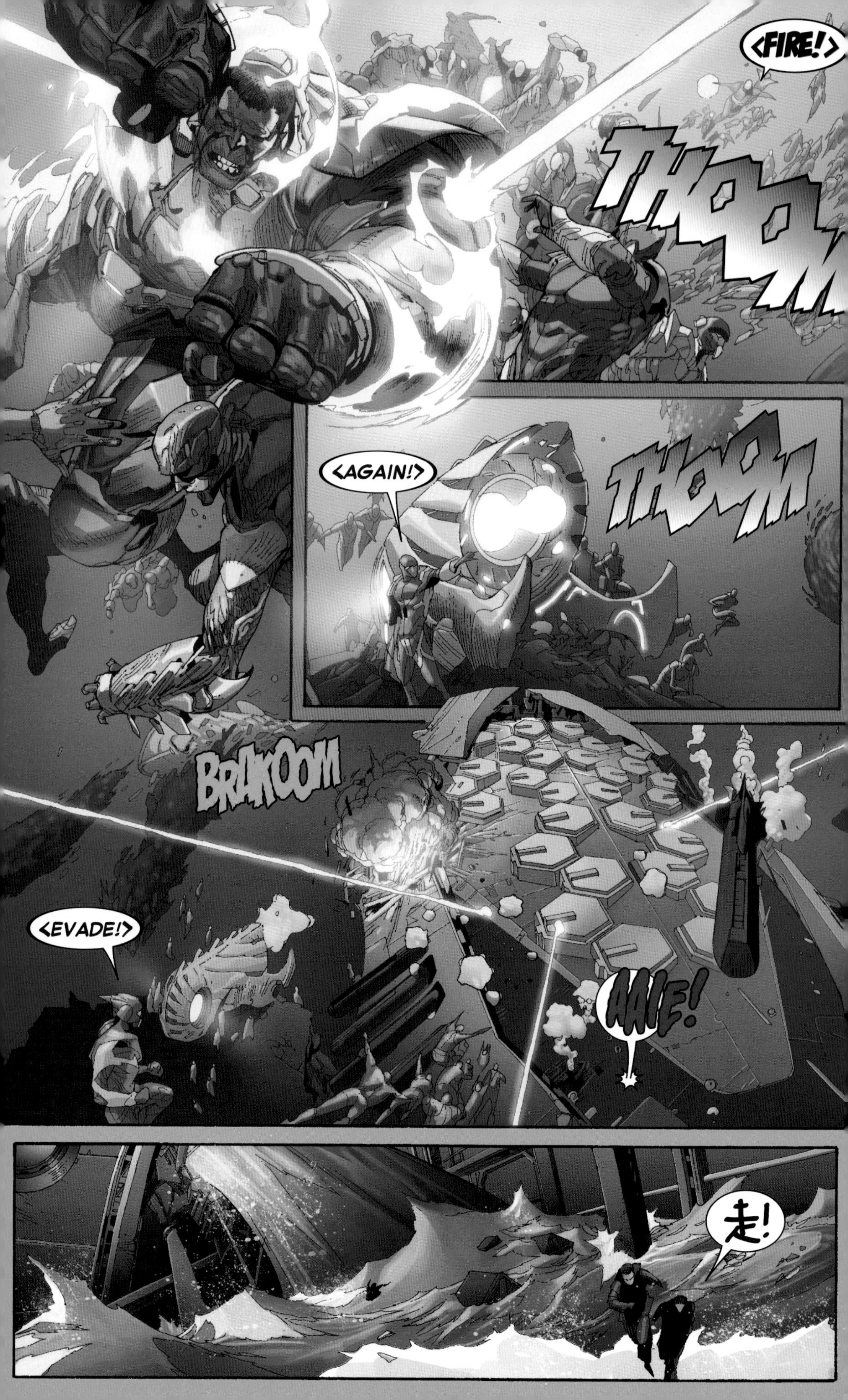
<FIRE!>
THOOM
<AGAIN!>
THOOM
BRAKOOM
<EVADE!>
AAIE!
走!

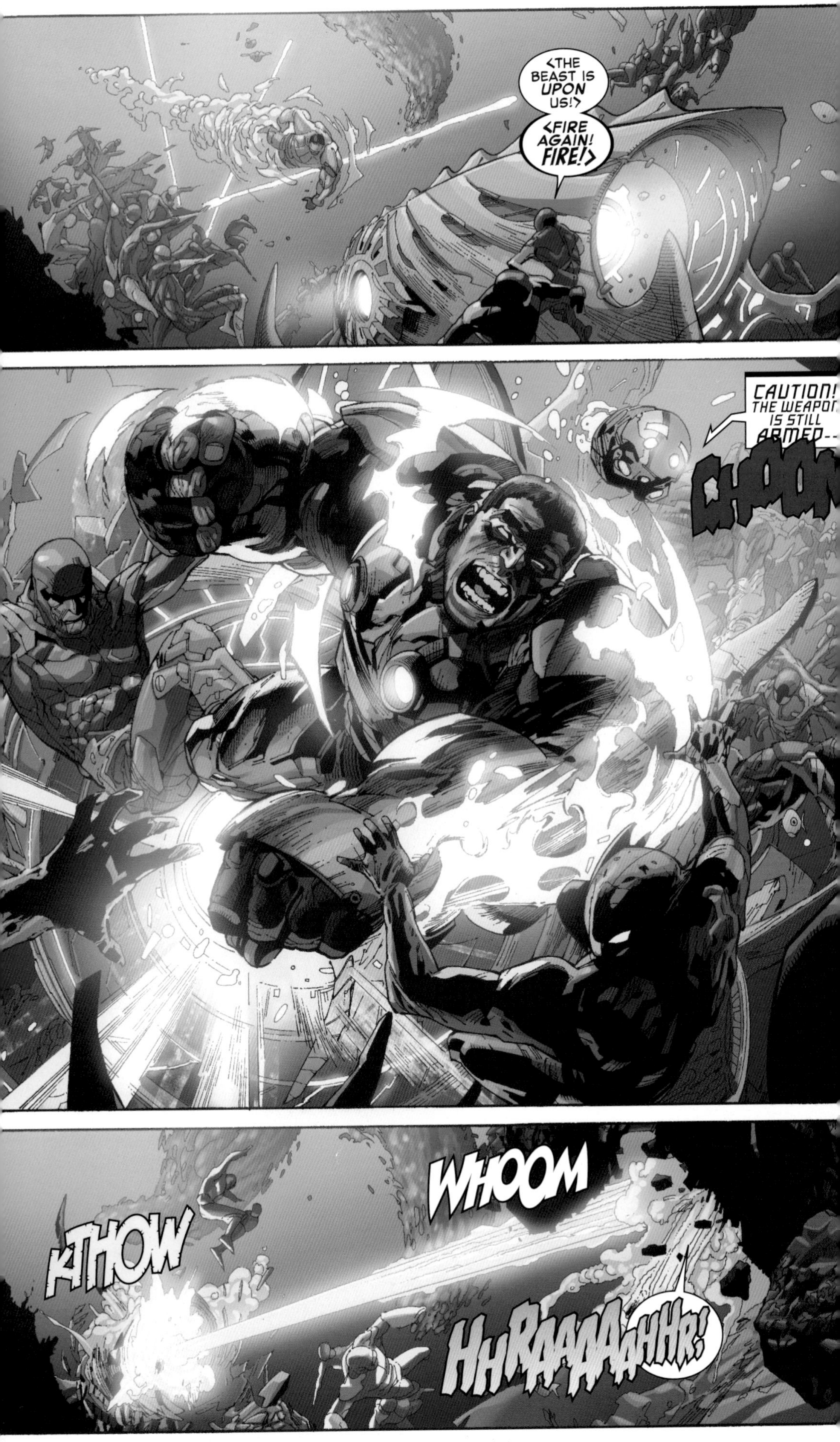
<THE BEAST IS UPON US!>
<FIRE AGAIN! FIRE!>
CAUTION! THE WEAPO IS STILL ARMED--
CHOOM
WHOOM
KTHOW
HHRAAAAAHHR!

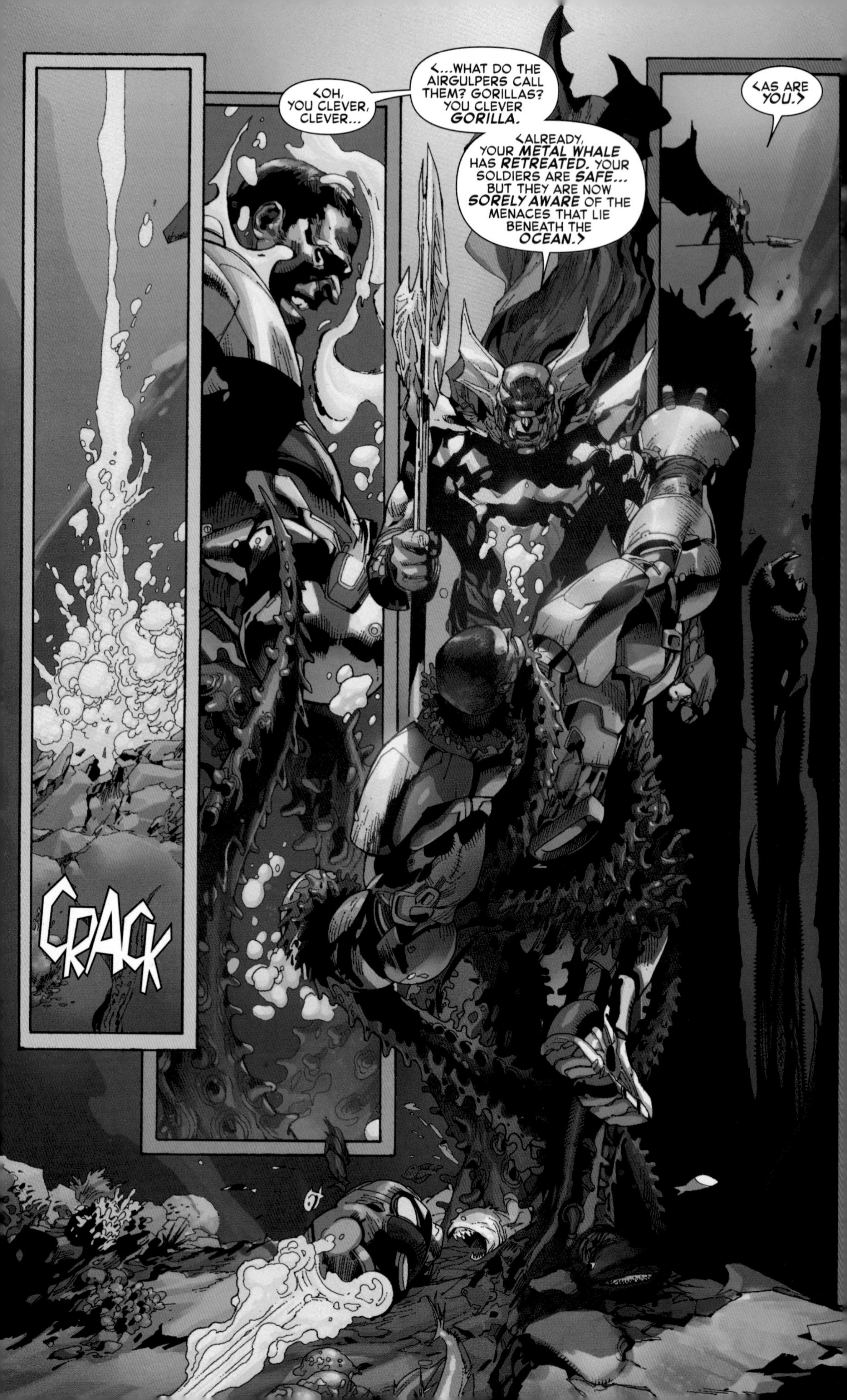

<OH, YOU CLEVER, CLEVER...
<...WHAT DO THE AIRGULPERS CALL THEM? GORILLAS? YOU CLEVER GORILLA.
<ALREADY, YOUR METAL WHALE HAS RETREATED. YOUR SOLDIERS ARE SAFE... BUT THEY ARE NOW SORELY AWARE OF THE MENACES THAT LIE BENEATH THE OCEAN.>
<AS ARE YOU.>
CRACK

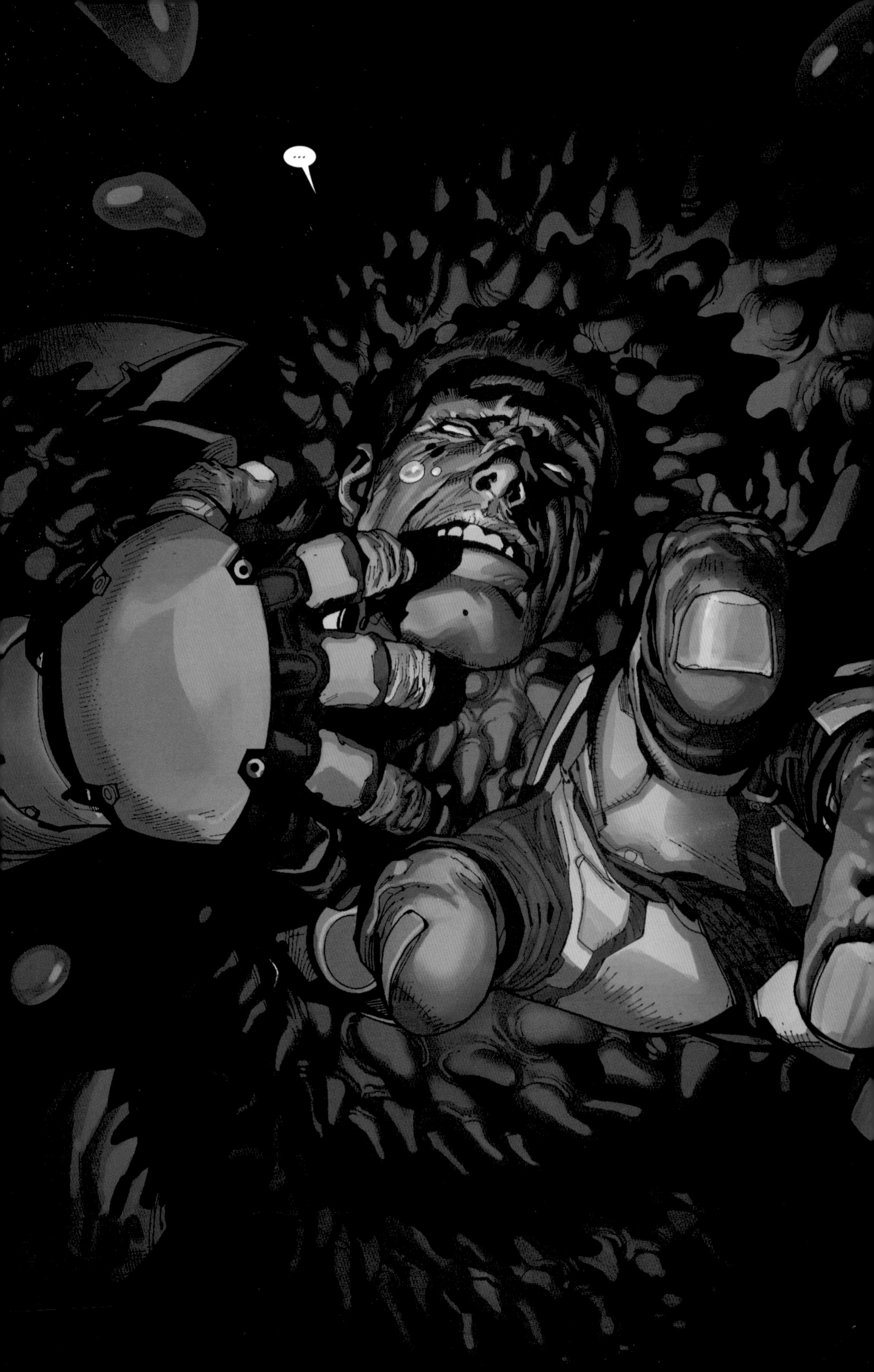
...

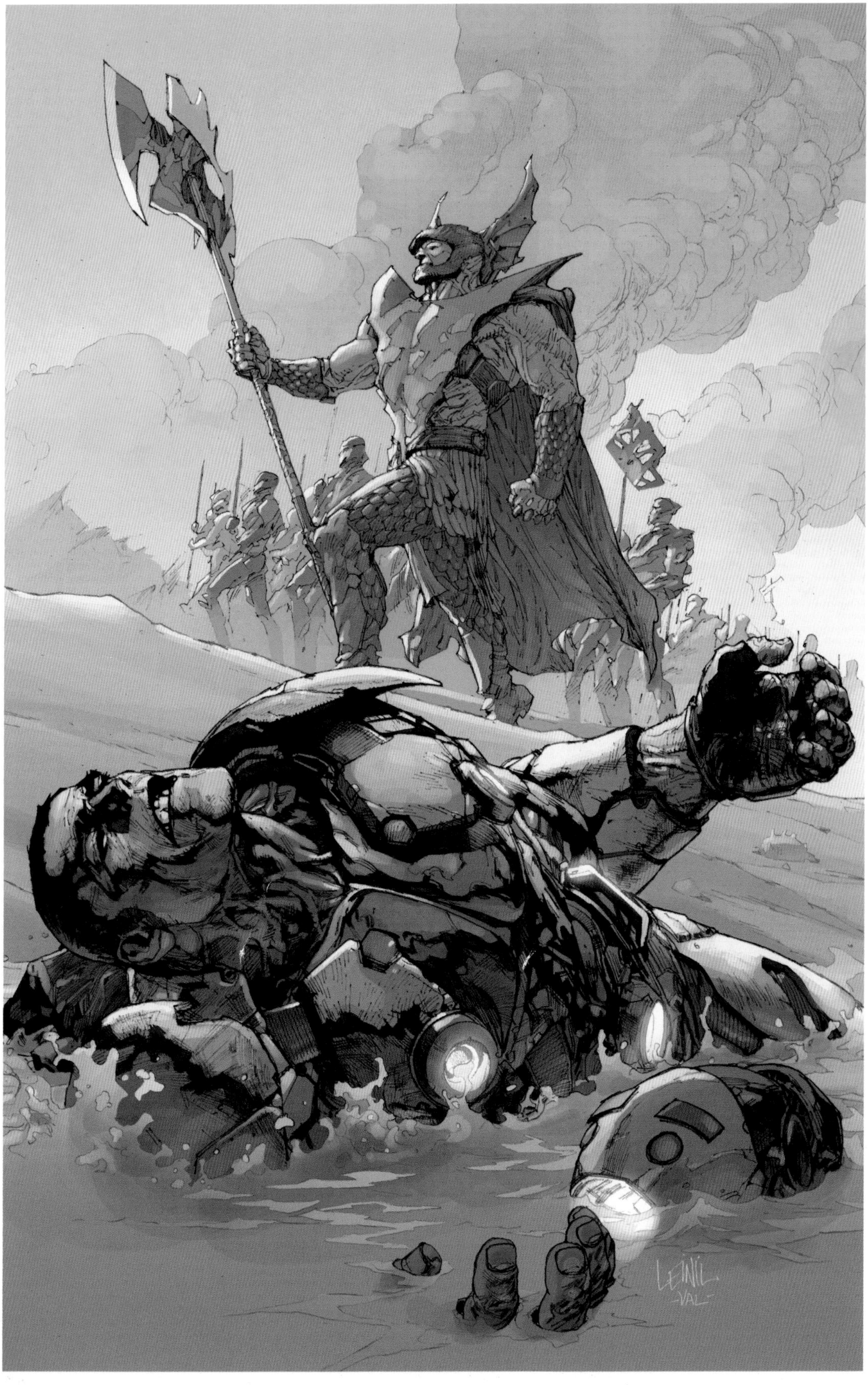
LEINIL
-VAL-

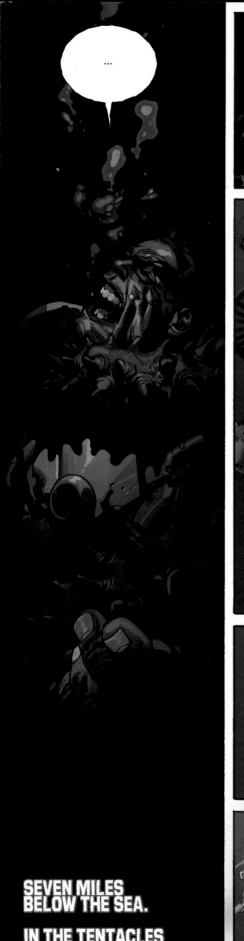

SEVEN MILES
BELOW THE SEA.

IN THE TENTACLES
OF AN ALIEN BEAST.

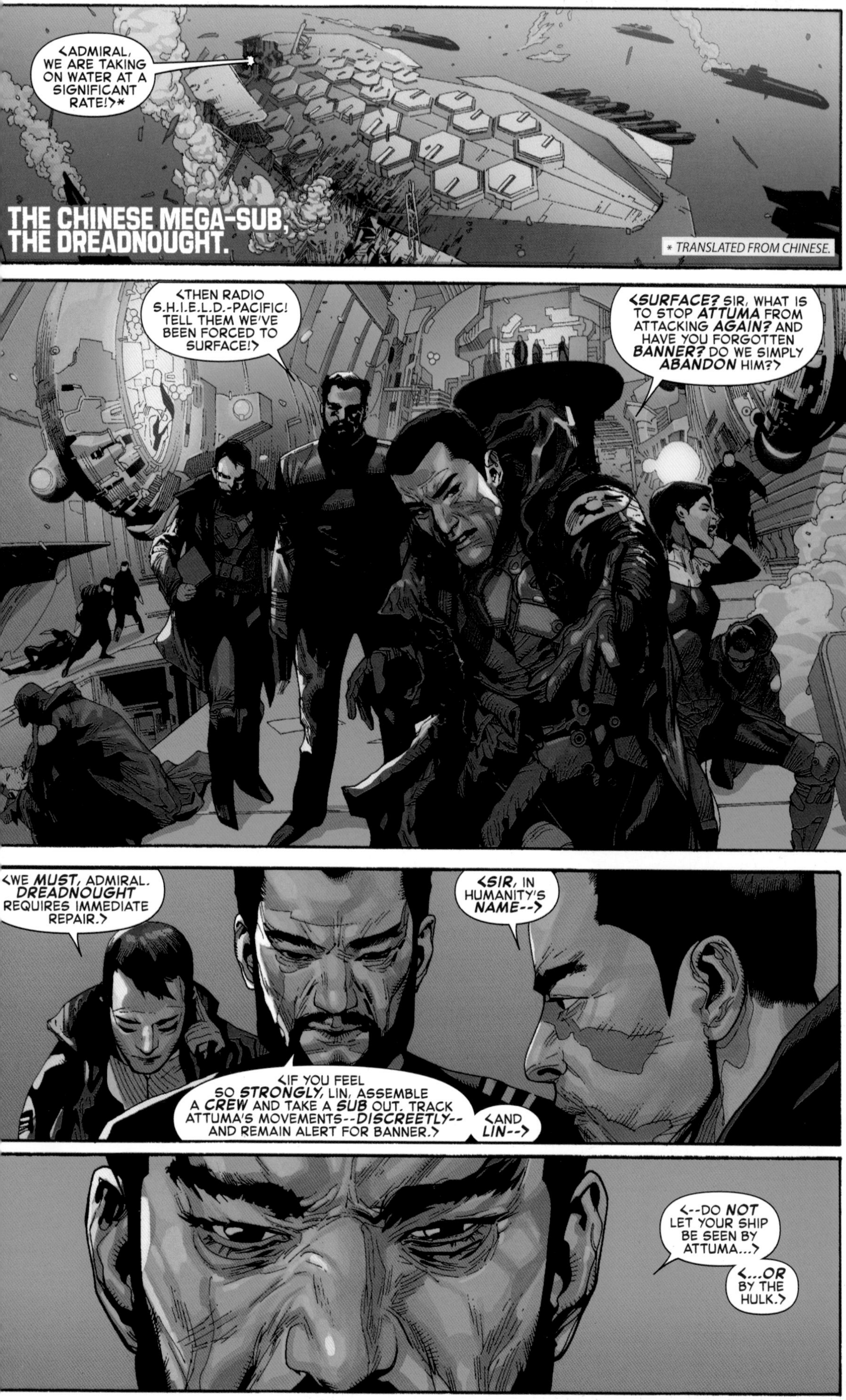
<ADMIRAL, WE ARE TAKING ON WATER AT A SIGNIFICANT RATE!>*
THE CHINESE MEGA-SUB, THE DREADNOUGHT.
* TRANSLATED FROM CHINESE.
<THEN RADIO S.H.I.E.L.D.-PACIFIC! TELL THEM WE'VE BEEN FORCED TO SURFACE!>
<SURFACE? SIR, WHAT IS TO STOP ATTUMA FROM ATTACKING AGAIN? AND HAVE YOU FORGOTTEN BANNER? DO WE SIMPLY ABANDON HIM?>
<WE MUST, ADMIRAL. DREADNOUGHT REQUIRES IMMEDIATE REPAIR.>
<SIR, IN HUMANITY'S NAME-->
<IF YOU FEEL SO STRONGLY, LIN, ASSEMBLE A CREW AND TAKE A SUB OUT. TRACK ATTUMA'S MOVEMENTS--DISCREETLY--AND REMAIN ALERT FOR BANNER.>
<AND LIN-->
<--DO NOT LET YOUR SHIP BE SEEN BY ATTUMA...>
<...OR BY THE HULK.>

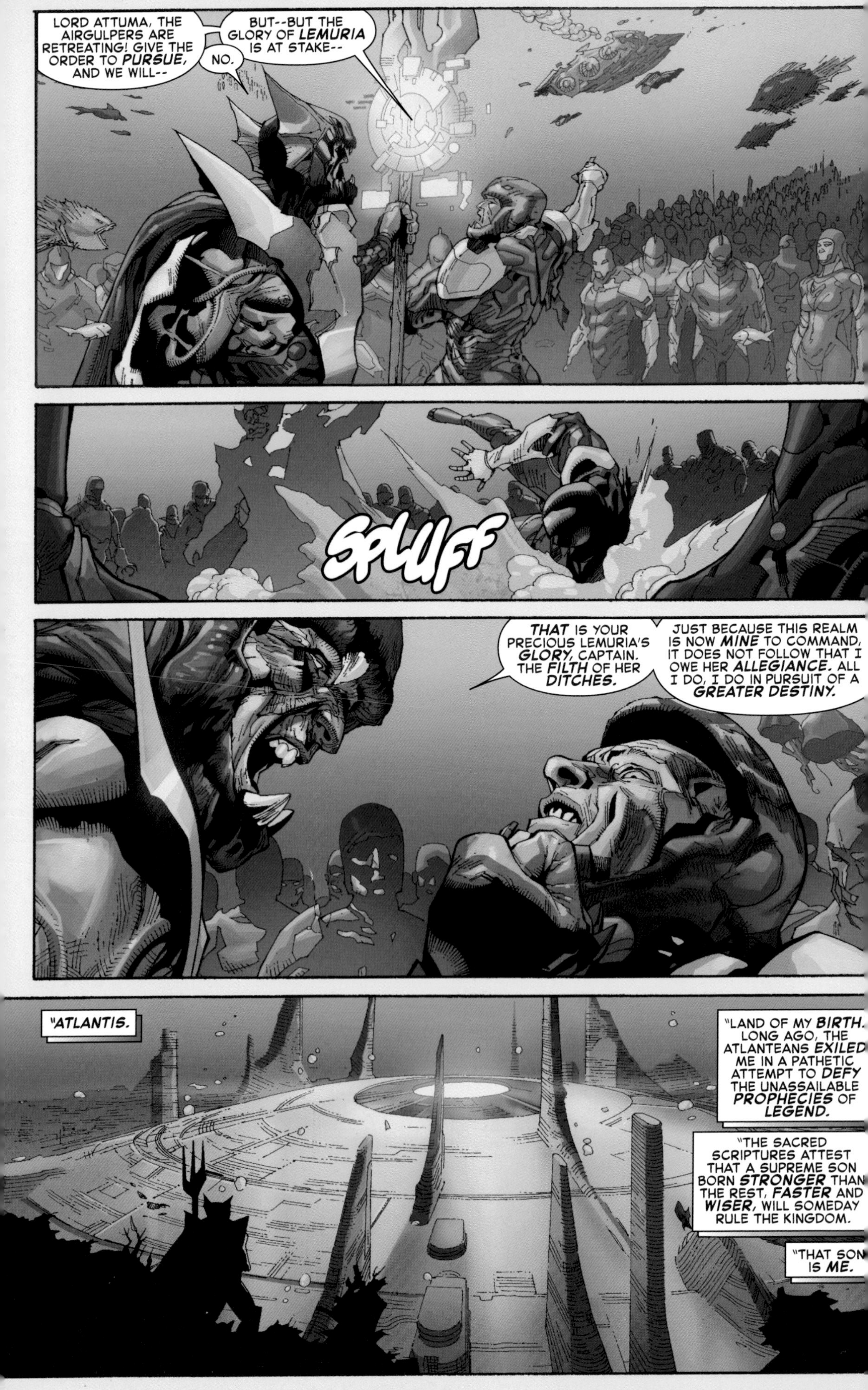
LORD ATTUMA, THE AIRGULPERS ARE RETREATING! GIVE THE ORDER TO *PURSUE,* AND WE WILL--
NO.
BUT--BUT THE GLORY OF *LEMURIA* IS AT STAKE--
SPLUFF
THAT IS YOUR PRECIOUS LEMURIA'S *GLORY,* CAPTAIN. THE *FILTH* OF HER *DITCHES.*
JUST BECAUSE THIS REALM IS NOW *MINE* TO COMMAND, IT DOES NOT FOLLOW THAT I OWE HER *ALLEGIANCE.* ALL I DO, I DO IN PURSUIT OF A *GREATER DESTINY.*
"*ATLANTIS.*
"LAND OF MY *BIRTH.* LONG AGO, THE ATLANTEANS *EXILED* ME IN A PATHETIC ATTEMPT TO *DEFY* THE UNASSAILABLE *PROPHECIES* OF *LEGEND.*
"THE SACRED SCRIPTURES ATTEST THAT A SUPREME SON BORN *STRONGER* THAN THE REST, *FASTER* AND *WISER,* WILL SOMEDAY RULE THE KINGDOM.
"THAT SON IS *ME.*

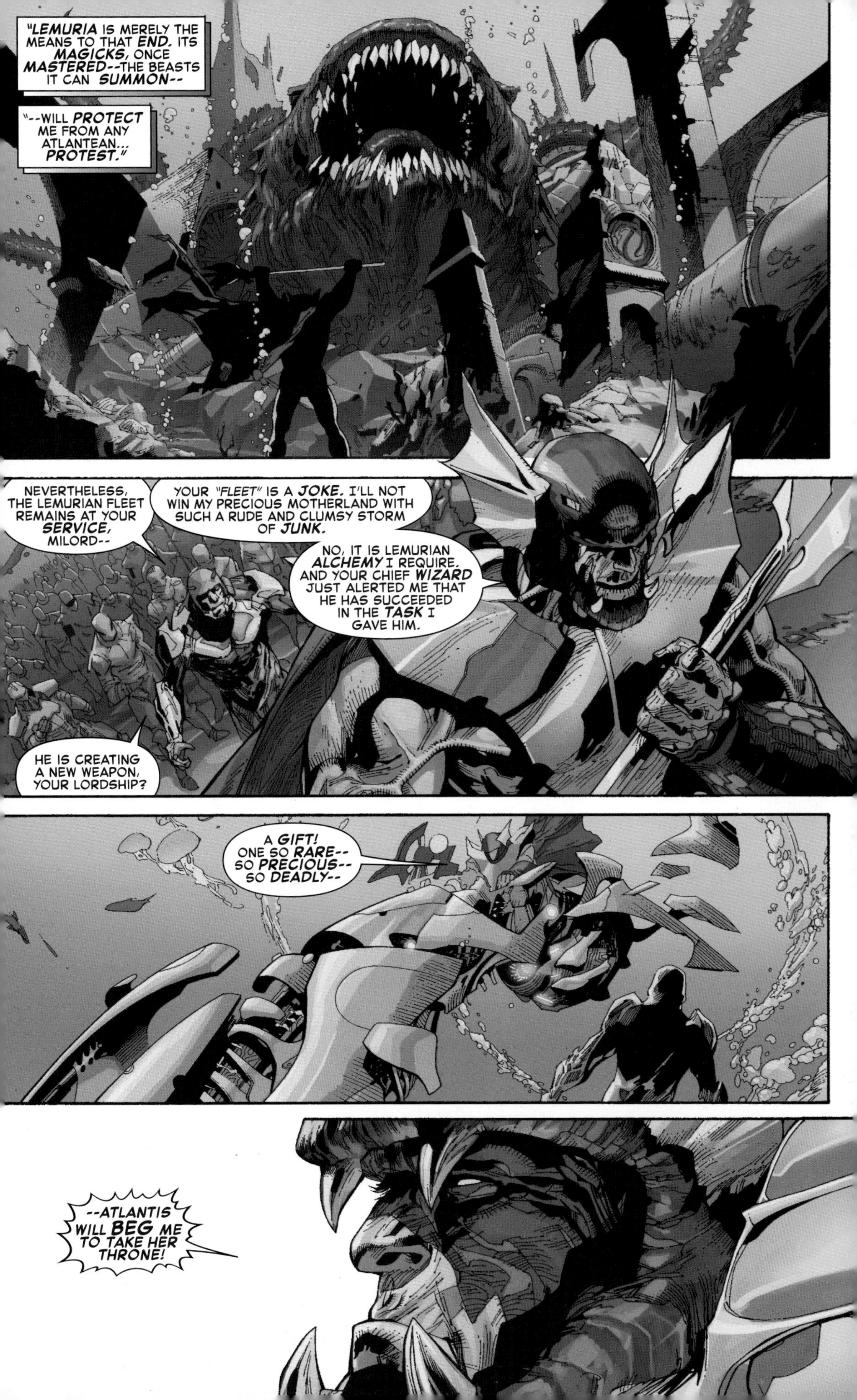
"LEMURIA IS MERELY THE MEANS TO THAT END. ITS MAGICKS, ONCE MASTERED--THE BEASTS IT CAN SUMMON--
"--WILL PROTECT ME FROM ANY ATLANTEAN... PROTEST."
NEVERTHELESS, THE LEMURIAN FLEET REMAINS AT YOUR SERVICE, MILORD--
YOUR "FLEET" IS A JOKE. I'LL NOT WIN MY PRECIOUS MOTHERLAND WITH SUCH A RUDE AND CLUMSY STORM OF JUNK.
NO, IT IS LEMURIAN ALCHEMY I REQUIRE. AND YOUR CHIEF WIZARD JUST ALERTED ME THAT HE HAS SUCCEEDED IN THE TASK I GAVE HIM.
HE IS CREATING A NEW WEAPON, YOUR LORDSHIP?
A GIFT! ONE SO RARE-- SO PRECIOUS-- SO DEADLY--
--ATLANTIS WILL BEG ME TO TAKE HER THRONE!

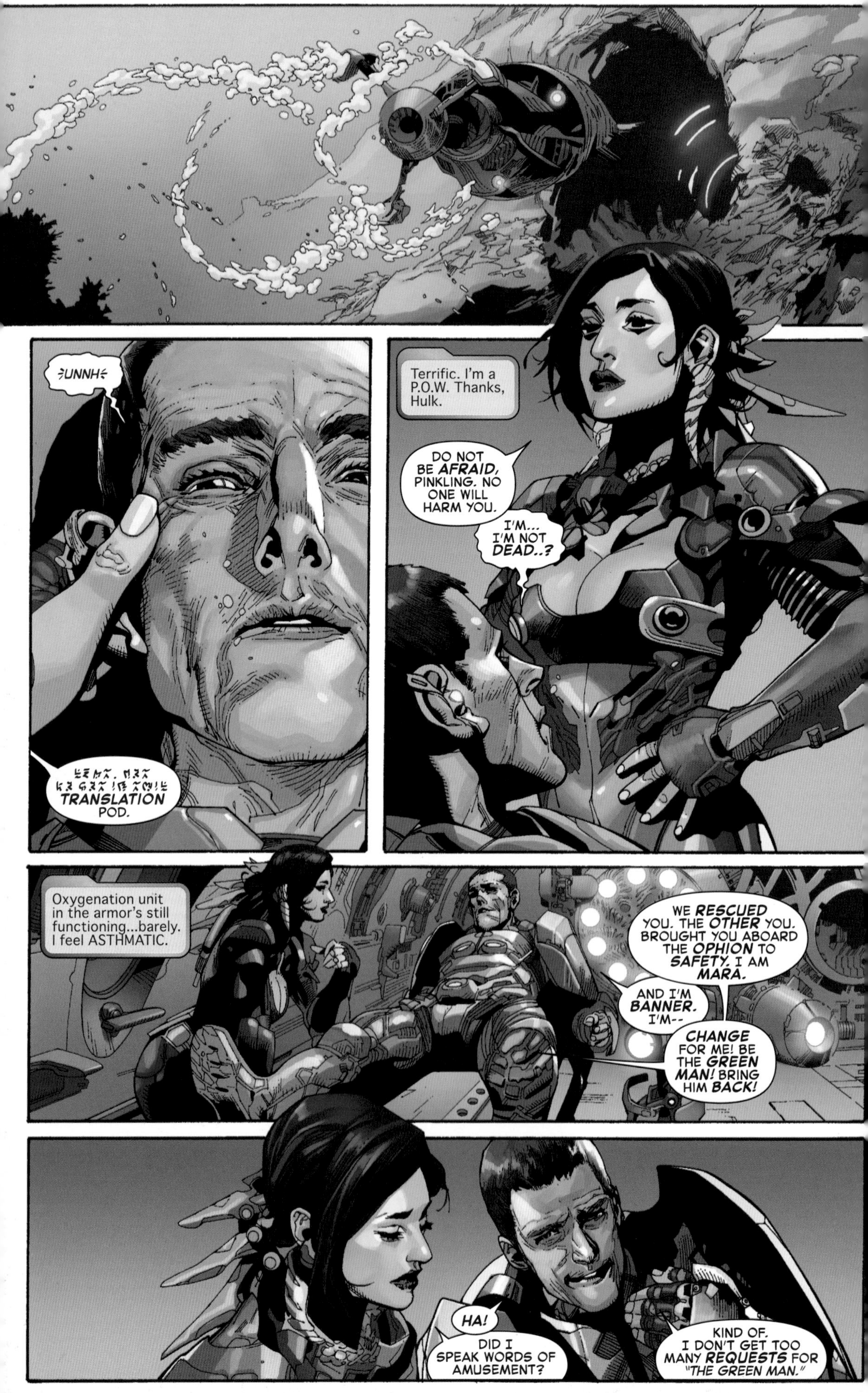
UNNH
Terrific. I'm a P.O.W. Thanks, Hulk.
DO NOT BE AFRAID, PINKLING. NO ONE WILL HARM YOU.
I'M... I'M NOT DEAD..?
TRANSLATION POD.
Oxygenation unit in the armor's still functioning...barely. I feel ASTHMATIC.
WE RESCUED YOU. THE OTHER YOU. BROUGHT YOU ABOARD THE OPHION TO SAFETY. I AM MARA.
AND I'M BANNER. I'M--
CHANGE FOR ME! BE THE GREEN MAN! BRING HIM BACK!
HA!
DID I SPEAK WORDS OF AMUSEMENT?
KIND OF. I DON'T GET TOO MANY REQUESTS FOR "THE GREEN MAN."

LET'S PLAN ON OPTION (A), NOT (B). I CAN *HELP.*

THIS, WE KNOW. WE SAW YOU--*HULK*--FIGHTING ATTUMA'S ARMY AND SAW IN YOU A POWERFUL *ALLY.*

SOMEWHERE IN YOU.

Mara goes on to explain that, despite it being one of the world's great repositories of SORCEROUS ARTIFACTS, Lemuria's merely a STEPPING STONE for Attuma.

That it's Lemuria's ALCHEMISTS he coveted, not its SOLDIERS or its MAGIC. And that it's rumored they've INVENTED something for him.

That he means to use it as his key to ATLANTIS.

HARDLY.

WELCOME TO THE HIDDEN GATHERPLACE OF THE *LEMURIAN REBEL ARMY*, BANNER...

...EXPATRIOTS MOURNFUL THAT OUR CITY HAS BEEN TURNED INTO A *FORTRESS*...AND SWORN TO *REGAIN* IT FROM ATTUMA'S GRASP OR DIE *TRYING*.

The rebel spies have obtained PLANS for this device, so I ask to take a LOOK, hoping that they're written in the UNIVERSAL language:

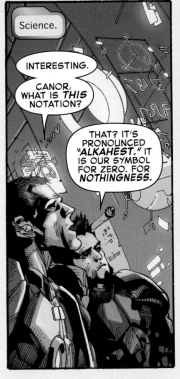

Science.

INTERESTING.

CANOR, WHAT IS *THIS* NOTATION?

THAT? IT'S PRONOUNCED *"ALKAHEST."* IT IS OUR SYMBOL FOR ZERO. FOR *NOTHINGNESS.*

WELL, THIS ISN'T *"NOTHING."*

THIS IS *QUANTUM ALCHEMY*...

"...AND WE ARE *SCREWED.*"

I PRESENT *"ATTUMA'S GIFT,"* MILORD. IT IS JUST AS YOU *DESIRED.*

WE SHALL *SEE,* RASA.

THE CREW OF A SURFACE *SPY CRAFT*--IGNORANT OF THE ABSOLUTE SURVEILLANCE *MAGIC* CAN PROVIDE--BELIEVES ITSELF TO BE *CLOAKED* IN ITS *APPROACH.*

DEMONSTRATE.

FWOOSH

<INCOMING! TOO SMALL TO BE A *MISSILE,* BUT-->

<SIR! SUGGEST EVASIVE ACTION!>

<SCAN SHOWS THE LIQUID IS-->

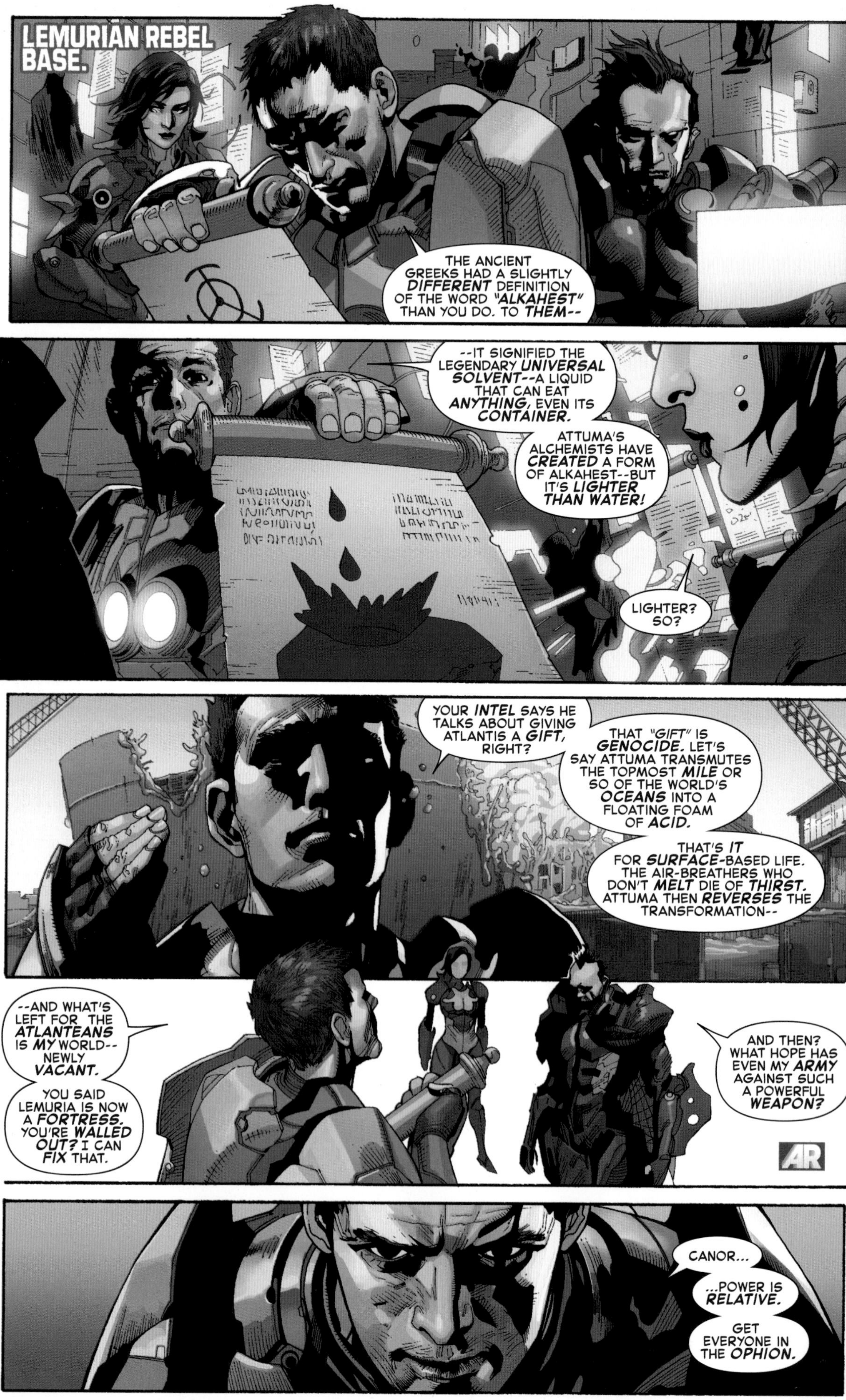
LEMURIAN REBEL BASE.
THE ANCIENT GREEKS HAD A SLIGHTLY DIFFERENT DEFINITION OF THE WORD "ALKAHEST" THAN YOU DO. TO THEM--
--IT SIGNIFIED THE LEGENDARY UNIVERSAL SOLVENT--A LIQUID THAT CAN EAT ANYTHING, EVEN ITS CONTAINER.
ATTUMA'S ALCHEMISTS HAVE CREATED A FORM OF ALKAHEST--BUT IT'S LIGHTER THAN WATER!
LIGHTER? SO?
YOUR INTEL SAYS HE TALKS ABOUT GIVING ATLANTIS A GIFT, RIGHT?
THAT "GIFT" IS GENOCIDE. LET'S SAY ATTUMA TRANSMUTES THE TOPMOST MILE OR SO OF THE WORLD'S OCEANS INTO A FLOATING FOAM OF ACID.
THAT'S IT FOR SURFACE-BASED LIFE. THE AIR-BREATHERS WHO DON'T MELT DIE OF THIRST. ATTUMA THEN REVERSES THE TRANSFORMATION--
--AND WHAT'S LEFT FOR THE ATLANTEANS IS MY WORLD--NEWLY VACANT.
YOU SAID LEMURIA IS NOW A FORTRESS. YOU'RE WALLED OUT? I CAN FIX THAT.
AND THEN? WHAT HOPE HAS EVEN MY ARMY AGAINST SUCH A POWERFUL WEAPON?
CANOR...
...POWER IS RELATIVE.
GET EVERYONE IN THE OPHION.

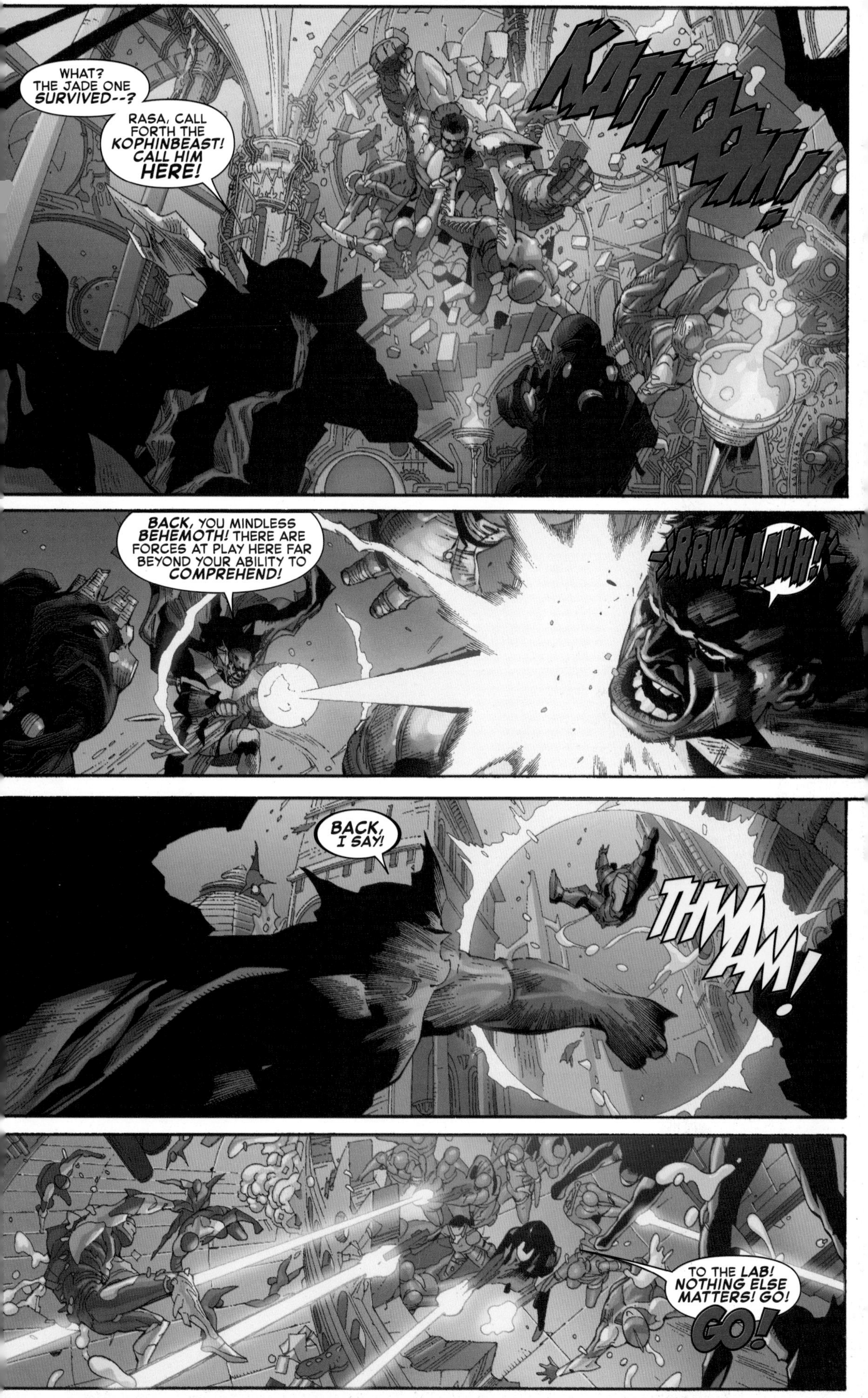

WHAT? THE JADE ONE SURVIVED--?
RASA, CALL FORTH THE KOPHINBEAST! CALL HIM HERE!
KATHOOM!
BACK, YOU MINDLESS BEHEMOTH! THERE ARE FORCES AT PLAY HERE FAR BEYOND YOUR ABILITY TO COMPREHEND!
RRWAAAHH!
BACK, I SAY!
THWAM!
TO THE LAB! NOTHING ELSE MATTERS! GO!
GO!

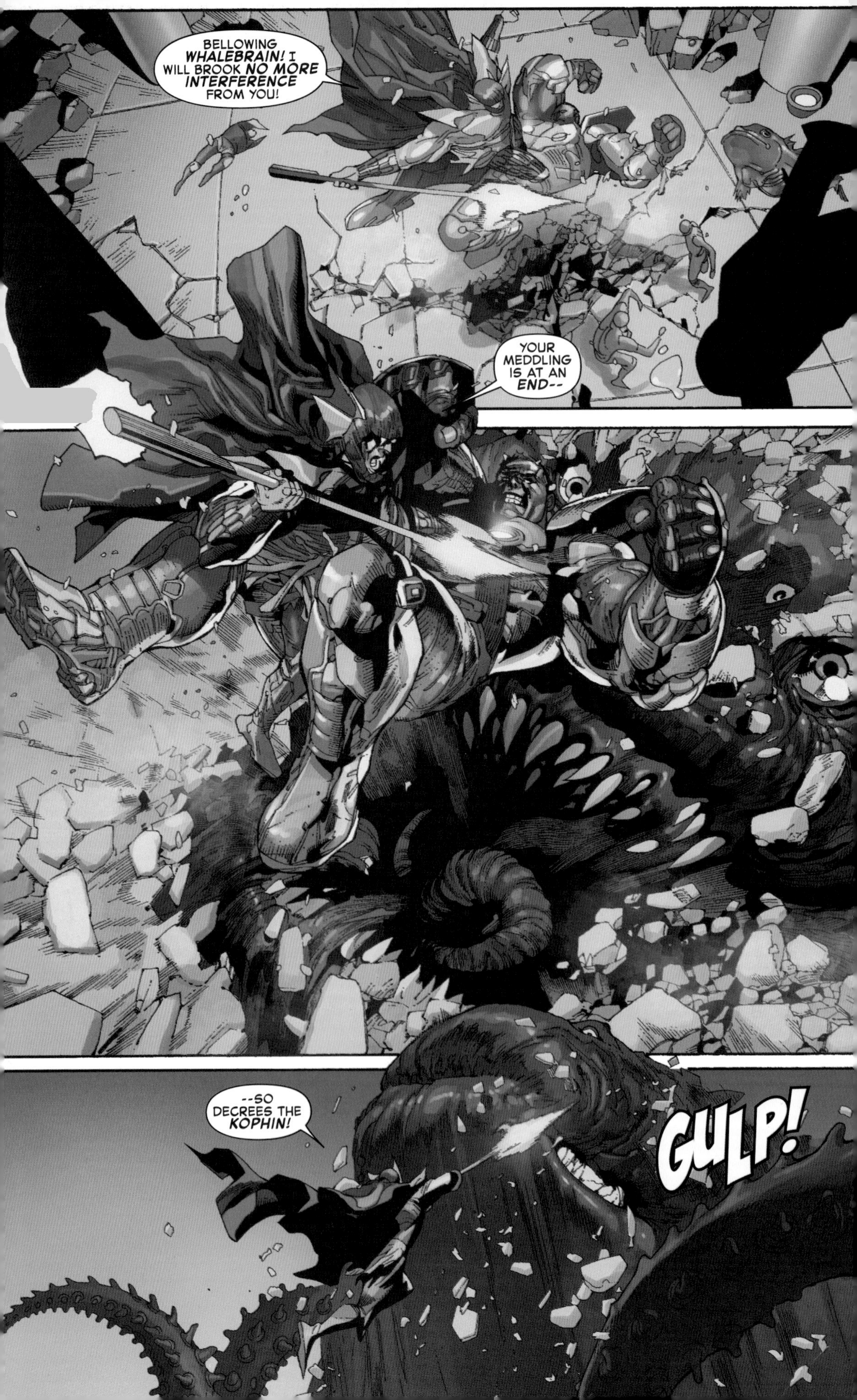
BELLOWING WHALEBRAIN! I WILL BROOK NO MORE INTERFERENCE FROM YOU!
YOUR MEDDLING IS AT AN END--
--SO DECREES THE KOPHIN!
GULP!

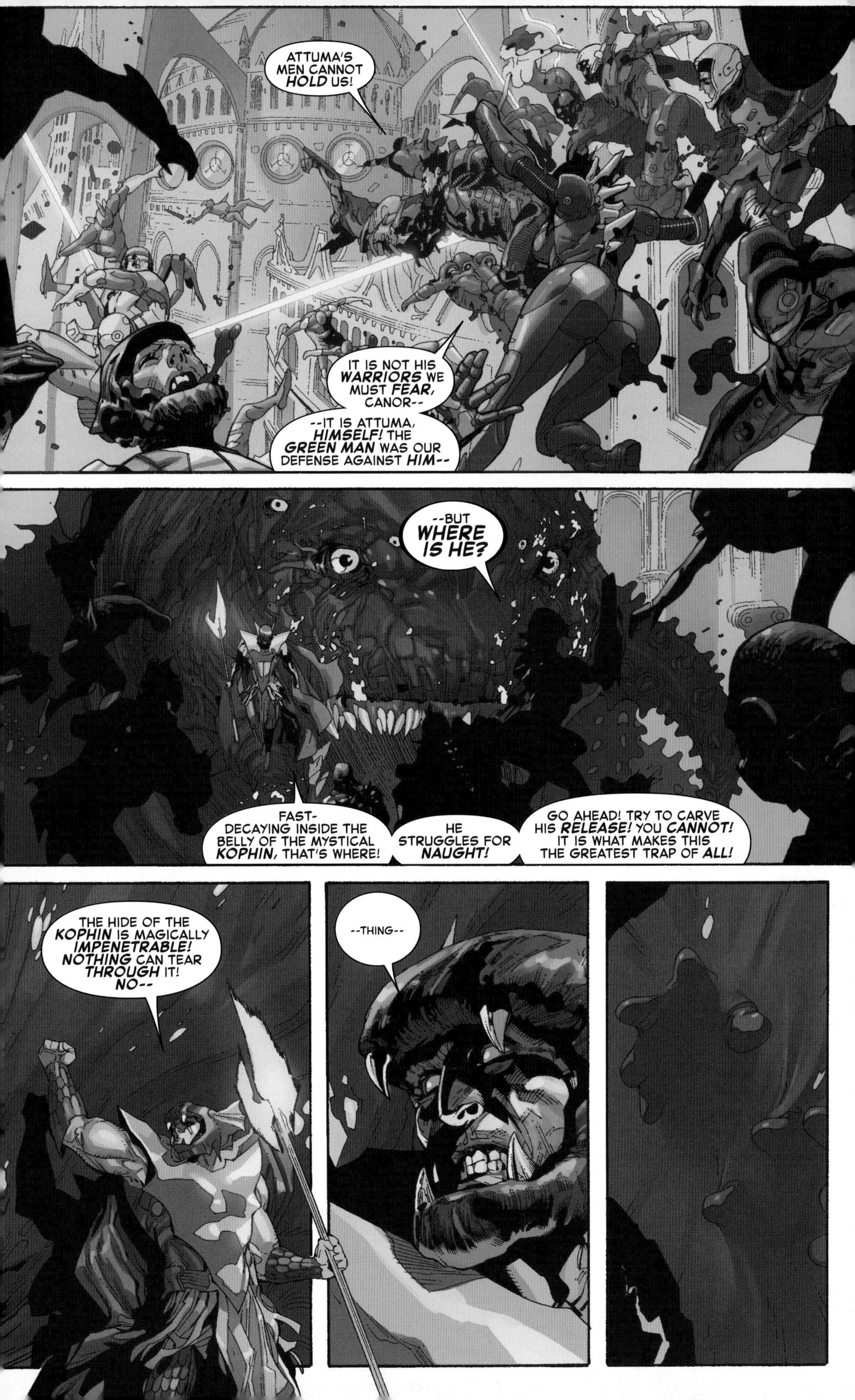
ATTUMA'S MEN CANNOT HOLD US!
IT IS NOT HIS WARRIORS WE MUST FEAR, CANOR--
--IT IS ATTUMA, HIMSELF! THE GREEN MAN WAS OUR DEFENSE AGAINST HIM--
--BUT WHERE IS HE?
FAST-DECAYING INSIDE THE BELLY OF THE MYSTICAL KOPHIN, THAT'S WHERE!
HE STRUGGLES FOR NAUGHT!
GO AHEAD! TRY TO CARVE HIS RELEASE! YOU CANNOT! IT IS WHAT MAKES THIS THE GREATEST TRAP OF ALL!
THE HIDE OF THE KOPHIN IS MAGICALLY IMPENETRABLE! NOTHING CAN TEAR THROUGH IT! NO--
--THING--

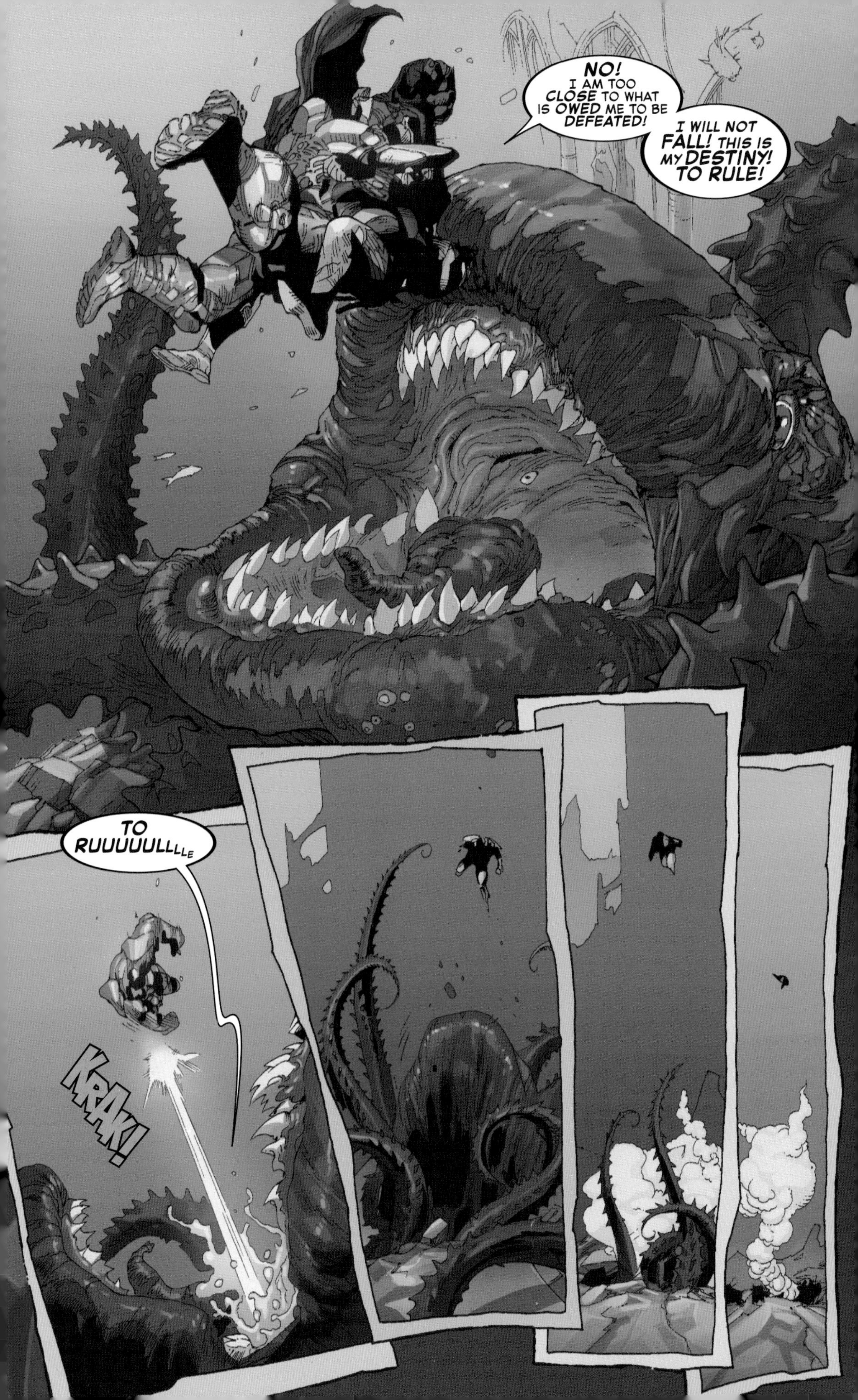
NO! I AM TOO CLOSE TO WHAT IS OWED ME TO BE DEFEATED!
I WILL NOT FALL! THIS IS MY DESTINY! TO RULE!
TO RUUUUULLLLLE
KRAK!!

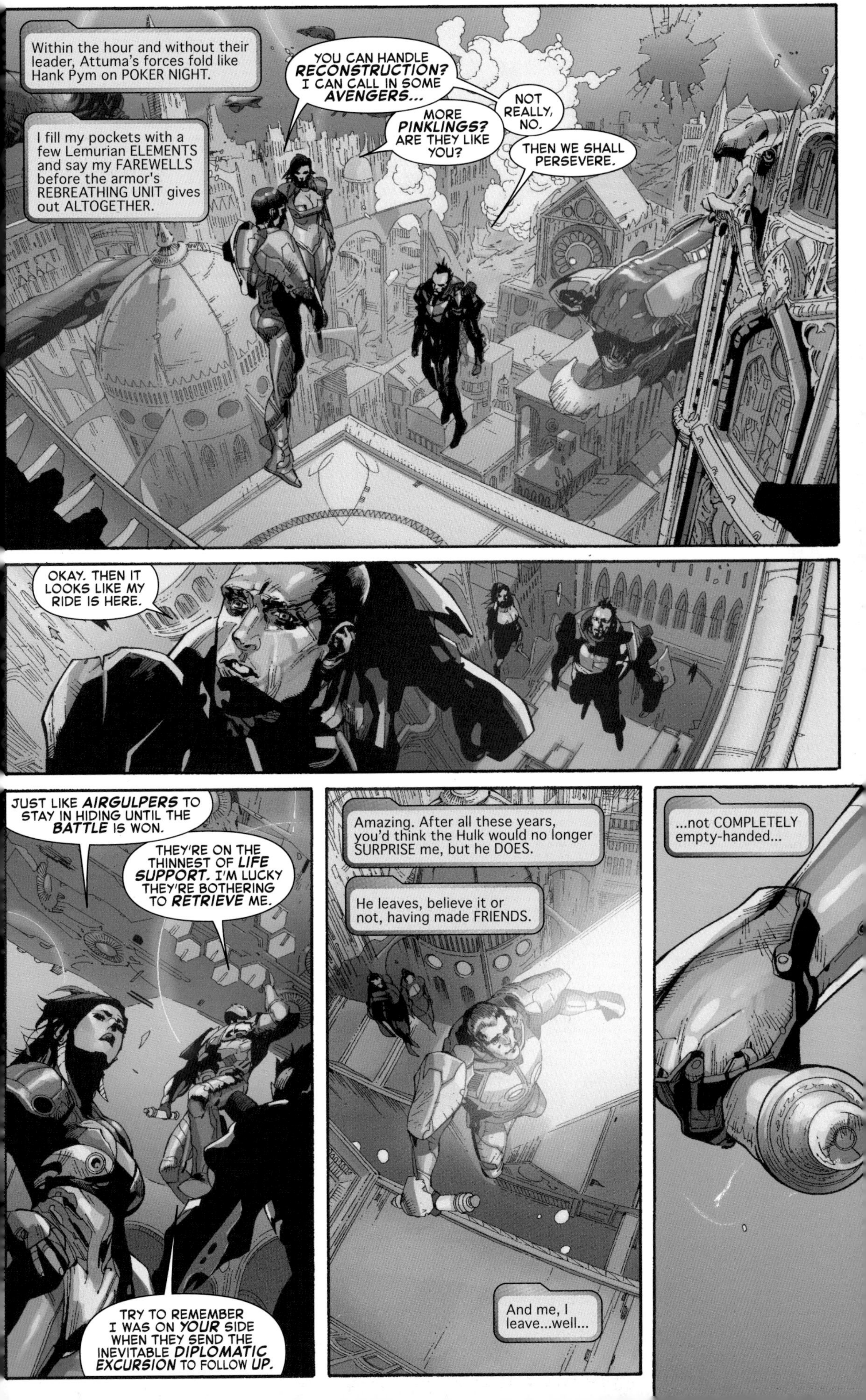

Within the hour and without their leader, Attuma's forces fold like Hank Pym on POKER NIGHT.
I fill my pockets with a few Lemurian ELEMENTS and say my FAREWELLS before the armor's REBREATHING UNIT gives out ALTOGETHER.
YOU CAN HANDLE RECONSTRUCTION? I CAN CALL IN SOME AVENGERS...
MORE PINKLINGS? ARE THEY LIKE YOU?
NOT REALLY, NO.
THEN WE SHALL PERSEVERE.
OKAY. THEN IT LOOKS LIKE MY RIDE IS HERE.
JUST LIKE AIRGULPERS TO STAY IN HIDING UNTIL THE BATTLE IS WON.
THEY'RE ON THE THINNEST OF LIFE SUPPORT. I'M LUCKY THEY'RE BOTHERING TO RETRIEVE ME.
TRY TO REMEMBER I WAS ON YOUR SIDE WHEN THEY SEND THE INEVITABLE DIPLOMATIC EXCURSION TO FOLLOW UP.
Amazing. After all these years, you'd think the Hulk would no longer SURPRISE me, but he DOES.
He leaves, believe it or not, having made FRIENDS.
And me, I leave...well...
...not COMPLETELY empty-handed...

INDESTRUCTIBLE HULK™ Variant Cover Gallery

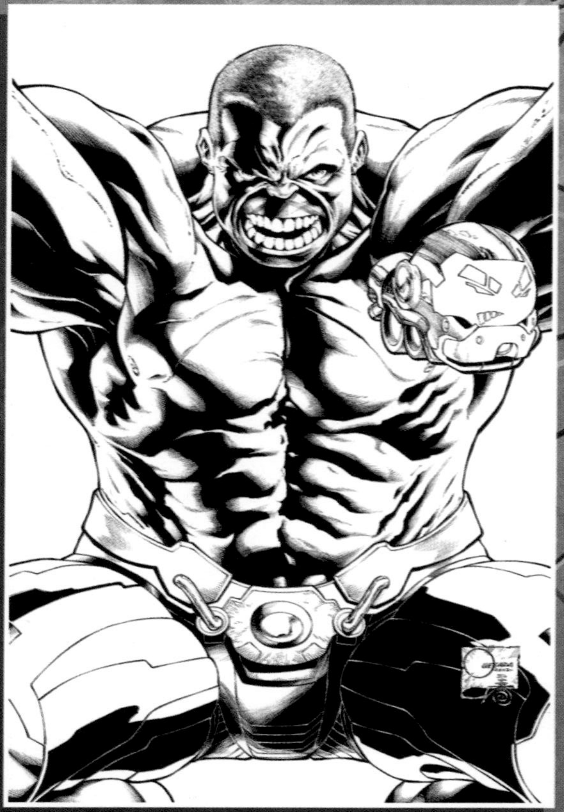

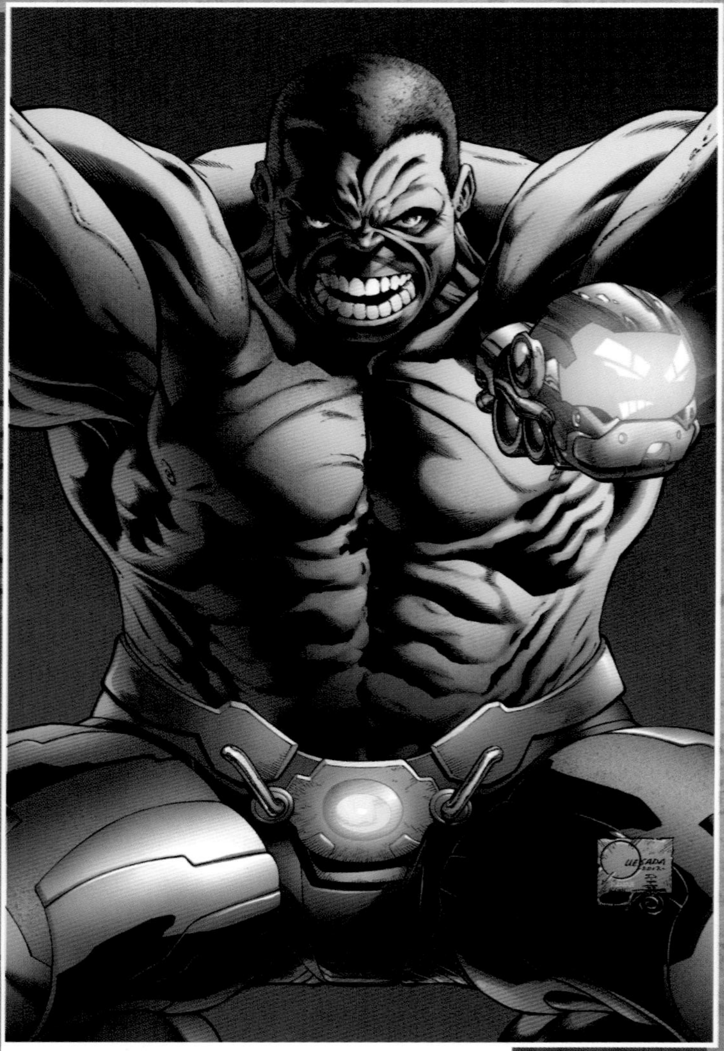

UNCANNY AVENGERS #1 BY JOE QUESADA

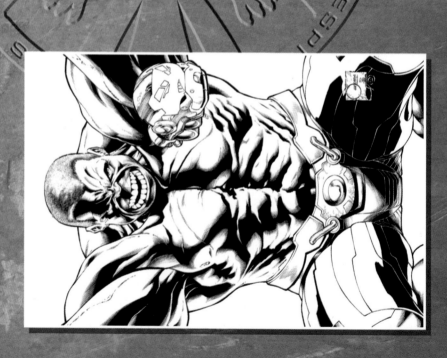

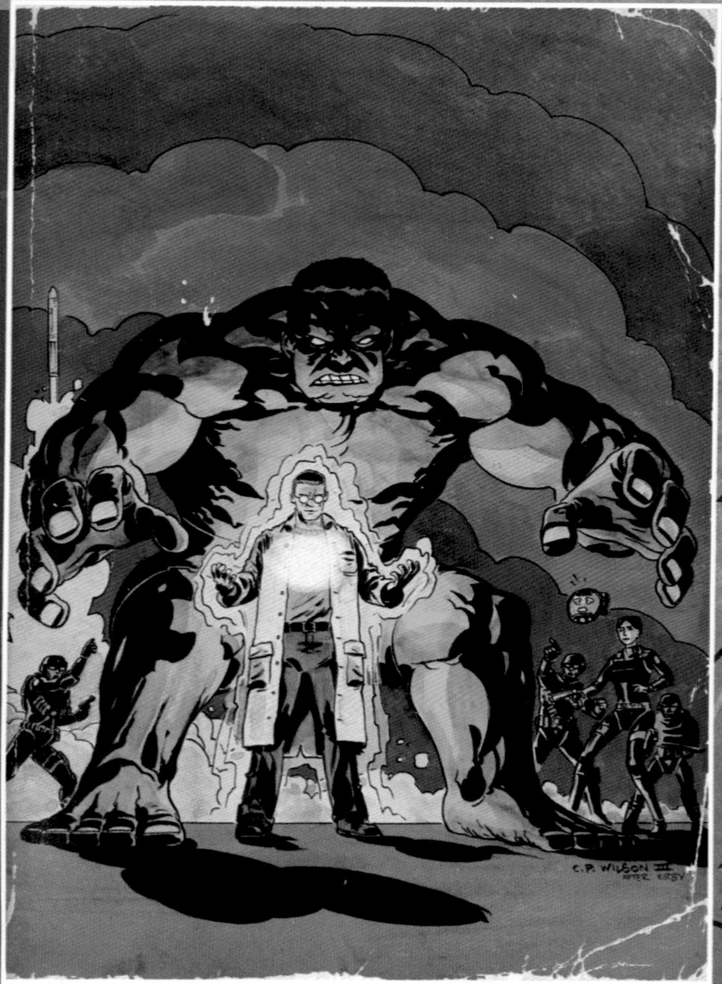
C.P. WILSON III
AFTER KIRBY

UNCANNY AVENGERS #1 BY CHARLES PAUL WILSON III

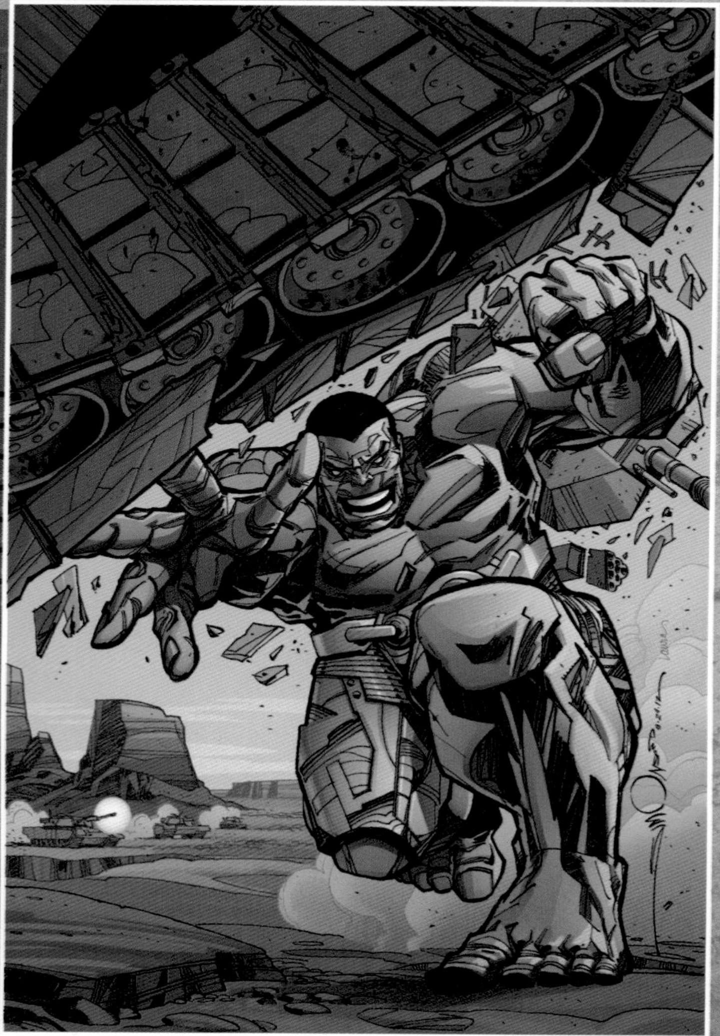

UNCANNY AVENGERS #1 BY WALT SIMONSON

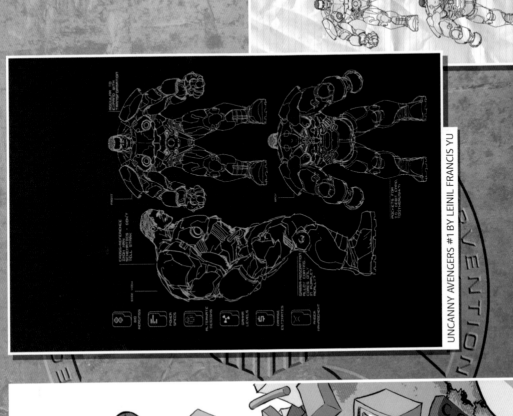

UNCANNY AVENGERS #1 BY LEINIL FRANCIS YU

UNCANNY AVENGERS #1 BY SKOTTIE YOUNG

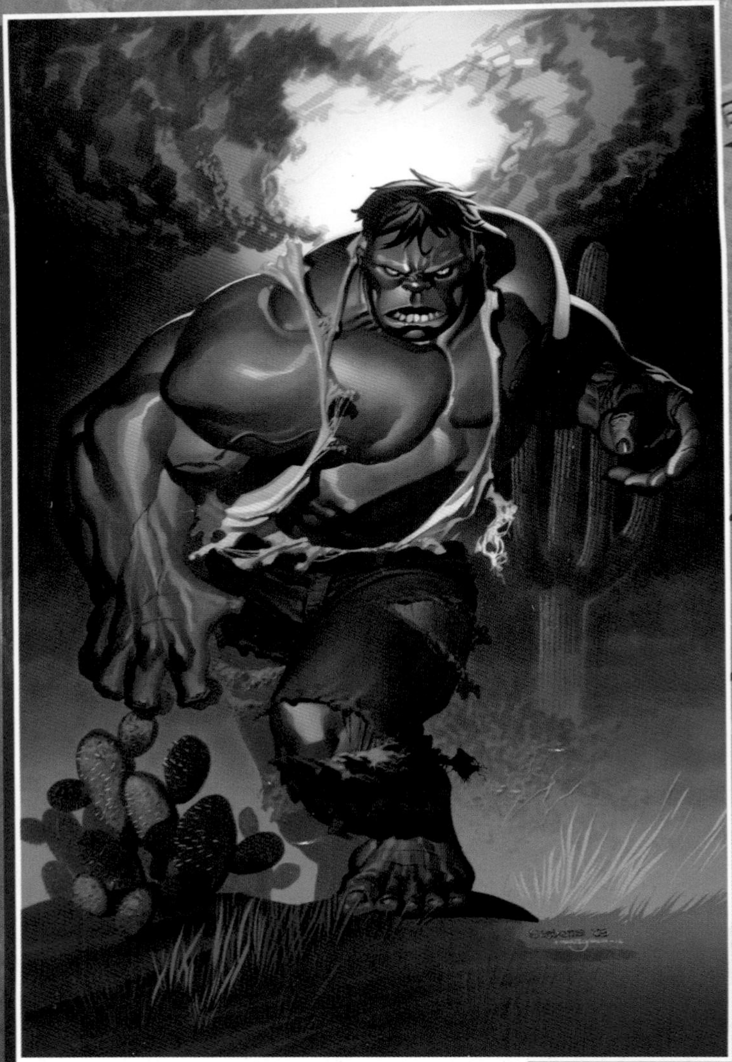

UNCANNY AVENGERS #5 BY CHRIS STEVENS

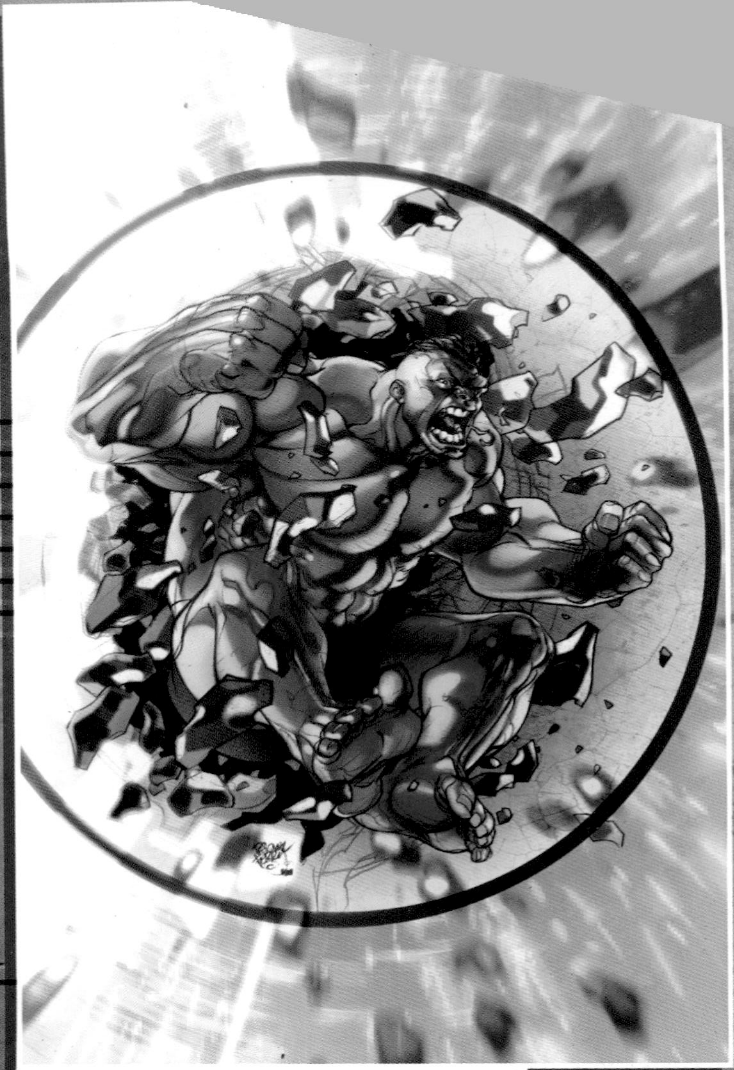

UNCANNY AVENGERS #4 BY PASQUAL FERRY

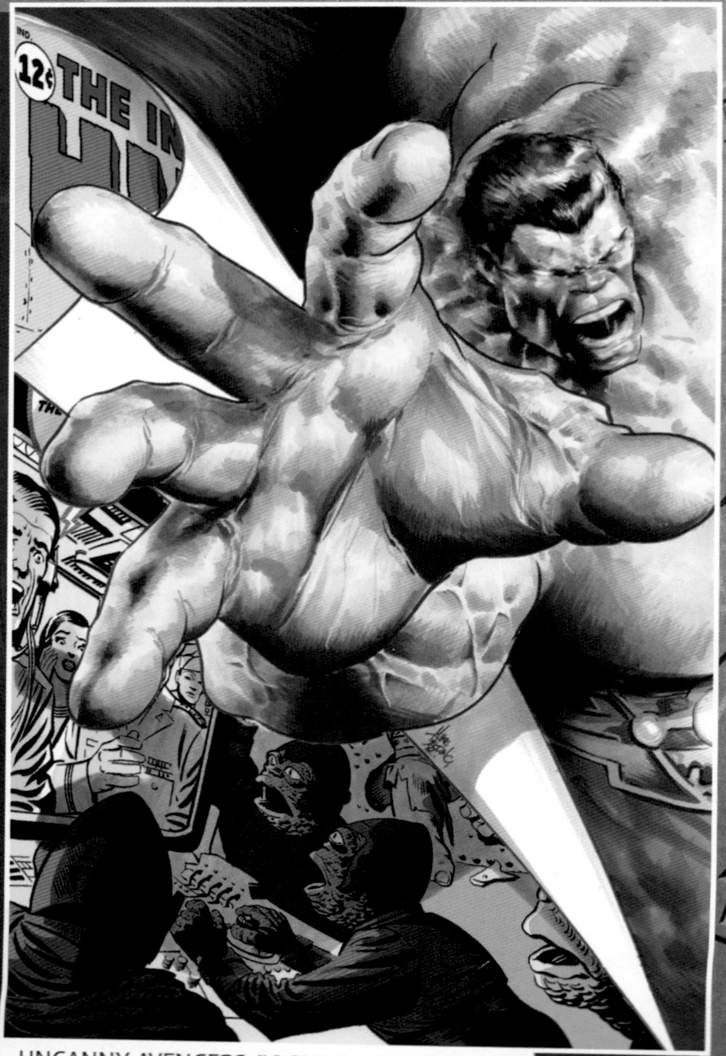
12¢
THE IN
UNCANNY AVENGERS #2 BY MIKE DEODATO JR.

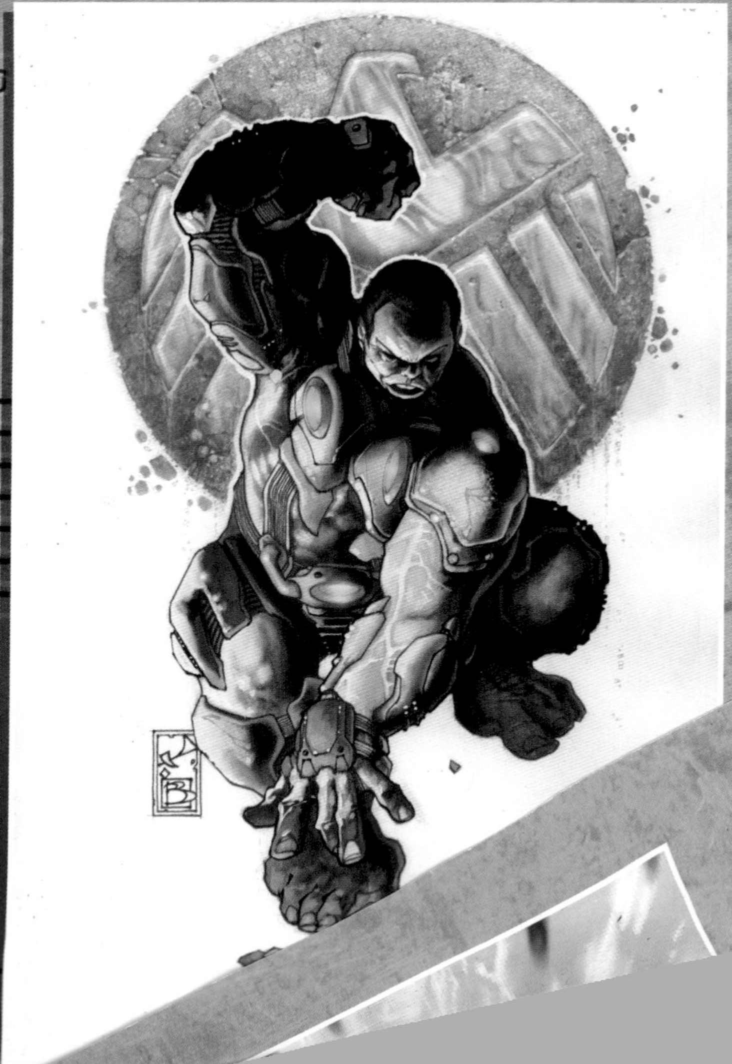